Education Governance
and Social Theory

Social Theory and Methodology in Education Research series

Edited by Mark Murphy

The Bloomsbury *Social Theory and Methodology in Education Research* series brings together books exploring various applications of social theory in educational research design. Each book provides a detailed account of how theory and method influence each other in specific educational research settings, such as schools, early childhood education, community education, further education colleges and universities. Books in the series represent the richness of topics explored in theory-driven education research, including leadership and governance, equity, teacher education, assessment, curriculum and policy studies. This innovative series provides a timely platform for highlighting the wealth of international work carried out in the field of social theory and education research, a field that has grown considerably in recent years and has made the likes of Pierre Bourdieu and Michel Foucault familiar names in educational discourse. Books in the *Social Theory and Methodology in Education Research* series offer an excellent resource for those who wish to use theoretical concepts in their research but are not sure how to do so, and who want to better understand how theory can be effectively applied in research contexts, in practically realizable ways.

Also available in the series
Foucault and School Leadership Research, Denise Mifsud

Forthcoming in the series
Education Research with Bourdieu, Julie Rowlands and Shaun Rawolle
International Perspectives on Theorizing Aspiration, edited by Garth Stahl,
Derron Wallace, Ciaran Burke and Steven Threadgold
Norbert Elias and the Sociology of Education, Eric Lybeck
The Future of Qualitative Research, edited by Matthew Thomas
and Robin Bellingham

Education Governance
and Social Theory

Interdisciplinary Approaches to Research

Edited by Andrew Wilkins and Antonio Olmedo

BLOOMSBURY ACADEMIC

LONDON • NEW YORK • OXFORD • NEW DELHI • SYDNEY

BLOOMSBURY ACADEMIC
Bloomsbury Publishing Plc
50 Bedford Square, London, WC1B 3DP, UK
1385 Broadway, New York, NY 10018, USA

BLOOMSBURY, BLOOMSBURY ACADEMIC and the Diana logo are trademarks of
Bloomsbury Publishing Plc

First published in Great Britain 2019

Series design by Louise Dugdale
Cover image © Ikon Images/Getty Images

A catalogue record for this book is available from the British Library.

A catalog record for this book is available from the Library of Congress.

ISBN: HB: 978-1-3500-4006-9
ePDF: 978-1-3500-4007-6
eBook: 978-1-3500-4008-3

Series: Social Theory and Methodology in Education Research

Typeset by Newgen KnowledgeWorks Pvt. Ltd., Chennai, India
Printed and bound in Great Britain

To find out more about our authors and books visit www.bloomsbury.com
and sign up for our newsletters.

Contents

Series Editor's Foreword   vii

Notes on Contributors   x

List of Abbreviations   xv

Foreword *Kenneth J. Saltman*   xviii

Introduction: Conceptualizing Education Governance: Framings, Perspectives and Theories *Andrew Wilkins and Antonio Olmedo*   1

Part One   Data Regimes

1   Digitizing Education Governance: Pearson, Real-Time Data Analytics, Visualization and Machine Intelligence *Ben Williamson*   21

2   Learning Personalization: Technics, Disorientation and Governance *Greg Thompson*   43

3   Dispositions and Situations of Education Governance: The Example of Data Infrastructure in Australian Schooling *Sam Sellar and Kalervo N. Gulson*   63

Part Two   Evaluation Regimes

4   Exploring the Role of School Inspectors in Implementing and Shaping Policy: A Narrative Approach *Jacqueline Baxter*   83

5   How Can Transnational Connection Hold? An Actor Network Theory Approach to the Materiality of Transnational Education Governance *Nelli Piattoeva*   103

Part Three   Knowledge Regimes

6   Revealing Market Hegemony through a Critical Logics Approach: The Case of England's Academy Schools Policy *Natalie Papanastasiou*   123

7   Test-Based Accountability and the Rise of Regulatory Governance
    in Education: A Review of Global Drivers *Antoni Verger and
    Lluís Parcerisa*   139

8   Making Education News in Chile: Understanding the Role of
    Mediatization in Education Governance through a Bourdieuian
    Framework *Eduardo Santa Cruz Grau and Cristian Cabalin*   159

Part Four Institutional Regimes

9   Preschool Teacher Agency and Professionalism: A Bourdieuian
    Approach to Education Governance *Ondrej Kaščák and
    Branislav Pupala*   177

10 Ever Greater Scrutiny: Researching the Bureaucracy of Educational
    Accountability *Mark Murphy*   193

11 Transformation and Control: What Role for Leadership and
    Management in a 'School-Led' System? *Howard Stevenson*   209

Index   227

Series Editor's Foreword

Education research has a long history of adapting ideas from social theory. While this has always been the case when it comes to educational foundations, in recent years there has been an enormous growth in the adoption of social theory in the field of educational research. The names of theorists such as Pierre Bourdieu, Jürgen Habermas, Judith Butler and Michel Foucault have become commonplace in the field, making social theory increasingly familiar to those who both conduct education research and utilize it in their teaching.

As its familiarity increases, so too does the desire to engage with social theory in more thoughtful and effective ways. There is currently a strong desire for applying social theory in educational research contexts, which makes sense, as without theory, much education research can be overly descriptive and/or restricted by narrow definitions of professional practice. Social theory can assist in efforts to transcend the everyday taken-for-granted understandings of education, while also reflecting erstwhile concerns in education around power, control, social justice and transformation.

The issue then becomes one of applying theory to method, with the focus shifting to a growing interest in the art of application itself. This interest comes with a set of key questions attached:

- How best to apply concepts such as habitus, subjectivation and performativity in educational research contexts?
- What are the ways in which methodological concerns meet theoretical ones?
- In what ways does social theory shape the quality of research outcomes?

These questions require thoughtful responses and the purpose of this book series is to help provide solutions to these issues, while also helping to develop the capacity, in particular of postgraduate and early career researchers, to successfully put social theory to work in research. This is especially important as theory application in method is a challenging and daunting enterprise. The set of theories developed by the likes of Foucault, Jacques Derrida, Bourdieu et al. could never be described as 'simple' or easy to navigate. On top of that there are a variety of issues faced when applying such ideas in research contexts, a field of complex interwoven imperatives and practices in its own right. These challenges – epistemological, operational, analytical – inevitably impact on researchers and our attempts to make sense of research questions, whether these be questions of governance and political regulation, social reproduction, power, cultural or professional identities (among others). So care needs to be taken when applying a challenging set of ideas onto a challenging set of practices, incorporating a strong consideration for intellectual arguments alongside the concerns of the professional researcher.

The series should hold a strong appeal to the growing numbers of researchers who are keen to apply social theory in their research, as evidenced by the growing audience for the editor's own website www.socialtheoryapplied.com. It will offer an excellent resource for those who wish to begin using theoretical concepts in their research, and will also appeal to readers who have a strong interest in better understanding how theory can be effectively applied in research contexts, in practically realizable ways.

In terms of output, this series is designed to provide a collection of books exploring various applications of social theory in educational research design. Each book will provide a detailed account of how theory and method influence each other in specific educational research settings, such as schools, early years, community education, further education colleges and universities. The series will represent the richness of topics explored in theory-driven education research, including leadership and governance, equity, teacher education, assessment, curriculum and policy studies. It will also provide a timely platform for highlighting the wealth of work done in the field of social theory and education research, a field that has grown considerably in recent years and has made the likes of Pierre Bourdieu and Michel Foucault familiar names in educational discourse.

Embedded in the design of the series is a strong pedagogical component – with a focus on the 'how' of applying theory in methods and an emphasis on operationalizing theory in research. This pedagogical remit will be addressed explicitly in the texts in different ways – the responsibility of addressing this will fall on the authors and editors, but can take the form of case studies, learning activities, 'focus' sections and glossaries detailing the key theoretical concepts utilized in the research.

Education Governance and Social Theory: Interdisciplinary Approaches to Research, co-edited by Andrew Wilkins and Antonio Olmedo, is a timely addition to the series, given the current interest in both the concept of governance and also the application of social theory in education policy research. 'Governance' as a form of description and/or explanation is currently in vogue in theoretical debates, yet this ubiquity can present a challenge to the researcher who aims to apply its more useful insights into education research projects. As the editors suggest, it is precisely because the term 'education governance' is aligned with different theoretical perspectives and research strategies that it is in danger of being rendered meaningless due to its multiple conceptual connotations. The fact that it is open to numerous theoretical points of view has implications for its application, especially among those unfamiliar with the interdisciplinarity of the field and the various theoretical perspectives imported through its use.

The book offers readers an important vantage point from which to navigate this conceptual and disciplinary diversity and engage with the field of educational governance. As an introductory text for postgraduate, doctoral and early career researchers, it is written and designed specifically to support and guide those researchers interested in pursuing educational governance as a conceptual framework and research method across a range of what the editors refer to as 'regimes' – including data, evaluation, knowledge and institutional regimes. It offers an excellent resource for those who wish to research educational governance in all its multifaceted forms, and provides case studies of applied social theory via engagement with the likes of Deleuze, Foucault, Bourdieu and Habermas. The book delivers a text that can be used to make sense of an important socio-theoretical concept while also allowing researchers to make effective links between social theory and research method. I thank both editors and the contributors for making such a valuable addition to the series.

Mark Murphy, February 2018

Contributors

Jacqueline Baxter is senior lecturer in Public Policy and Management at The Open University Business School, UK. Her research interests lie in the area of public management and governance and her most recent funded projects investigate strategic decision-making in multilevel school boards (Leverhulme) and trust in accountability systems in education in South Africa (DfID). Her most recent publications include *School Inspectors: Policy Implementers, Policy Shapers in National Policy Contexts* (2017) and *School Governance: Policy, Politics and Practices* (2016). She is co-editor in chief of the Sage journal *Management in Education*.

Cristian Cabalin is assistant professor at the Institute of Communication and Image and associate researcher with the Centre for Advanced Research in Education at the University of Chile, Chile. He is also a researcher at the Universidad Central de Chile, Chile. He obtained his PhD in Educational Policy Studies from the University of Illinois at Urbana-Champaign, USA. His research areas include cultural studies in education, mediatization of education and political communication. He has published articles in *Discourse: Studies in the Cultural Politics of Education, Critical Studies in Education, Studies in Higher Education* and *Policy Futures in Education*, among other journals.

Kalervo N. Gulson is associate professor in the School of Education, University of New South Wales, Australia. His work draws on human geography, education policy studies, and science and technology studies. His current research investigates whether new knowledge, methods and technologies from life and computing sciences will substantively alter education policy and governance. His recent publications include *Education Policy and Racial Biopolitics in Multicultural Cities* (with P. Taylor Webb, 2017).

Ondrej Kaščák is associate professor and head of the Department of School Pedagogy at Trnava University, Slovakia. He is also senior research fellow at Centre for Research in Education at Slovak Academy of Sciences in Bratislava. He is the lead editor of *Journal of Pedagogy*. His research interests cover the education policy (focusing on neo-liberal governmentalities within the post-communist contexts), sociology of childhood and sociology of education.

Mark Murphy is reader in Education & Public Policy and Co-Director of the Robert Owen Centre for Educational Change, University of Glasgow, UK. He has published widely in the field of social theory and applied research, with recent books including *Habermas and Social Research: Between Theory and Method* (2017), *Theory as Method: On Bourdieu, Education and Society* (with C. Costa, 2016) and *Bourdieu, Habitus and Social Research: The Art of Application* (with C. Costa, 2015). Mark is the editor for the book series *Social Theory and Methodology in Education Research* (Bloomsbury Academic) and is co-editor of the multi-authored website www.socialtheoryapplied.com.

Antonio Olmedo is reader in Education Policy Sociology at the University of Bristol and honorary reader at UCL Institute of Education, University College London, UK. His research rests within the fields of education policy analysis and sociology of education, with a specific focus on the role of the private sector in education; neo-liberal policies and the creation of quasi-markets; and global networks, international organizations, policy advocacy, philanthropy and edu-businesses. He has recently completed a research project funded by the British Academy entitled 'Philanthropy, business and education: Market-based solutions to educational problems in developing countries'. He is currently developing a research project on philanthrocapitalism and the role of edu-businesses in global education policy funded by Education International.

Natalie Papanastasiou is a postdoctoral researcher currently based at the Universitat Autònoma de Barcelona, Spain, and holds a 2-year research grant from the Leverhulme Trust. Her research explores the politics of education governance and policymaking in local, national and European settings. Natalie's theoretical interests draw on political geography, critical policy studies and political discourse analysis. She holds a PhD in Social Policy from the University of Edinburgh and her work has been published in the *Journal of Education Policy, Environment and Planning A, European Educational Research Journal* and *Critical Policy Studies*. Her forthcoming monograph *The Politics of Scale in Policy: Scalecraft and Education Governance* will be published in April 2019.

Lluís Parcerisa is a doctoral candidate in the Department of Sociology at Universitat Autònoma de Barcelona, Spain. He has been a member of the GEPS research centre since 2013 where he participates in the European research project REFORMED: Reforming Schools Globally: A Multiscalar Analysis of

Autonomy and Accountability Policies in the Education Sector (ERC StG 2016–2021). He has also collaborated with UNESCO, Education International and the Jaume Bofill Foundation. His research interests include comparative education, cultural political economy, school autonomy with accountability reforms and teacher professionalism.

Nelli Piattoeva is lecturer in Education Sciences at the University of Tampere, Finland and Adjunct Professor in International and Comparative Education Policy Research at the University of Oulu, Finland. Nelli's current research interest is mainly focused on the transnationalization and datafication of education policy. She is particularly concerned with national and international large-scale assessments as sources of evidence for policymaking and new technologies of governance at a distance, examining these through the lenses of Science and Technology Studies (STS) and Actor-Network Theory (ANT). Nelli's primary geographical focus is Russia and the post-Soviet space. Her scholarship also spans changes in citizenship education policies and curricula in result of nation- and state re-building after the Cold War, Russia as a re-emerging aid donor, and socialist and postsocialist memories of childhood and schooling.

Branislav Pupala is professor of Education at Trnava University, Slovakia, senior research fellow at the Slovak Academy of Sciences, Slovakia, and co-founder of the Centre for Research in Education, Bratislava, Slovakia. His research focuses on policy in ECEC, curriculum development and comparative/international studies in ECEC. He was the head of the team developing and implementing the new national curriculum for ECEC in Slovakia.

Kenneth J. Saltman is professor in the Department of Educational Leadership at the University of Massachusetts Dartmouth, USA, where he teaches in the Educational Leadership and Policy Studies PhD program. He is the author most recently of *Scripted Bodies: Corporate Power, Smart Technologies, and the Undoing of Public Education* (2017), *The Politics of Education: A Critical Introduction* Second Edition (2018) and co-author of *Toward a New Common School Movement* (2016). He is a fellow of the National Education Policy Center and received a Fulbright Chair in Globalization and Culture.

Eduardo Santa Cruz Grau is a postdoctoral researcher at the Centre for Advanced Research in Education at the University of Chile, Chile. He is also researcher at the Interdisciplinary Research Program in Education (PIIE). He obtained his PhD in Education at the University of Granada, Spain. He has published several articles and contributions to journals and books in the field of Sociology of Education, Educational Policy and Ethnography.

Sam Sellar is reader in Education Studies at Manchester Metropolitan University, UK. His current research focuses on four interrelated issues in schooling: data infrastructures, large-scale assessments, commercialization and new accountabilities. Sam works closely with teacher associations around the world to explore the effects of datafication and commercialization for schools and communities. He has published widely on the growing influence of large-scale assessments in school systems, including the education work of the OECD and its Programme for International Student Achievement (PISA). He is a co-author of *Globalizing Educational Accountabilities* (2016) and *The Global Education Race: Taking the Measure of PISA and International Testing* (2017) and a co-editor of *National Testing in Schools: An Australian Assessment* (2016).

Howard Stevenson is director of research and professor of Educational Leadership and Policy Studies in the School of Education, University of Nottingham, UK. His research interests focus on teachers' work and teacher professionalism, with a particular interest in teachers' unions and education sector industrial relations. He is currently researching European Union policy processes with a specific focus on the role of teacher unions in shaping education policy at a European level.

Greg Thompson is associate professor of Education Research at Queensland University of Technology (QUT), Australia. Prior to becoming an academic, he worked as a high school teacher in Western Australia for 13 years. Thompson's research focuses on educational theory, education policy and the philosophy/sociology of education assessment and measurement with a particular emphasis on large-scale testing. Recent research projects include reconceptualizing test validity, Instructional Rounds as Professional Learning, education policy and teachers' perceptions of time and the impending impact of learning personalization/Big Data on schools. He is the Australasian editor of *The Journal of Education Policy* and an associate editor of *Discourse: Studies in the Cultural Politics of Education*. He is also the editor of two book series, Local/Global Issues in Education, and Deleuze and Education Research. Recent books include *The Global Education Race: Taking the Measure of PISA and International Testing*, and *National Testing in Schools: An Australian Assessment*.

Antoni Verger is associate professor at the Department of Sociology of the Universitat Autònoma de Barcelona, Spain, and general deputy of the

European Masters program Education Policies for Global Development. A former postdoctoral fellow at the Amsterdam Institute for Social Science Research, Verger's research analyses the relationship between global governance institutions and education policy. He has specialized in the study of public–private partnerships, quasi-market mechanisms and accountability policies in education. Currently, he coordinates the ERC-funded project REFORMED – Reforming Schools Globally: A Multiscalar Analysis of Autonomy and Accountability Policies in the Education Sector. He is one of the lead editors of the *Journal of Education Policy* and of the *World Yearbook of Education*.

Andrew Wilkins is reader in Education at the University of East London, UK. His research interests are in areas of sociology of governance and sociology of education with a focus on risk, bureaucracy, democracy and technocratic cultures and their influence on education structures and processes. He is a member of several editorial boards including Critical Studies in Education, Journal for Critical Education Policy Studies, British Journal of Sociology of Education, and Journal of Applied Social Theory. His book *Modernising School Governance: Corporate Planning and Expert Handling in State Education* (2016) was awarded joint-second prize by the Society for Educational Studies (SES) for books published in 2016.

Ben Williamson is lecturer and researcher in the areas of education technology and policy at the University of Stirling, UK. His recent research has focused on digital data in educational policy and practice, the role of Silicon Valley entrepreneurs and venture philanthropists in education reform, and on the cross-sector policy networks that introduced computer science and coding into the school curriculum. His book *Big Data in Education: The Digital Future of Learning, Policy and Practice* was published in 2017.

Abbreviations

A4L	Access 4 Learning
ACER	Australian Council for Educational Research
ACT	Actor-Network Theory
AIEd	AI in education
CDDAAL	Center for Digital Data, Analytics and Adaptive Learning
CICED	Center for International Cooperation in Education Development
DIBELS	Dynamic Indicators of Basic Early Literacy Skills
EAOKO	Eurasian Association for Educational Assessment
EGRA	Early Grade Reading Assessment
EIU	Economist Intelligence Unit
ETIN	Education Technology Industry Network
FTAA	Free Trade Area of the Americas
FTI	Education for All Fast-Track Initiative
GAL	Global Alliance for Monitoring Learning
GMS	Grant Maintained Schools
HMI	Her Majesty's Inspectorate
ICT	Information and Communication Technology
IEA	International Association for the Evaluation of Educational Achievement
ITS	Intelligent Tutoring Systems
LA	Local Authority
LMS	Local Management of Schools

LSA   Learning Services Architecture

MAT   Multi Academy Trust

NAPLAN   National Assessment Program – Literacy and Numeracy

NCLB   No Child Left Behind

NCSL   National College of School Leadership

NLE   National Leaders of Education

NPM   New Public Management

NPQH   National Professional Qualification for Headteachers

NSIP   National Schools Interoperability program

OECD   Organisation for Economic Co-operation and Development

Ofsted   The Office for Standards in Education, Children's Services
               and Skills

PAL   Network People's Action for Learning Network

PISA   Programme for International Assessment

PISA-D   PISA for Development

PLE   Personalized Learning Environments

QUANGO   Quasi-Autonomous Non-Government Organization

READ   Russia Education Aid for Development Trust Fund

RTC   Russian Training Center

SABER   Systems Approach to Better Education Results

SACMEQ   Southern and Eastern African Consortium for Monitoring
               Educational Quality

SAM   Student Achievements' Monitoring

SDG   United Nations Sustainable Development Goal

SIF   Schools Interoperability Framework

SIIA   Software & Information Industry Association

SKU	Slovak Chamber of Teachers
SPB	Student Information System Baseline Profile
TBA	Test-Based Accountability
TIMSS	Trends in International Mathematics and Science Study
TSA	Teaching School Alliances
UNDP	United Nations Development Programme
UNESCO	United Nations Educational, Scientific and Cultural Organization
USAID	United States Agency for International Development
WoS	Web of Science
ZMOS	Association of Slovak Towns and Villages

Foreword

Kenneth J. Saltman

Around the world, democracy is under siege and democratic forms of education governance have been severely threatened. Threats to democracy have involved the extreme concentration of wealth among the elite and widening economic inequality, the rise of authoritarian politics and cultural projects antithetical to critical intellectual culture, public culture, social theory and democratic dispositions for dialogue, dissent, debate and curiosity. The fate of education governance matters for not just the quality of education institutions but their capacity to foster and contribute to democratic, just and equal societies.

In the past thirty years, on a global scale, the rich have succeeded in concentrating their ownership and control of wealth. As economic inequality has expanded, Keynesian welfare state protections that ameliorated the vicissitudes of markets have been dismantled and privatized, capital has been deregulated and union power has been weakened drastically. Public goods and services including schools have been privatized. These economic changes represent the political triumphs of ruling class people as well as a shift in ownership and control of public institutions. In education, these changes have been expressed through neo-liberal privatization and corporate managerial reforms that effectively transfer ownership and control of schools from the public to rich private individuals and corporations. This redistribution of ownership and control has a dire effect on democracy by conveying education governance from citizens to investors and market ideologues. As well, in the post-Fordist era social and cultural reproduction has been revised in ways that repurpose the use of public education for the pursuit of profit. In the Fordist era, public schools in part compelled the public to subsidize the reproduction of the labour force by teaching skills and know-how in ways that ideologically reproduced relations of production. Fordist schooling represented a long-term investment in making workers whose future labour could be exploited. In the post-Fordist era, students have become short-term profit opportunities whose bodies can be exploited through contracting and privatization. These profit-seeking activities have heavily involved standardization of pedagogy and curriculum and the merging of techniques of Foucauldian disciplinary self-regulation with a Deleuzian 'societies of control' biopolitical management of life and bodies.

These radical economic transformations have been accompanied by and depended upon a radical cultural symbolic project operating on a global scale that has reimagined society as a private domain and eviscerated the very concept of the public, projected the individual as primarily an economic actor, and promoted the ideologies of corporate culture, social Darwinism and consumerism under the aegis of an allegedly efficient and competitive market. Markets, in this neo-liberal ideological perspective, will replace the allegedly bureaucratic and inefficient public sector with shiny market efficiencies and there is no alternative. Under the guise of clear-cutting stodgy and inefficient public bureaucracy, a new market-style bureaucracy has been rolled out in multiple domains including education promoted by corporate philanthropies, consultancies and think tanks. In education, the radical cultural shift involved a renewal of positivist ideology linked to transmissional models of pedagogy and test-based – 'accountability' tied to for-profit business. A resurgent positivism has involved a hostility to theory in higher education, teacher education and K–12 schooling as well as a turn to radical empiricism. Education governance has become modelled heavily on corporate culture and military models of authority. These are highly hierarchical and anti-democratic models of institutional governance.

These radical economic and cultural shifts have been joined by a radical political shift that attacks democratic governance in both formal politics and throughout social institutions. Rightist movements are unified in their efforts to roll back liberal and social democratic traditions and institutions as the distinction between public and private sphere has been eroded. Neo-liberal post-politics effaced competing values and ideologies under the guise of a falsely neutral managerialism. Rising political authoritarianism (neo-liberalism with the gloves off) is imbricated with and fuelled by a broader crisis of knowledge, truth and education that is defined against both theory and democratic dispositions.

The contemporary crisis of knowledge, truth and fact is characterized by a contradiction in education policy and practice between, on the one hand, an endlessly espoused imperative for empirical data (data-driven teaching, data-driven leadership, data-driven policy) and, on the other hand, the pursuit of policies that are unsupported by empirical data and rely instead upon market metaphors and baseless assertion of truth – chartering, vouchers, turnaround and portfolio models, to name a few. This contradiction with regard to knowledge, fact, truth and education I call 'the alienation of fact'. This contradiction can be comprehended through the legacy of positivist ideology and a hostility to theory: positivism treats truth as a collection of facts that speak for themselves and do not require theory or context. The legacy of positivism makes facts appear almighty yet unmoored and estranged. This contradictory understanding of facts explains the mistaken faith in data 'driving practice' in multiple fields including policing, education, journalism and technology. The positivist legacy represents antipathy for comprehension of how theories undergird facts, organize facts and make facts meaningful through practices of interpretation. Facts appear omnipotent and ungrounded, a mystical inexplicable force. In such a context, theory, argumentation and evidence are replaced by an aura of authority that is frequently grounded through reference to decontextualized numbers, essentialized bodies, institutional authority and cults of personality.

As Theodor Adorno observed, the allure of numbers in the era of positivism is a false promise of certainty and solidity in a world experienced as floating and unmoored by everything being subject to market exchange and equivalencies. If fact comes estranged from theory, history or argument, then fact appears as the result of emphatic assertion. This contradiction around fact and the positivist legacy explains not only the emergence of education profiteering that is unsupported by evidence and the lie of disinterested objectivity and neutrality at the centre of the testing, standards and accountability movement in education but also the replacement of empirical evidence with faith, particularly in market metaphorics. The alienation of fact also explains the contemporary broader crisis of truth found, for example, in the growth of conspiracy, the capacity of politicians to dismiss empirically verifiable truths as 'fake news', the problem of allegedly disinterested, objective and neutral journalism, and the authoritarian tendency of equating the authority of a truth claim with the social authority of the claimant. The alienation of fact helps explain how public sector pillage is increasingly interwoven with the recent tendency of politics to ground assertions in numbers, bodies and essentialized identities – false guarantees of certainty due to their association with materiality. The false guarantees of material grounding have a particular attraction when evidence, argument and theory have been wiped out and fact appears to come from nowhere. Rising material precarity amplifies the collective demand for definitive explanations just as the alienation of fact undermines people's use of knowledge for agency. As a consequence, people are turning to irrational social explanations that appear to be grounded specifically in forms that falsely promise certainty and solidity – especially numbers and bodies (essentialized identities).

Social theory and the institutionalization of it in critical education projects are a crucial antidote to the alienation of fact and hostility to theory. The direction of education governance is a manifestation of broader political governance trends but it is also a force for the production of counter-hegemonic social relations and formations. How do we comprehend education governance in relation to these broader radical shifts in economics, culture and politics?

First, we should recognize that neo-liberal privatization and deregulation represent de-democratization of education systems and roll-out of systems of hierarchical control.

The move away from egalitarian forms of education governance and towards hierarchical forms of governance takes a number of forms including the militarization of schools, the corporatization of schools and the employment of technologies (like adaptive learning and personalized learning) that falsely frame hierarchical control as automated and beyond human agency while concealing particular interests and ideologies that are enacted through these falsely disinterested efficacy reforms.

Educative institutions have been organized to a tremendous extent in ways that undermine democratic social relationships: from authoritarian pedagogies and approaches to knowledge such as transmission models of learning and competitive individualism, to authoritarian teacher–student and administrator relations, to standardization and the replacement of human agency with the machinery of bureaucracy and the replacement of agency with machines themselves. Educative institutions, however, do not have to defeat democracy. They can instead model democracy by being organized in egalitarian forms. They can be places that foster egalitarian social relations and modes of learning as well as democratic dispositions for questioning, curiosity, dissent and dialogue. They can also be places in which social theory plays a central role in giving students, teachers and administrators the means to analyse and interpret truth claims in relation to power, politics, ethics and history. Education governance arrangements can foster such critical education practices that create the conditions for broader egalitarian social relations. Such critical education practices can also use social theory to facilitate, as C. Wright Mills and Zygmunt Bauman emphasize, the translation of private problems into public problems and counter the ways that public problems get translated into private worries.

Social theory ought to be comprehended as a crucial instrument for democratic forms of collective governance – a means of understanding and acting together. If social theory allows people to think about the education governance practices that they do and participate in, then it would be valuable to identify some of the 'techniques' that are employed to keep people from thinking about education governance and the kinds of values, ideologies and social relations that are promoted by those governance arrangements. In other words, social theory allows people to think about how some of these hierarchical forms are employed to delink understanding from the possibilities for collective control and agency. Some of the most significant of these anti-thinking techniques include claims to neutral, universally valuable and disinterested forms of governance that claim 'efficacy'. The employment of standardized testing and test-based accountability is used to justify often market-based and anti-democratic governance reforms. Here numbers are alleged to represent the truth of quality and progress, yet the numbers conceal the values, ideologies of the knowledge on the tests and the social positions of those who made the tests. In other words, the tests conceal the values, ideologies and cultural and class positions of those social actors in the position to administer and tabulate the tests. Test-based accountability like grades does not only conceal the unequal system of cultural capital distribution but also participate in misframing the unequal distribution of life chances as merit, talent and hard work.

Just as all practices are undergirded by theoretical assumptions, all education governance practices and organizations are undergirded by theoretical assumptions as well. Social theory provides educators, administrators and other cultural workers with the tools to interpret experience and social phenomena, reconceptualize them and act thoughtfully. Theory allows people to draw from traditions of thought to think about what they do, to denounce current arrangements that are unjust and to announce alternatives that theory helps them to imagine. Theory helps us not only to solve problems and answer questions but also to take apart the questions that we are asking and examine the assumptions behind our own questions. Take, for example, the commonly posed question of how schooling can 'close the achievement gap' – a concept that is linked to both test-based accountability and justifications for education privatization. More important than answering this question is taking the question apart to show what is falsely presumed and in fact concealed by the question, for example, that knowledge is not transmitted and consumed, that knowledge 'deficits' presume that knowledge and culture are not contested and hence political, that there are falsely universalized knowledge norms that are applied to everyone, that knowledge claims are generated by particular people who come from particular class and cultural positions and so on.

Social theory helps us reveal what is often concealed in dominant rhetoric and ideology. Sometimes what is concealed is the relationship between education governance and the broader social forces and systems that produce it. One of the most crucial uses of social theory to examine education governance involves contextualizing education governance arrangements in terms of the broader social forces and structures that produce these arrangements as well as the material and symbolic interests that drive the actors who participate in these arrangements.

A number of chapters in this volume address what Stephen Ball has termed the shift from *government to governance* in education. The shift recognizes that as a consequence of neo-liberal globalization the governing power of the nation state has become at least partially replaced by other education governing institutions – corporations, philanthropies, consultancies, think tanks, non-profit organizations and non-governmental organizations. Some contributors here ask the reader to see the networks between these extra-state organizations and the discourses that they produce and are produced by as governors. This volume suggests as well that as a consequence of technological development, new education forces that represent privatization and deregulation, such as data analytics, artificial intelligence and personalized learning software, govern education or rather participate in an education governance matrix. The movements for test-based accountability and market-based reform appear as governance forces.

As the editors and some contributors emphasize, education governance is subject to struggle and contestation. This collection raises some crucial questions about the relationship between social theory and education governance: 1) How do we comprehend struggles over education governance within broader political, economic and cultural forces and contests? In part this is a question about determining the objects of critical analysis. This is also a question about comprehending education governance as both a structural effect and a potential force for remaking these aspects of the social by agents; 2) Who exactly is struggling over education governance and what are they struggling for? This question is not only about agents of education governance and their agency but also about the inevitability that practices enact particular social visions and political values; 3) What should be the points of intervention for these agents – scholars, teachers, students, administrators and other culture and knowledge workers – to use social theory to foster just, egalitarian, emancipatory and genuinely democratic forms of education and social governance? This question is about how people can do good cultural education work to intervene in public problems and academic discourse about those problems; and 4) What theories or whose theories should we appropriate to theorize the subject, the society and relations and social and education governance?

Social movements and activism are necessary but insufficient responses to the present crises of democracy, social and education governance. Social theory is a crucial tool that needs to be integrated into educative institutions and social movements to enable collective agency by allowing individuals, as Henry Giroux advocates, to interpret social contexts, institutions and their own self-formation such that they can intervene socially. Social theory is necessary to enable students, teachers, administrators, scholars and activists to comprehend and act reflectively in ways that expand egalitarian and just forms of governance. This volume provokes a valuable and provocative dialogue for just this kind of necessary thought and reflective action.

Introduction: Conceptualizing Education Governance: Framings, Perspectives and Theories

Andrew Wilkins and Antonio Olmedo

The term 'education governance' is one of the most cited concepts in contemporary parlance used to describe and understand changing patterns in the organization of education in the twenty-first century. It dominates the vernacular of big supranational organizations such as the European Community and Free Trade Area of the Americas (FTAA), the United Nations Development Programme (UNDP), the Organisation for Economic Co-operation and Development (OECD) and the World Bank. It functions as a key reference point for national governments, state authorities, local governments, municipalities and regional offices, provincial and district departments, parastatal agencies, and school boards. Moreover, it forms the everyday language of specialists and 'experts' (governors, leaders, consultants, inspectors, auditors and business partners) involved in practices of appraising, credentialing, brokering, mediation, monitoring, and purchasing or commissioning. Yet despite such pervasive use, the term 'education governance' lacks precise meaning due to its polyvalence as a *policy strategy, political-economic project, mode of intervention, problematizing activity, vehicle of empowerment, scaling technique* and *discourse* or *normative description*.

Polyvalence

Such polyvalence is indicative of a slippery concept that also speaks to different sets of grievances, discontents and hopes. Education governance is experienced by some as a part of the dangerous and mischievous practice of the 'hidden hand' of the market or neoliberalism more generally, while those who fear the tyranny of hierarchies and are distrustful of top-down systems celebrate it as an empowering tool for democratic change, innovation and improved effectiveness or transparency. Education governance makes possible new institutional forms and practices that subvert and hollow out traditional political structures and processes, including the discretionary powers of civil servants and elected councillors, and therefore works to 'disable or disenfranchise or circumvent some of the established policy actors and agencies' (Ball 2008: 748). On this account, education governance creates opportunities for new agents and agencies to intervene in and profit from the delivery of public policy, from social enterprises to businesses and charities. On the other hand, education governance is shaped by decentralizing education reforms designed to increase horizontal accountability and empower communities and citizens as 'intermediary associations' (Ranson et al. 2005: 359) who can successfully hold others to account.

According to Rose (1999), governance more generally has been traditionally approached from two different, though interlinked, angles. The first one, what he calls the *normative* theme, tackles the problem of determining whether specific political strategies represent instances of *good versus bad* governance. According to its advocates, most notoriously the World Bank, *good* governance implies less government, or at least the exercise of government power through steering rather than rowing, and greater privatization to scale back the political apparatus and introduce new agents as managers and overseers of public provision. The second approach to governance studies is *descriptive*. Here, governance is understood as the resulting product of the interplay of old and new policy actors, which takes the shape of 'self-organizing policy networks' (Rose 1999: 17). Studies within this area attempt to describe the organization, structures and operations of the multiple and complex exchanges that constitute and reshape such policy networks.

Unable to concur with any of those approaches and adding to this polyphony, or at least with the intention of identifying a running thread, we loosely characterize education governance as a heuristic device, discourse and technology of government. In this sense, we want to avoid any comfortable domestication of education governance within a single definition or elevate it to a fixed concept. Instead, we propose to view education governance in Deleuzian terms as a 'modulation', 'like a self-transmuting moulding continually changing from one moment to the next, or like a sieve whose mesh varies from one point to another' (Deleuze 1995: 178–179).

Without claiming to be exhaustive, this book reflects our attempt to think through these different possibilities for framing and debating conceptualizations of education governance with a view to offering readers a set of entry points and orienting positions for engaging with education governance as an object of critical inquiry and a tool or method of research. The point of this mapping exercise is, first, to trace the systems of signification through which education governance is co-opted and translated into practice and acquires meaning as a dominant or contested concept. This includes a focus on the different stakes, dilemmas, motives, interests and normative commitments mobilized through discourses and programmes of education governance. Second, by mapping specific trends and tendencies in this way, the book serves an important pedagogic function, namely to provide researchers with practical tools, empirical examples and conceptual resources to help situate and enrich their understanding and analyses of education governance.

Struggles over meaning

Education governance can be reduced to something procedural and programmatic – a technique or technology of government, for example. The introduction of new public management systems captures the intensity and encroachment of these techniques and technologies 'on the ground' where they appear deeply ingrained in the everyday practices inhabited and performed by frontline staff in schools. Public management systems work to reconfigure the internal dynamic within schools through redefining the roles of senior and middle school managers; embedding new forms of accountability that bolster choice and competition; setting priorities and directives that complement new provision models, key among them being charter schools, academies and free schools; and rearticulating meanings and practices of professionalism, professional judgement or 'success', now intimately linked to performance pay indicators. Viewed in another way, education governance can be conceptualized as a field of contestation where different interests and motives conflict, collide and sometimes converge to produce struggles over meaning that involve choosing between values of an incommensurable kind. School governance, for example (not to be confused with the broader, more multifaceted term 'education governance'), aims at building relations of trust between schools and various stakeholders through empowering members of the public, be they community members, parents, teachers, staff members, students or business leaders, to bring lay and professional judgements to bear upon the actions of those who run schools, namely head teachers and middle leaders (Karlsson 2002; Prieto-Flores et al. 2017; Wilkins 2016). Governance, therefore, is underpinned by decisions and judgements that are framed by norms and values: 'Implicitly or explicitly, governance means choosing between them' (Kooiman and Jentoft 2009: 818).

Studies of education governance therefore span and become inflected through different kinds of empirical and conceptual work, as judiciously theorized and evidenced by the contributing authors to this book. The result is a rich resource for thinking through possibilities for engaging with education governance at the level of theory and practice. Following a Foucauldian toolbox approach, this is best achieved, we argue, through combining a plurality of perspectives, analytical strategies and research approaches, thus aligning education governance more closely and rigorously to an interdisciplinary field of critical inquiry and scholarship.

In this sense, the book is a first approximation of the multiplicity of meanings shaping education governance in policy and practical terms. Moreover, it demonstrates the efficacy of using social theory to 'capture' such multiplicity, even if only provisionally and tendentially, and to develop theoretically robust approaches to tracing the configuration and dynamics of specific policy programmes, discourses, objects, practices, relations, subjectivities and their conditions and effects within 'spatio-temporal fixes' (Jessop and Sum 2016: 108). But theory, however fashionable and fanciful, must be practical in the sense that it enriches our understanding of the events, processes and discursive categories we experience and relate to, even if only temporarily and partially, and shores up possibilities for intervention and change. This is important if education governance is to avoid 'hypostatization' – excess theory and theorizing – where it risks becoming a detached signifier devoid of critical purchase as a model for praxis in the transformation of society and individuals.

At the same time, our approach to education governance is 'diagnostic' rather than 'descriptive', with the aim to develop

> an open and critical relation to strategies for governing, attentive to their presuppositions, their assumptions, their exclusions, their naiveties and their knaveries, their regimes of vision and their spots of blindness. (Rose 1999: 19)

To do so, it is paramount to avoid making any rigid claims to the precise meaning and practice of education governance in order to maintain its flexibility and receptivity to be adapted and revised over time. Hence the importance of theory to this project: 'the absence of theory leaves the researcher prey to unexamined, unreflexive preconceptions and dangerously naïve ontological and epistemological a prioris' (Ball 1995: 265–266). Naturally, therefore, we regard education governance as a continually evolving, mutating project – not just for governments, parastatal authorities and communities, but for researchers too. In what follows we tentatively sketch the different ways education governance can be conceptualized and researched in studies of education structures and education more generally.

The governance turn

Education governance can be broadly characterized as a response to the failure of state and market forms of welfare planning (Jessop 2000). Libertarians and neoconservatives, for example, tend to be critical of top-down government to the extent it exerts a limiting, constraining effect on the capacity of organizations to self-innovate and the liberty of individuals to pursue their own self-interest and freedom (state failure). Conversely, social justice activists and those broadly situated on 'the Left' draw attention to the fallacy that citizens as consumers of welfare services share equal opportunities and capacities to secure their own competitive self-advantage in a field of choice (market failure). Education governance is a *movement or trend* that seeks to overturn some of these failures by intervening to create devolved systems of education planning managed through the interaction, cooperation and co-influence of multiple stakeholders (Sørensen and Torfing 2007). The 'governance turn' in education (Ball 2009: 537) therefore designates new modes of government and governing where power is not confined to the state or to the market but is exercised through a plethora of networks, partnerships and policy communities who 'consensually' work with stakeholders to produce more flexible, fluid, diverse and responsive forms of service delivery.

From this perspective, education governance describes a *policy strategy* for governing acentred, polycentric systems of education – that is, education systems in which central steering mechanisms at the federal, state or regional level are supplemented, substituted even, by self-organization or 'heterarchy' (Olmedo et al. 2013). A further role of education governance concerns the replacement of the formal authority of government with improved conditions for the development of informal relations of 'trust', diplomacy and cooperation between welfare providers, users, funders and regulators (Rhodes 1997). This has deep implications for education policy research which is required to focus on 'the complexity of interacting forces rather than assuming that governmental practice in a plurality of sites flows uniformly' (Newman 2007: 54). Education governance therefore has as its focus the problematics of governing highly fragmented, devolved systems of education planning where power is not applied at particular points or reducible to the actions of a single actor or apparatus. Instead power tends to be disaggregated, co-produced and interdependent among numerous actors and organizations (Stoker 1998) to complement the distribution of power outwards to parastatal organizations (inspection, credentialing and commissioning bodies) and downwards to communities and stakeholders, thereby undercutting the costs and constraints associated with top-heavy bureaucracy and traditional government structures, including 'clunky command or instrumental contract relationships' (Davies and Spicer 2015: 226).

Complexity, anxiety and mistrust

This is not to say that education governance as a policy strategy is not concerned with the governing of centralized education systems and their formal operations and activities, typically those in 'late-developing' countries, for example. 'Complexity' is not restricted to the vicissitudes and exigencies that accompany decentralized education system planning, namely coordination through a mixture of hierarchies, markets and networks (Crouch 2011). Indeed, the goal of education governance more generally is to enhance organizational preparedness and response to complexity in all its forms (Olmedo 2017). 'Governance failure' (Jessop 2000) therefore is a recurring problem in education systems where significant instructional, financial and operational powers have shifted away from the centre and shifted towards schools and those charged with the responsibility of running schools, often bypassing traditional policy actors in the process, say, municipal authorities and local governments.

The decommissioning of certain intermediate structures and activities in favour of power being devolved directly to schools and communities has also given rise to a regulatory gap (or 'missing middle') formerly occupied by government-employed authorities and actors. Related to this are heightened government concerns over the suitability of schools and their 'governors' to discharge their responsibilities as assessors and appraisers at a time of increased decentralization and 'disintermediation' (Lubienski 2014: 424). (Here we mobilize the term 'governor' in a very general sense to refer to school-based managers and overseers of education, from leaders and trustees to business directors and parent governors.) Ironically, then, the shift from government to governance has ameliorated some anxieties (the spectre of 'state monopoly', for example, see Wilkins 2017) while intensifying others, namely how best to govern the governors. Education governance captures elements of a neurotic government (distrustful, anxious, maladjusted) unable to fully accept the vagaries of its own reform. Hence governments in favour of decentralized education planning typically pursue forms of 'hard governance', 'things like target-setting, performance management, benchmarks and indicators, data use to foster competition, and so on' (Clarke and Ozga 2012: 1). Education governance is a 'self-contradictory form of regulation-in-denial' (Peck 2010: xiii).

On this account, education governance can be described as a 'technology of mistrust' (Rose 1999: 154) since it concerns the struggle to maintain control in the face of 'contradictory systems, contested positions and contentious subjects' (Clarke 2004: 3). But rather than concede incomplete and imperfect control, governments typically pursue techniques and strategies that may enhance their capacity to govern at a distance. In some cases, the generation of attrition and compliance through inspection, managerial deference and high-stakes testing is monitored and regulated by third-party organizations and agents to strengthen accountability to the centre. Education governance therefore entails elements of 'soft governance', namely 'attraction-drawing people in to take part in processes of mediation, brokering and "translation" and embedding self-governance and steering at a distance through these processes and relations' (Clarke and Ozga 2012: 1).

Freedom through control

The involvement of charities, businesses and social enterprises as new policy actors does not always undermine traditional organization structures and bureaucratic modes of governance, however. Soft governance appears to be less about disrupting state power or curtailing the encroachment of state officialdom and more about upholding the dominance of certain rule-bound hierarchies and building legitimacy with the government through extra-governmental relations and practices that sustain practices of 'extrastatecraft' (Easterling 2014). On this account, Davies (2011: 2) argues that it is more appropriate to talk of 'governance hegemony' and the persistence of 'unwarranted assertions and silences of dominant paradigms'. The broader aims of education governance therefore concern the optimization of techniques and strategies by which subjects may be successfully called upon and incentivized to regulate themselves voluntarily in accordance with certain directives, priorities or provisos (funding agreements, national targets, contractual obligations, statutory guidelines, pedagogical strategies and performance benchmarks). This includes bringing the gaze of government to bear more firmly upon the actions of others and their horizon of intelligibility and morality or 'common sense', namely what counts as 'good', 'fair' or 'just'. This is evident when we look at the formation of education systems where 'deregulation' and 'decentralization' are drivers of reform.

In Australia, the Independent Public Schools (IPS) initiative claims to free schools up from the constraints of top-heavy bureaucracy so they may govern themselves, but which introduces further regulation through tight centralized accountability made possible through a competitive performative culture that compels and obligates school leaders to acquiesce to the demands of the National Assessment Program – Literacy and Numeracy (NAPLAN) and the enterprise form more generally (Gobby 2013). These forms of intervention can be characterized as 'key fidelity techniques in new strategies of government' (Rose 1999: 152): they are integral to the discursive, political work of joining up external evaluation and self-evaluation with the aim of 'linking political objectives and person conduct' (ibid.: 149). Similarly, the academies programme in England aims to extricate state-funded schools from the politics and bureaucracy of local government so that they become 'state-funded independent schools', but which also intervenes to place limits on meanings and practices of 'good governance' so that, despite their 'autonomy' and professional discretion, schools are amendable to the statistical mapping, administration and scrutiny of government and non-government authorities (Wilkins 2016).

Supranational organizations like the OECD administer the Programme for International Assessment (PISA) to achieve similar results on a global scale. The purpose of PISA is to collect and compare data on student achievement from different countries to enable national governments to determine their international economic competitiveness. These global testing regimes constitute a new form of biopolitics and 'metapolicy', steering educational systems in particular directions with great effects in schools and on teacher practices, on curricula, as well as upon student learning and experiences of school' (Lingard, Martino and Rezai-Rashti 2016: 540). These reforms can therefore be described as the function of 'introducing additional freedom through additional control and intervention' (Foucault 2008: 67). Education governance involves 'improving steering functions at the centre' and 'improving the quality regulation', as indicated in the OECD report 'Governance in Transition' (1995). On this understanding, education governance is a *political-economic project* that echoes and redeems elements of 'neoliberal governmentality': a 'flowing and flexible conglomeration of calculative notions, strategies and technologies aimed at fashioning populations and people' (Wacquant 2012: 69). As Eagleton-Pierce (2014: 16) astutely observes, the term 'governance' vacillates between

> the intuitive sense of hierarchical ordering (long tied to state rule) and the modern appeal to horizontal networking . . .Governance thus seems to be a kind of bridging concept between the bureaucratic and post-bureaucratic visions of politics.

Complexity regulation

On this account, education governance can be described as a *mode of intervention* for 'coping with complexity' (Jessop 2003: 3), perhaps because complexity and plurality are not conducive to regulation. Indeed, complexity is counterproductive to regulation inasmuch as it undermines the capacity of external authorities (regulators and funders) to hold schools to account for specific purposes, agendas or priorities. Any person, process or unquantifiable outcome that resists or evades capture from the 'lure of the explicit' (Green 2011: 49) and the 'cult of efficiency' (Stein 2001: 7) is counterintuitive to a system of complexity regulation. Complexity therefore needs to be grasped at the level of 'representation' and 'meta-analyses' so that it is amenable to cognitive, conceptual, visual and statistical mapping by league tables, data-driven audit cultures, accountability infrastructures, comparative-competitive frameworks and standardized testing regimes.

Education governance functions to superficially 'stabilize' elements of complexity within interoperable, complementary systems of signification and quantification, thus helping to secure the always unstable and provisional as navigable and calculable sites of 'commensurability, equivalence and comparative performance' (Lingard, Martino and Rezai-Rashti 2016: 542). In other words, education governance strives to render the internal operation of schools calculable and 'appropriable' – that is, amenable to rituals of verification and instruments of objective measurement so that they can be replicated across organizations and contexts and compared for the purpose of inscribing organizations within systems and sorting mechanisms of ranking and grades. Described in another way, these forms of intervention constitute 'metagovernance' which, according to Marsh (2011: 43), 'is a process by which the state shapes both the particular form that hierarchy, networks or markets, as modes of governance, take within a policy area/political process, and the way in which each form articulates with other forms of governance'.

Interconnectivity and problematization

Education governance therefore is also a *scaling technique* since it works to produce greater interconnectivity and overlap between the local, the regional and the national, but more broadly and ambitiously aims to produce alignments and interdependency between national and international or global education priorities (Lingard, Martino and Rezai-Rashti 2016). The production of statistical data on the educational performance of different national education systems not only helps to digitally render diverse education systems 'inscribable and comparable in numerical form' (Rose 1999: 153); they also create new opportunities for policy intervention, profit-making by large multinational corporations and the designation of 'problems' and potential solutions (Williamson 2015). Viewed in another way, education governance works to reduce complexity to causal relations between units in a fluid chain reaction, with the implication that diagnosis and programmatic solutions are possible for the purpose of intervening upon and even predicting specific 'problems'. Education governance is the use of post hoc evaluation to determine efficacy of knowledge to achieving specified goals or principles and enhancing different accountability frameworks, for example.

On this account, education governance is a 'problematizing activity' (Rose and Miller 1992: 181) and therefore more than a doctrine and set of rules about how to cope with complexity and respond to problems. It is a *discourse* or *normative description* about 'what works' and what is thinkable and practical to achieving specific outcomes. Education governance works to constitute 'problems' rather than simply reflect them (Fischer 2003). From this perspective, education governance needs to be differentiated from education management which has as its focus the implementation of policy and an operational focus on the mobilization of resources and staff to achieve a set of predetermined goals and outcomes. In contrast, education governance is concerned with the design of parameters and disciplinary frameworks under which behaviour management and administrative systems operate successfully, sometimes located within a 'neo-corporatist ideology' (Fusarelli and Johnson 2004: 118).

Checks, balances and self-regulation

Education governance therefore relates to the development of strategies, techniques and frameworks (training and evaluative tools, for example) to help embed self-governance and steer actors towards fulfilling the requirements of 'good' or 'strong' governance, for example. This may include a focus on improved resource allocation and monitoring, resource-use efficiency, digital data use, performance appraisals, professional guidelines, quality controls, and target setting to future-proof the long-term sustainability of schools as 'high-reliability' organizations (Reynolds 2010: 18). Education governance is about strengthening the transparency (or visibility) of the internal operations of schools through engendering a culture of evaluation and self-review that makes use of optimizing-information-gathering technologies such as data tracking instruments to capture, digitize and make 'known' staff and pupil performance.

Such developments are designed to enhance upward and downward accountability to different stakeholders through processes of coordination, priority-setting and consensus-building as well as to ensure organizations act prudently, professionally, morally, efficiently, and legally. On this account, education governance is designed as a *vehicle of empowerment* since it concerns developing the capacities and skills of others to self-regulate and pursue their own freedom in the absence of any overarching authority or safeguards, albeit self-regulate in line with certain priorities, prerogatives and provisos. Moreover, education governance constitutes a *heuristic device* or *method of analysis* which can be put to use by researchers in their studies of education systems and their concomitant relations, practices and discourses, as illustrated in the chapters that follow.

Structure of the book

Despite the pedagogic design of the book, there is no attempt here at theoretical closure and suturing the meanings and practices of education governance. In fact, one of the strengths of the chapters that follow is the different theoretical and methodological approaches taken by the authors. For instance, some authors engage with more well-established theoretical perspectives (e.g. Bourdieu, Habermas, Actor Network Theory or ANT) while others focus on specific concepts (e.g. dispositions and situations) or analytical frameworks (e.g. narrative approach or political discourse theory). Far from a criticism, we understand the multifarious epistemological and empirical approaches to education governance adopted by the different authors in this book as an attempt to problematize unidimensional and seemingly bounded exploratory research approaches; to render porous those boundaries separating different modes of explanation; and to revise and rethink the utility of traditional theoretical models that have dominated the field of education research for decades. In doing so, inconsistencies and unsteadiness may surface and become apparent. This is, from our perspective, the everyday life of the elucidative challenge of the social scientist who has chosen the wobbly and rickety intellectual terrains instead of the steady, domesticated comforts of apparently coherent schools of thoughts.

Each chapter in this book demonstrates the utility and operationalization of specific conceptual tools, theoretical frameworks and methodological approaches to generate original insight into education governance and its different operations, conditions and effects across diverse geopolitical contexts. From digital data and accountability infrastructures to public–private partnerships and inspection policy, each chapter engages with contemporary issues that can be read as both conditions and effects of education governance. Moreover, each chapter combines theory and methodologies with case study material to interlink theory and method through an exploration of real-world issues, and therefore offers readers a theoretically and empirically rich resource for thinking through the possibilities and dilemmas of researching education governance in all its multifaceted, multi-scalar forms.

The book is divided into four parts in order to bring some thematic coherence (data regimes, evaluation regimes, knowledge regimes and institutional regimes), although the chapters could have been arranged differently according to other organizational logics. In Part 1, Williamson focuses on the growth of digital data-processing technologies and non-governmental organizations in processes of education policy and governance. Developing the concept of 'algorithmic governance', Williamson analyses Pearson's efforts to position itself as a site of expertise in the generation and analysis of educational data and as an authoritative source for narrating its meanings. Thompson tackles what he calls the 'promise of digital learning personalisation'. Using Steigler's work, Thompson discusses some of the wide-ranging implications of learning personalization and related technologies – learning analytics and Big Data – to pedagogy and the ritualized practices that typically make up teacher–learner interaction. Finally, within this part, Sellar and Gulson examine the development of data infrastructure in Australian schools and school systems. Drawing on infrastructure studies, post-structuralism and interpretivist governance studies, Sellar and Gulson show, on the one hand, how data infrastructures in Australian schooling are producing a standardized national space of education governance and new market opportunities for commercial providers. On the other hand, their analysis reveals how these very same data infrastructures are creating new opportunities for these providers to shape education governance through moral and technical narratives that operate alongside, and potentially modify, their commercial objectives.

In Part 2, 'Evaluation Regimes', Baxter's chapter focuses on the role of the quasi-autonomous non-governmental organization (or QUANGO) and how they are used by government to not only evaluate standards in education but also, through the act of inspection, govern standards in education. Using a narrative approach to reveal the tensions inherent within instruments and processes of governance, Baxter unravels the hidden discourses of inspection and the conflicted nature of school inspector's work. From a different perspective, Piattoeva tackles the ways in which global governance manifests a transnationally networked structure that builds on allies and connections to spread particular policy messages. Piattoeva asks how such a structure is held in place, how it expands and how it wields influence, and concludes by arguing that global education governance and numerical assessments co-evolve and co-produce relationally.

Part 3, 'Knowledge Regimes', opens with Papanastasiou's endeavour to explain how market discourses have become powerful shapers of education governance. Drawing on a 'critical logics approach', Papanastasiou focuses on England's school landscape, which has steadily become a quasi-market steeped in the promotion of individual choice and self-interest. The chapter considers the impact of market discourses on education governance and highlights how a critical logics approach reveals possibilities for resisting or destabilizing the hegemonic grip of the market on education. Within this part, Verger and Parcerisa offer an analysis of test-based accountability (TBA) as an emergent powerful device to steer public services at a distance. TBA allows the state to retain regulatory powers over the broader range of education actors that operate in increasingly complex and multilayered education systems, for example. Verger and Parcerisa also demonstrate how international organizations promote the use of TBA to achieve different, sometimes conflicting, sets of goals and outcomes, thus pointing to the different sets of interests, motives and stakes served by these policy technologies. Finally, Santa Cruz Grau and Cabalin offer an account of the mass media as a key site where the production, circulation and contestation of education policy discourses takes place. According to Santa Cruz Grau and Cabalin, the process of news structuring is defined by the interrelationships between the rationale of the journalistic profession, the characteristics of the media field and the powerful interests of the dominant elites. Moreover, in a context of growing societal mediatization, this dynamic appears to affect processes of education governance through legitimizing those voices that bolster a neoliberalized education agenda.

Kaščák and Pupala open Part 4, 'Institutional Regimes', with an exploration of the conditions and opportunities made available for the Slovak teaching community to engage in education governance. Based on the work of Bourdieu and developing the concept of 'participatory governance', Kaščák and Pupala explore the kinds of conditions necessary for teachers to actively engage in political debate and shape education governance. Murphy's chapter explores the relevance of Habermas to research on education governance and, in particular, research on education accountability. In Murphy's view, Habermas offers critical tools to explore the limits of accountability as well as document the damage it can cause to interpersonal relations in an education context. While his chapter highlights some of the limitations of Habermas' theory, it concludes by making a case for Habermas as an exemplar of hybridization in the field of social theory and education governance research. Closing this final part, Stevenson analyses the changing role of education leadership in the English school system following a sustained period of system reform. Stevenson claims that while governance structures associated with post-war welfarism have been progressively dismantled, a set of new actors and a more complex relationship between the state and private sector has emerged. Drawing on 'labour process theory' and a framework grounded in scientific management, he challenges the orthodoxy of a new transformational leadership in schools and argues that school leaders play a key role in advancing the 'frontier of control' whereby state and managerial authority is asserted at the expense of teachers' autonomy and their space to exercise professional judgement.

Intendedly, this book does not have a 'conclusion chapter'. This is our way of refusing to exert the 'editorial right' to have the last word. We regard education governance as something always unfinished and incomplete due to its overt political construction. Education governance is, for us, a hegemonic project and therefore continually in the making, remaking and unmaking subject to the histories, narratives and struggles of those who partake in and write it. To omit a conclusion chapter, as we have done, is to retain this open-endedness and search for impermanence and unbounded hope in the face of indissoluble truths, post-truths and authoritarian claims to 'good governance' for all.

References

Ball, S. J. 1995. 'Intellectuals or technicians? The urgent role of theory in educational studies'. *British Journal of Educational Studies* 43 (3): 255–271.

Ball, S. J. 2008. 'New philanthropy, new networks and new governance in education'. *Political Science* 56 (4): 747–765.

Ball, S. J. 2009. 'The governance turn!'. *Journal of Education Policy* 24 (5): 537–538.

Clarke, J. 2004. Subjects of doubt: In search of the unsettled and unfinished. Paper prepared for CASCA annual conference, 5–9 May, London, Ontario.

Clarke, J., and Ozga, J. 2012. Working Paper 4. Inspection as governing. Taken from http://jozga.co.uk/GBI/tag/working-paper/ (1 June 2013).

Crouch, C. 2011. *The Strange Non-Death of Neoliberalism*. Cambridge: Polity.

Davies, J. 2011. *Challenging Governance Theory: From Networks to Hegemony*. Bristol: Policy Press.

Davies, J. S., and Spicer, A. 2015. 'Interrogating networks: Towards an agnostic perspective on governance research'. *Environment and Planning C: Government and Policy* 33 (2): 223–238.

Deleuze, G. 1995. *Negotiations*. New York: Columbia University Press.

Eagleton-Pierce, M. 2014. 'The concept of governance in the spirit of capitalism'. *Critical Policy Studies* 8 (1): 5–21.

Easterling, K. 2014. *Extrastatecraft: The Power of Infrastructure Space*. London and New York: Verso.

Fischer, F. 2003. *Reframing Public Policy: Discursive Politics and Deliberative Practices*. Oxford: Oxford University Press.

Foucault, M. 1980. *Power/Knowledge: Selected Writings and Other Interviews 1972–1977*. Brighton: Wheatsheaf.

Foucault, M. 2008. *The Birth of Biopolitics: Lectures at the Collége de Franc, 1978–79*. Basingstoke: Palgrave.

Fusarelli, L. D., and Johnson, B. 2004. 'Educational governance and the new public management'. *Public Administration and Management: An Interactive Journal* 9 (2): 118–127.

Gobby, B. 2013. 'Principal self-government and subjectification: The exercise of principal autonomy in the Western Australian Independent Public Schools programme'. *Critical Studies in Education* 54 (3): 273–285.

Green, J. 2011. *Education, Professionalism and the Quest for Accountability: Hitting the Target but Missing the Point*. London: Routledge.

Jessop, B. 2000. 'The dynamics of partnership and governance failure'. In G. Stoker (ed.), *The New Politics of British Local Governance*, pp. 11–32. Basingstoke: Macmillan.

Jessop, B. 2003. Governance, governance failure, and meta-governance. Paper presented at International Seminar Polices, Governance and Innovation for Rural Areas, Universitá della Calabria, 21–23 November. Available at: http://www.ceses.cuni.cz/CESES-136-version1-3B_Governance_requisite_variety_Jessop_2002.pdf

Jessop, B., and Sum, N.-L. 2016. 'What is critical?' *Critical Policy Studies* 10 (1): 105–109.

Karlsen, G. E. 2000. 'Decentralized centralism: Framework for a better understanding of governance in the field of education'. *Journal of Education Policy* 15 (5): 525–538.

Karlsson, J. 2002. 'The role of democratic governing bodies in South African schools'. *Comparative Education* 38 (3): 327–336.

Kooiman, J., and Jentoft, S. 2009. 'Meta-governance: Values, norms and principles, and the making of hard choices'. *Public Administration* 87 (4): 818–836.

Lingard, B., Martino, W., and Rezai-Rashti, G. 2016. 'Testing regimes, accountabilities and education policy: Commensurate global and national developments'. *Journal of Education Policy* 28 (5): 539–556.

Lubienski, C. 2014. 'Re-making the middle: Dis-intermediation in international context'. *Educational Management Administration & Leadership* 42 (3): 423–440.

Marsh, D. 2011. 'The new orthodoxy: The differentiated polity model'. *Public Administration* 89 (1): 32–48.

Newman, J. 2007. 'Governance as cultural practice: Text, talk and the struggle for meaning'. In M. Bevir and F. Trentmann (eds), *Governance, Consumers and Citizens: Agency and Resistance in Contemporary Politics*, pp. 49–68. New York: Palgrave Macmillan.

OECD. 1995. *Governance in Transition: Public Management Reforms in OECD Countries*. Paris: OECD.

Olmedo, A. 2017. 'Something old, not much new, and a lot borrowed: Philanthropy, business and the changing roles of government in global education policy networks'. *Oxford Review of Education* 43 (1): 69–87.

Olmedo, A., Bailey, P. L., and Ball, S. J. 2013. 'To Infinity and beyond . . .: Heterarchical governance, the teach for all network in Europe and the making of profits and minds'. *European Educational Research Journal* 12 (4): 492–512.

Peck, J. 2010. *Constructions of Neoliberal Reason*. Oxford: Oxford University Press.

Prieto-Flores, O., Feu, J., Serra, C., and Lázaro, L. 2017. Bringing democratic governance into practice: policy enactments responding to neoliberal governance in Spanish public schools. Cambridge Journal of Education. iFirst.

Ranson, S., Arnott, M., McKeown, P., Martin, J. and Smith, P. 2005. 'The participation of volunteer citizens in school governance'. *Educational Review* 57 (3): 357–371.

Reynolds, D. 2010. *Failure Free Education? The Past, Present and Future of School Effectiveness and School Improvement*. London: Routledge.

Rhodes, R. A. W. 1997. *Understanding Governance: Policy Networks, Governance, Reflexivity, and Accountability*. Buckingham: Open University Press.

Rose, N. 1988. 'Calculable minds and manageable individuals'. *History of the Human Sciences* 1 (2): 179–200.

Rose, N. 1999. *Powers of Freedom: Reframing Political Thought*. Cambridge: Cambridge University Press.

Rose, N., and Miller, P. 1992. 'Political power beyond the state: Problematics of government'. *British Journal of Sociology* 43 (2): 173–205.

Sørensen, E., and Torfing, J. 2007. 'Governance network research: Towards a second generation'. In E. Sørensen and J. Torfing (eds), *Theories of Democratic Network Governance*, pp. 1–24. Basingstoke: Palgrave-Macmillan.

Stein, J. 2001. *The Cult of Efficiency*. Toronto: House of Anansi Press.

Stoker, G. 1998. 'Governance as theory: Five propositions'. *International Social Sciences Journal* 50 (155): 17–28.

Wacquant, L. 2012. 'Three steps to a historical anthropology of actually existing neoliberalism'. *Social Anthropology/Anthropologie Sociale* 20 (1): 66–79.

Wilkins, A. 2016. *Modernising School Governance: Corporate Planning and Expert Handling in State Education*. London: Routledge.

Wilkins, A. 2017. 'Rescaling the local: Multi-academy trusts, private monopoly and statecraft in England'. *Journal of Educational Administration and History* 49 (2): 171–185.

Williamson, B. 2015. 'Governing methods: policy innovation labs, design and data science in the digital governance of education'. *Journal of Educational Administration and History* 4 (3): 251–271.

Part One

Data Regimes

1

Digitizing Education Governance: Pearson, Real-Time Data Analytics, Visualization and Machine Intelligence

Ben Williamson

Digital technologies have become significant non-human actors in education governance. This chapter examines emerging techniques of *digital governance* in education. The global education company Pearson has become a key actor in contemporary education governance (Hogan et al. 2015), with aspirations to become a 'digital-first' company using data-processing techniques to govern educational institutions and individuals (Williamson 2016). Pearson's ambitions involve generating massive databases of educational data, producing data visualizations and utilizing real-time data analytics, machine learning algorithms and artificial intelligence to monitor, measure, make calculations and produce objective facts and knowledge about education. Its strategic business objective since 2016 has been to create a 'global digital learning platform' utilizing cloud services, data analytics and machine learning across all its products and services (Ismael 2016).

Pearson exemplifies how digital data, real-time analytics and machine intelligence are being recruited to the task of enacting education governance. Moreover, Pearson's activities in education are characteristic of an emerging 'data politics' (Ruppert et al. 2017), whereby power has been distributed to non-human systems and to those human actors able to translate what digital data are 'saying' for public audiences, political agents and states (Davies 2017). Through both its technological innovations and its narration of the impacts of digital data in education, Pearson is seeking to not only speed up conventional techniques of governance, such as data-driven performance measurement, but also circumvent conventional modes of policymaking by making educational processes of improvement and reform into real-time, automated tasks performed with non-human computational systems rather than administrative tasks enacted via bureaucratic organs of state. In so doing, it is seeking 'data monopoly' over the production and narration of educational data. This chapter provides a case study of Pearson's efforts to digitize education governance, focusing on its data visualization, machine learning and artificial intelligence developments, and theorizes its activities as a form of 'algorithmic governmentality' (Rouvroy and Berns 2013) that enmeshes educational institutions, teachers and students in the computational logics of algorithmic data analysis. Methodologically, the chapter draws on 'policy network analysis' (Gulson et al. 2017) and 'software studies' (Kitchin and Dodge 2011) approaches to analyse Pearson's influence network and its digital product development.

Governance and governing

The term 'governance' signifies two distinctive but related ways of analysing the circuits and functions of power in contemporary states, and has been taken up as a key concept in understandings of contemporary educational policy processes. Firstly, governance signifies a structural shift from centralized state government control to distributed and interactive networks of actors and experts working together across sectors on policy problems and policymaking (Ozga et al. 2011). Contemporary governments are increasingly seeking to 'decentralize' powers away from central bureaucratic agencies and 'devolve' processes of 'state monopoly', in some cases with new 'private monopolies' of business networks supplementing or supplanting the formal authority of government (Wilkins 2017). The second definition of governance is inspired by Michel Foucault's influential conceptualization of techniques of governing. In the term 'governmentality' Foucault (2007) captured the historically grounded techniques, calculations, analyses and procedures employed by specific authorities and political powers for directing human behaviour, as captured in the phrases 'conduct of conduct' or 'acting upon action'. Importantly, for authorities to govern, studies of governmentality insist, it is essential to possess knowledge of whatever they wish to govern in order to then administer and intervene in the lives of individuals or activate and manage populations (Rose 1999).

The task of studying governance methodologically involves tracing the networks of authorities and experts, which together administer society and the state, and examining the specific ideas and techniques they enact to know, analyse and guide human behaviour to achieve their objectives. Education governance, then, can be understood as the increasingly devolved ways in which educational policies are influenced and generated – through networks and relations between state, civil society and private sector actors – and refers to the manifold techniques being developed through these relations to establish new practices, routines, technologies and discourses within the institutions of state education. In order to examine the specific issue of education governance, education researchers therefore address and 'follow' how 'policy actors, discourses, conceptions, connections, agendas, resources, and solutions of governance' increasingly move across sectors and spaces, and how they are exerting 'significant impact on the formulation and reformulation of teaching and learning, assessment and the curriculum, and the general directions and conceptualization of education policy and governance' (Ball 2016: 1–2).

In order to articulate how Pearson is involved in both a structural shift to 'de-governmentalized' governance (Gulson et al. 2017) and designing techniques to govern conduct within education, the focus for the chapter is on the 'policy networks' (Ball 2016) that Pearson occupies, and on the 'policy instruments' (Lascoumes and le Gales 2007) it has produced to intervene into, manage and activate the actions of policymakers, teachers and students to achieve desired outcomes. Methodologically, network analysis has been conducted on Pearson to identify its key actors, events, connections and partnerships, and then to follow some of its activities, its products and its technical developments over a period from 2011 to 2017. Network analysis involves mapping actors and their connections, and then 'studying the chains, circuits, networks, and webs in and through which policy and its associated discourses and ideologies are made mobile and mutable' (McCann and Ward 2012: 43). As such, policy networks produce what McCann and Ward (2012: 43) describe as 'policy assemblages', using the term ' "assemblage" in a descriptive sense to encourage both an attention to the composite and relational character of policies . . . and also to the various social practices that gather, or draw together, diverse elements . . . into relatively stable and coherent "things" '. A 'software studies' approach is also employed to examine the specific digital policy instruments that Pearson and its partners have produced as part of these assemblages. This involves tracing the evolution and contextual unfolding of ideas, decisions, constraints, actions and actors that shape software projects, in order to 'excavate 'the social lives of ideas into code' (Kitchin and Dodge 2011: 255). The examples of Pearson's policy instruments reveal how specific ideas, assumptions, values and intentions structure the software products they produce or form partnerships to promote. Taken together, policy network analysis and software studies methodologies allow us to trace the organizational webs that produce composite policy assemblages, and then to excavate the social practices, values and expert knowledges that have informed the development of the digital 'things' these policy networks are seeking to embed into educational settings and practices.

Digitizing governance

In order to approach and understand Pearson as a key actor of digital education governance, it is important to locate their activities in the broader context of shifts in the ways that governance is structured and practised. One key shift is the temporal acceleration and spatial distribution of policy processes, termed 'fast policy' (Peck and Theodore 2015). Peck and Theodore (2015) argue that modern policymaking may still be focused on centres of political authority, but is also distributed to sprawling networks of human and non-human actors. As such, policy is increasingly accomplished through connected webs of consultants, think tanks, research institutes, guru performers as well as websites, blogs, social media and other non-human technologies and material objects.

The non-human actors of fast policy can be approached as 'policy instruments'. Policy instruments are defined as any kind of device, method, tool or technique designed to put a particular policy into practice (Lascoumes and le Gales 2007). Importantly, policy instruments are not value-neutral. Because they are designed in particular settings, they carry values and worldviews that then may partly shape policies. Policy instruments constitute 'a condensed form of knowledge about social control and ways of exercising it' and 'are not neutral devices: they produce specific effects . . . which structure public policy according to their own logic' (Lascoumes and Gales 2007: 3). With digital policy instruments – software programs designed to operationalize key policy ideas – particular values and ways of approaching problems and solutions can therefore be understood to be coded-in to their functioning. Fast policy is partly the accomplishment of digital policy instruments, with technologies of measurement, ranking and comparison creating new continuities and flows that can overcome physical distance in an increasingly interconnected and accelerating digital world (Lewis and Hogan 2016).

The adoption of digital policy instruments to accomplish particular policy objectives is part of a wider and ongoing transformation in the organization of the state termed 'digital governance' (Dunleavy and Margetts 2015). In the era of social media, automation and big data, governments, organizations and individuals alike leave digital traces of everything they do. Digital governance describes the use of these digital data to generate insights to inform future policy development and political intervention. Digital education governance is part of this turn to the use of digital data to generate the knowledge required to govern the state. Techniques of digital governance can already be seen in the expansion of highly complex technical data infrastructures required for the collection, storage, analysis and dissemination of test data at national and international scales (Sellar 2015). The test data collected from schools are themselves the products of chains of decisions about what should be collected, and how it should be processed and reported, with these decisions made not just by actors within the formal education system but by various testing companies, software firms, consultancies, university consortia and philanthropic foundations. As a consequence, educational data are 'the products of complex assemblages of technology, people and policies that stretch across and beyond the boundaries of our formal education system' (Anagnostopoulos et al. 2013: 2).

The existing infrastructure of test-based performance measurement, however, is beginning to evolve to include algorithmic data analytics in which huge quantities of continuously collected 'big data', real-time analysis and automated feedback – and the technical and statistical experts that handle it – are to play a crucial role (Hartong 2016; Mayer-Schonberger and Cukier 2014). The role of computer algorithms to make sense of massive quantities of digital data is ushering in a new condition of 'algorithmic governmentality' whereby individuals can be 'known' from digital data traces of their activities and then acted upon on the basis of that knowledge. Rouvroy and Berns (2013: 7) have detailed how algorithmic governmentality is enacted through the collection and automated storage of vast 'data warehouses' from various sources. These data can then be subjected to 'data mining', or 'the automated processing of these big data to identify subtle correlations between them', leading to 'action on behaviours', or the application of this knowledge to infer 'probabilistic predictions' that might be used to 'anticipate individual behaviours' (Rouvroy and Berns 2013: 7–8).

The use of statistical knowledge to govern populations has a long genealogy stretching back to nineteenth-century censuses, surveys, accounting and other bureaucratic practices of state management and control (Foucault 2007). Statistical knowledge of the population was a key source of modern governmental power, enabling 'a machinery of government to operate from centres that calculate' (Rose 1999: 213). Algorithmic governmentality registers a shift from population data to fine-grained individual data and its use for purposes of precise behaviour management. While digital governance conceptualizes the changing practices of the state – and the technical institutions that increasingly co-constitute state power – as digital data become available to conduct a constant audit of the population (Ruppert et al. 2017), algorithmic governmentality registers in a more Foucauldian sense how algorithms that process digital data may be used to intervene in and govern people's lives (Rieder and Simon 2016). This algorithmic governmentality has been described by Cheney-Lippold (2011: 167) as a 'soft biopolitics' whereby algorithmic sorting of users' data may be used 'to determine the new conditions of possibilities of users' lives'. Digital education governance, then, signifies how policy and governance are becoming more accelerated and distributed to include non-human technical instruments and networked systems that collect, process and communicate data. Education might therefore be measured through digital data to allow state governments and other organizations to know and intervene in education at scales from the classroom to the nation state, while new and emerging forms of algorithmic analysis of data may enable individuals to be tracked, traced, anticipated and even pre-empted through automated real-time systems.

The Pearson network

Pearson is an exemplary case of digital education governance in practice. Pearson is the world's most successful education business and has positioned itself as a policy influencer, yet remains the subject of relatively little research. Watters (2017) has detailed the timeline of Pearson's activities since its establishment in 1844, demonstrating how it has transformed itself from a publishing company into the world's largest education company through strategic partnerships, acquisitions and network-building at a massive global scale. In recent years, Pearson has extended beyond publishing to testing and assessment, e-learning, data analysis, evidence production, philanthropic funding, and partnerships and contracts with other businesses, governments and international organizations such as the OECD, thereby transforming itself from 'a media holding company to an edu-business' and also a 'legitimate policy actor' and a 'morally authoritative agency in educational matters' (Hogan et al. 2015: 49). As a global 'edu-business' with links to government, commercial and multilateral agencies, Pearson also has 'business ambitions . . . to find new markets and to create new spaces of education for Pearson's products' (Junemann and Ball 2015: 49). By 2016, however, Pearson was experiencing falling revenue and reputational decline, with a growing number of activists actively trying to disrupt its business (Hogan 2016).

In 2016, Pearson announced its ongoing strategic business priority to be a 'digital-first' company. Alongside major corporate restructuring, it disclosed the creation of a 'digital learning platform' combining cloud-based services with analytics and machine learning capabilities into a single digital architecture to cover both the internal running of the business and its digital learning products. As its chief information officer (Ismael 2016) stated:

> So when you look at the use of social media and Facebook, when you look at the use of Amazon for the retail environment, when you look at the use of Netflix for the media environment, we want to create a platform that has a number of those attributes associated with it.

Although its global digital learning platform remains in development at present, previous activities by Pearson indicate how it is seeking to involve itself in educational policymaking and governance via digital means and a vast partner network spanning the academic, technical, political and media fields. These partners and activities are prototypical of how Pearson is seeking to mobilize large data and visualizations, machine learning and artificial intelligence as digital policy instruments and techniques of education governance. Pearson is building vast networks to support its position as a policy actor and a source of governing expertise, and assembling discourses, practices and technologies that might govern directly the activities of policymakers, schools, teachers and students.

Data visualization

The Learning Curve was launched by Pearson in November 2012 as a visually accessible portal to international educational data under the leadership of Pearson's Chief Education Adviser Michael Barber, a former head of the UK prime minister's delivery unit and author of reports on evidence-based policymaking for the consultancy McKinsey's (Barber and Ozga 2014). The Learning Curve consists of a databank of 60 comparative indicators from 50 countries, encompassing over 2500 data points. As stated on its website, it is intended to 'help positively influence education policy at local, regional and national levels. The data and analysis on this website will help governments, teachers and learners identify the common elements of effective education' (http://thelearningcurve.pearson.com/). The 'internationally comparable' data in the Learning Curve are compiled from sources including the OECD, IEA and UNESCO into a global index of educational performance – ranked as a league table of national 'cognitive skills' and 'educational attainment' measures – which maps correlations between the inputs to and outputs of education, the inputs to education and socio-economic environment indicators (as a proxy for wider society) and the outputs of education and socio-economic environment indicators. These data are presented on the website as ranked league tables and visual tools and inscribed in reports. In the foreword to the 2012 report, Michael Barber wrote that the Learning Curve would become 'an open, living database which we hope will encourage new research and ultimately enable improved . . . evidence-informed education policy' (Economist Intelligence Unit 2012: 3).

Understood as a policy assemblage created through the relations of a network of actors that Pearson has coordinated, importantly, the Learning Curve was produced by the Economist Intelligence Unit (EIU), part of the Economist Group of which Pearson owned 50 per cent until 2015. The EIU is an expert centre in econometric data analysis and forecasting for both businesses and governments. Many of its econometric methods are utilized in the Learning Curve, in its global index of ranked countries; its production of country profiles detailing their social, political and demographic indicators; its generation of visualizations to make the data easy to use and interpret; and its attempt to correlate the inputs to and outputs of education with socio-economic environment indicators.

The Learning Curve is especially notable for its interactive data visualizations, which are employed to make visible and comprehensible complex datasets that would otherwise be difficult to interpret. Michael Barber has claimed it supports 'evidence-based policy' through data visualization 'to make it easy for people . . . to use quickly without undermining the integrity of the data' (Barber and Ozga 2014: 77). Countries' educational performance is represented on the site as heat maps and graphical time-series trend tools. It permits the user to generate country infographic profiles to visually compare multiple education input, output and socio-economic indicators. Through the application of visual analytics, it allows the user to manipulate the images in order to reveal patterns and associations, to conduct comparisons by altering variables and to build visual models and explanations.

As an instrument of education governance, the interactive elements of the Learning Curve invite users to become data experts, able to manipulate the data to develop their own governing knowledge. In this sense, and in line with the theory of governmentality, the Learning Curve creates alliances between those expert centres of calculation that have generated the data – Pearson, the OECD, UNESCO, IEA and the EIU – and its users who are incited by the software to perform their own analyses and interpretations, thus taking control of the data and its narration. Michael Barber claims it allows the public to 'play' with the 'co-creation' of educational data and 'connect the bits together' in a way that is more 'fun' than preformatted policy reports (Barber with Ozga 2014: 84). However, consonant with the comparative economic methods of the EIU, global comparison and forecasting are coded-in to the user interface to shape interpretation, make visible particular educational realities and encourage particular kinds of responses. The design of the Learning Curve interface configures the research user as a comparative analyst and a data co-producer. As Hogan et al. (2016: 2) argue, the Learning Curve is an important element 'in Pearson's present transformation and involves the representation of its education policy analysis work as a positive benefit to policy debates and to individual learners', while also increasing the value of the company.

Through its digitally rendered data visualizations and accompanying reports, Pearson is making complex statistical and comparative data relevant and accessible to inform evidence-based policymaking and thereby reshape the ways education systems are understood and acted upon. Based on a 'metric realist' assumption that numbers present reality as it is (Desrosieres 2001), the Learning Curve is designed as a fast policy instrument that might accelerate the transnational movement, diffusion and uptake of 'best practice' models and 'common elements of effective education'. In so doing, the Learning Curve acts as a vehicle for Pearson to insert itself and its realist quantitative expertise and private authority into public policy debates, and to act as a key profit-making participant in processes of education governance. This demonstrates how education governance is being practised through extended relationship networks that are able to assemble discourses, best practice models and technologies that might exert profound influence on policy processes. In particular, through the alliances it has brokered to produce the Learning Curve, Pearson has sought to make data visualization into a key policy instrument of education governance that invites user participation and which subtly encourages policymakers to become engaged comparative analysts who are able to 'play' with numbers in order to guide their decisions and priorities for intervention.

Machine learning

Pearson has also begun to promote machine learning technologies as hyper-accelerated digital policy instruments. Machine learning, simply put, consists of programs that can be 'trained' on historic data to then detect patterns in new datasets; though an automated process, it requires training, checking and calibrating by technical engineers (Mackenzie 2015). Machine learning can generate descriptive, predictive and prescriptive analytics, where descriptive analytics provide insight into what happened, predictive analytics generate probabilistic outcomes and prescriptive analytics offer 'actionable intelligence' about what to do next. Some advanced machine learning can automatically act on its own actionable intelligence, as is the case with 'adaptive learning platforms' which respond automatically to students' digitally recorded activities by 'personalizing' subsequent content and adapting their 'learning pathways'. Pearson has begun to actively involve itself in learning analytics and adaptive learning platform development, as part of a proliferation of the concept of 'personalized learning' in education policy that it has assisted into circulation (Roberts-Mahoney et al. 2016).

In 2011 Pearson began investing in Knewton, a learning analytics and adaptive learning infrastructure provider, and began embedding Knewton technology in its courseware products in order to 'diagnose each student's proficiency at every concept, and precisely deliver the needed content in the optimal learning style for each. These products will use the combined data power of millions of students to provide uniquely personalized learning' (Knewton 2011). Based on consolidating data science, statistics, psychometrics and machine learning, Knewton (2013: 8) is 'a flexible, scalable system for delivering adaptive learning experiences and predictive analytics across arbitrary collections of content in different learning environments' (Wilson and Nichols 2015: 4). Its analytics methods include 'sophisticated algorithms to recommend the perfect activity for each student, constantly', based on its automated analysis of 'data that reflects cognition' – that is, vast quantities of 'meaningful data' recorded during student activity 'that can be harnessed continuously to power personalized learning for each individual' (Knewton 2013: 13).

The strategic relationship with Knewton exemplifies Pearson's ambitions to become a global centre of expertise in educational big data analysis and product development. Pearson's own in-house Center for Digital Data, Analytics and Adaptive Learning (CDDAAL) was established in 2012 to use data science methods to capture stream or trace data from learners' interactions with learning materials; enable computer analysis to detect new patterns that may provide evidence about learning; and take a learner's profile of knowledge, skills and attributes in order to determine the best subsequent activity (DiCerbo and Behrens 2014). Pearson's aspirations go beyond the application of machine learning to the production of new knowledge and theories of learning processes.

The founding director of CDDAAL, John Behrens (2013), has articulated how educational big data will challenge current theoretical frameworks in educational research, as 'new forms of data and experience will create a theory gap between the dramatic increase in data-based results and the theory base to integrate them'.

At the core of Pearson's ambitions for big data and machine learning is an attempt to disrupt existing practices of standardized testing and policymaking based on test results, since if 'learning becomes digital, data will be available not just from once-a-year tests, but also from the wide-ranging daily activities of individual students' (DiCerbo and Behrens 2014). In 2014 Pearson published a report on using 'intelligent software and a range of devices that facilitate unobtrusive classroom data collection in real time' and 'the application of data analytics and the adoption of new metrics to generate deeper insights into and richer information on learning and teaching' (Hill and Barber 2014: 8). Such systems, they argued, could instantiate a revolution in education policy, shifting the focus from the governance of education through the institution of the school to 'the student as the focus of educational policy and concerted attention to personalising learning' (Hill and Barber 2014: 2).

Machine learning, from this perspective, could be utilized as a real-time digital policy instrument. Whereas existing policy instruments such as standardized tests demand lengthy intervals of data collection, analysis and reporting before they might inform subsequent policymaking, machine learning could short-circuit this process. Machine learning could generate real-time descriptive and predictive analytics that detect patterns in individual student performance and generate probabilistic outcomes based on comparative analysis against huge populations of other students. Immediate feedback could then be provided via prescriptive analytics and adaptive learning platforms that would personalize students' subsequent encounters with content and their pathways through courses. In other words, the infrastructure of machine learning that Pearson has sought to construct would transform the existing infrastructure of test-based performance measurement that has dominated public education through international testing organizations – a testing industry in which Pearson has itself been a key actor, but which has experienced rising levels of criticism.

Pearson's shift towards real-time digital data analytics as a core part of its business, then, is at least partly animated by commercial concerns about its future profit-making potential, since the company is ultimately accountable to its shareholders and actively needs to seek out new markets for its products and services. In this sense, as an edu-business with commercial ambitions, Pearson exemplifies how being an actor in the policy networks of contemporary education governance is itself a market opportunity, giving private sector organizations competitive leverage to design and sell new products to schools and universities.

Pearson's CDDAAL and other digital data activities were restructured in 2016, as part of its ongoing streamlining transition to digital products, services, cloud adoption and the roll-out of a global learning platform across its entire portfolio of products. In 2017, Pearson announced it was phasing out its partnership with Knewton to focus on its own in-house global digital learning platform, amid rising concerns that Knewton had overstated the capacity of its adaptive platform (Young 2017). These developments are all part of Pearson's strategic plan to move the business to a '21st century digital platform body' and 'provide a very rich and personalised media experience that's delivered using analytics, and through understanding learner behaviour' (Ismael 2016). At about the same time, however, Pearson announced a new deal with IBM to begin embedding advanced cognitive computing and artificial intelligence in its courseware, representing the next stage in its development as a for-profit actor of digitized education governance.

Artificial intelligence

Early in 2016, Pearson produced a report on the potential of artificial intelligence in education. Its vision is of augmented educational systems, spaces and practices where humans and AI work symbiotically, and refers to advances in machine learning algorithms, computer modelling, statistics, artificial neural networks and neuroscience, since 'AI involves computer software that has been programmed to interact with the world in ways normally requiring human intelligence' (Luckin et al. 2016). In these ways, through its new AI projects Pearson is establishing itself as a site of algorithmic governance, capable of real-time algorithm-driven diagnostics and analytics at the level of the individual. In other words, Pearson has sought to extend its activities from the kind of statistical techniques of education governance represented by the Learning Curve to a new big data-driven logic of algorithmic education governance whereby student data are captured and calculated continuously in order to direct automated systems. According to Rieder and Simon (2016), the algorithmic logics of big data include: (1) extending the reach of automation, from data collection to storage, curation and analysis; (2) capturing massive amounts of data and focusing on correlations rather than causes, thereby reducing the need for theory, models and human expertise; (3) expanding the realm of what can be measured, in order to trace and gauge movements, actions and behaviours in ways that were previously unimaginable; and (4) aspiring to calculate what is yet to come, using smart, fast and cheap predictive techniques to support decision-making and optimize resource allocation across many sectors.

In this vein, Pearson's vision of AI in education (AIEd) includes Intelligent Tutoring Systems which use AI techniques to simulate one-to-one human tutoring and deliver learning activities matched to individuals' cognitive needs, 'all without an individual teacher having to be present'. As with its personalized learning platforms, AIEd is presented as a technical means of achieving whole-scale reform of education systems:

> Once we put the tools of AIEd in place as described above, we will have new and powerful ways to measure system level achievement. . . . AIEd will be able to provide analysis about teaching and learning at every level, whether that is a particular subject, class, college, district, or country. This will mean that evidence about country performance will be available from AIEd analysis, calling into question the need for international testing. (Luckin et al. 2016: 48)

In other words, Pearson is proposing to bypass conventional techniques of governance based on test results, and instead focus on real-time intelligent analytics conducted up-close, using algorithmic systems, within the pedagogic routines of the AI-enhanced classroom. In this sense, Pearson's ambitions exemplify the potential emergence of algorithmic governance in education, whereby automated data-mining is to be conducted to generate real-time knowledge about both individual and system-level performance and to prescribe pre-emptive intervention where calculated as necessary.

At about the same time, IBM released its own report on the use of cognitive computing for personalized education. In recent years IBM has restructured its business to focus on 'cognitive computing' and has developed innovations such as 'neurosynaptic chips' and 'neuromorphic systems' modelled on the capacity of the human brain for efficient information processing and analysis. Its cognitive technologies are specifically brain-based, utilizing expert knowledge about brain plasticity 'to learn dynamically through experiences, find correlations, create hypotheses and remember – and learn from – the outcomes, emulating the human brain's synaptic and structural plasticity (or the brain's ability to re-wire itself over time as it learns and responds to experiences and interactions with its environment)' (IBM Research 2011). Translated into the educational context, IBM proposes that 'deeply immersive interactive experiences with intelligent tutoring systems can transform how we learn' (King et al. 2016: 8). Instead of being hard-programmed in code and defined by human inputs, its authors claim, 'cognitive systems are in a wholly different paradigm of systems that understand, reason and learn. In short, systems that think' (King et al. 2016: 9).

The most publicly visible product of its cognitive R&D is IBM Watson. In 2016 IBM began marketing IBM Watson Education, which consists of an analytics platform for generating 'critical insights about each student – demographics, strengths, challenges, optimal learning styles, and more – which the educator can use to create targeted instructional plans, in real-time' and an adaptive platform to support teachers in generating appropriate, relevant 'personalized learning content and activities' (https://www.ibm.com/watson/education/). Instead of seeking to displace the teacher, IBM sees cognitive systems as optimizing and enhancing the role of the teacher, as a kind of 'natural' brain-based cognitive prosthetic of human qualities. The promise of cognitive computing for IBM is a fundamental reimagining of the 'next generation of human cognition, in which we think and reason in new and powerful ways', as claimed in its white paper on 'computing, cognition and the future of knowing': 'It's true that cognitive systems are machines that are inspired by the human brain. But it's also true that these machines will inspire the human brain, increase our capacity for reason and rewire the ways in which we learn' (Kelly 2015: 11). Studies of policy networks tend to focus on the human actors that participate in contemporary techniques of education governance, but for IBM, as for Pearson, the policy actor may now be a non-human artificial intelligence. Education governance, in other words, is being displaced to algorithmic machine learning systems that are able to scrape individual students for objective data and automatically adapt to 'optimize' their cognitive skills.

The similarities between the two reports anticipated a partnership between Pearson and IBM Watson announced in late 2016. Although Pearson claims to be 'in-housing' much of its data analytics and adaptive learning R&D, commentators have suggested that it is more plausible that it will do so through its partnership with IBM Watson (Wan 2017). Pearson announced their partnership would 'make Watson's cognitive capabilities available to millions' as a 'flexible virtual tutor' enabled to 'search through an expanded set of education resources to retrieve relevant information to answer student questions, show how the new knowledge they gain relates to their own existing knowledge and, finally, ask them questions to check their understanding' (Pearson 2016). IBM added that Watson would be 'embedded in the Pearson courseware' to 'spot patterns and generate insights', act as 'a digital resource' and 'assess the student's responses to guide them with hints, feedback, explanations and help identify common misconceptions, working with the student at their pace to help them master the topic' (IBM 2016).

Through their partnership, AI is being positioned as a non-human governing technique that can monitor, quantify, analyse and then adapt to guide student behaviour and cognitive activities. Through Pearson and IBM, algorithmic governance which emphasizes automation, data analytics and action on individual behaviours is being introduced into educational settings and practices. As with machine learning algorithms, however, AI is not just technical but a combination of technologies, human actions, social arrangements and meaning, since 'AI always performs tasks that serve human purposes and are part of human activities' (Johnson and Verdicchio 2017: 3). Approached in this way, Pearson's AIEd ambitions and partnership with IBM Watson are invested with institutional values, intentions and purposes. A key indication of these purposes is provided in IBM's report on cognitive systems in education (King et al. 2016), which states:

> There is a growing disconnect between what education delivers and the skills being demanded in today's ever-changing global marketplace. . . . At the same time, we are seeing unprecedented levels of change across industries and professions, with digital technologies serving as agents of transformation.

For IBM, the capacity for human capital development and the production of labour for this technological context lie in the 'rewiring' of the brain itself in order to boost cognition. Far from being neutral and objective, the AI systems Pearson and IBM are seeking to introduce into schools and colleges privilege particular models of personalized learning and enhanced cognition that are concerned with maximizing efficiency and effectiveness for particular purposes of future economic productivity.

Through techniques of algorithmic governance, these companies are seeking real-time capture of student data which can then be used for targeted and automated intervention designed to modify neural processes for the purposes of optimizing the cognitive skills by which national education systems are judged and evaluated at a global scale. Thus, for Pearson, while its Learning Curve databank functions as a benchmarking tool for countries' overall 'cognitive skills', its machine learning applications and proposed AIEd tutors are intended to maximize the development of those measurable human capacities deemed appropriate to the global marketplace.

Education data power

Pearson is working in digital networks of technical and commercial organizations that are seeking to influence and intervene in education governance. It is enacting this task through producing and promoting digital policy instruments, including data visualization, machine learning and artificial intelligence systems, which are intended to govern by guiding the actions and behaviours of policymakers, leaders, teachers and students. In the process, Pearson and its partners are undertaking the task of digitizing education governance, both by involving far more digitally focused organizations in processes of policymaking and enactment and by introducing far more digital policy instruments, software packages and digital database programs into policy processes and practical settings alike. In so doing, Pearson is seeking to influence the conceptualization and direction of education policy itself. Through machine learning and artificial intelligence, Pearson is seeking to make policy into a real-time process whereby algorithms and data analytics software conduct a continuous audit of actions and behaviours in classrooms, which can then automatically adapt in response to the activities of teachers and students. Real-time feedback and adaptive technologies, in Pearson's view, can accelerate the cumbersome process of bureaucratic policymaking by changing the pedagogy and content of the classroom without the need for long-term policy processes such as those based on test scores and performance rankings.

The digitization of education governance exemplified by Pearson needs to be understood as a significant manifestation within the education sector of the growing power and politics of data and metrics in advanced states (Beer 2016). Updating Foucauldian insights into the historical use of statistics to know and administer the state, Ruppert et al. (2017) argue that data have now become a major object of economic, political and social investment for governments, corporations and other diverse agencies and authorities to collect, analyse and deploy. While state agencies and authorities have historically maintained 'effective monopoly on data regimes concerning whole populations', the 'monopoly of the state over data production, collection, and even interception is increasingly challenged', including 'by corporations, agencies, authorities, and organizations that are producing myriad data' (ibid.: 3–4). In an era of 'data politics', data have become 'an object whose production interests those who exercise power' (ibid.: 3).

Similarly, Davies (2017: 2) argues that traditional forms of expertise, authority and judgment have experienced diminishing levels of public trust in recent years, with 'experts' and 'elites' critiqued over their lack of 'objective judgment over the "facts" of what is taking place'. Instead, computational systems which can process big data, and those who manage them and report what the numbers mean, are gaining increasing public status and authority. As a consequence, 'elite power' now increasingly resides in a combination of non-human, real-time feedback technologies and the human intermediaries who can translate and narrate the flow of data to make it intelligible for 'public audiences' and 'political agents and states' (ibid.: 17). In other words, 'the rise of big data privileges those capable of mediating between mathematical analytics and empirical narratives about what is being represented' (ibid.: 18).

Education governance, too, is increasingly being delegated to computational systems that can process large numbers and to the human experts who can narrate them. A new kind of data politics is opening up in education, with organizations such as Pearson staking their claim to elite power and authority over educational data and its analysis. Pearson has developed its own systems to conduct real-time analyses of massive quantities of data, and has also positioned itself as a data translator –particularly through public figures such as Michael Barber – able to narrate the meanings, potential and impacts of educational data and digital technologies for different audiences, the public, the media, practitioners, policymakers and states alike. Though centres of political authority still retain a strong role in education governance, organizations such as Pearson are seeking to consolidate their power within education through both the production and the narration of digital data. As policy processes extend to permit more digital-first organizations to join influential policy networks, it is likely that some digital organizations and the digital policy instruments they produce and promote will attain privileged status in the governance of state education, able to exercise elite power through their capacity to both generate and narrate data. Pearson's ambitions to create a single global digital learning platform suggest it is seeking a form of data monopoly in education, and is positioning itself at the centre of the networks of digitized education governance.

Conclusion

This chapter has shown how techniques of education governance are increasingly being digitized. The structural shift to governance by cross-sector networks has allowed more 'digital-first' companies, such as Pearson, Knewton and IBM, to seek to influence the direction of educational policy and practice. While Pearson products such as the Learning Curve have been designed as accessible portals to complex data to shape the practices of evidence-based policymaking, new big data technologies such as adaptive platforms insert non-human and algorithmic decision-making systems – as techniques of algorithmic governmentality – more directly into pedagogic practices where they might guide classroom conduct. Even more advanced cognitive AI is intended to interact 'naturally' with students and so shape their cognitive capacity towards particular instrumental ends. Through these actors, education is becoming subject to algorithmic governance – the use of automated systems of data collection and analysis to predict and intervene in the behaviours and actions of individuals towards pre-specified ends and purposes.

Pearson's technologies function as digital policy instruments and as practical techniques of digital education governance that are programmed to guide and shape practices in policymaking centres, leaders' offices and classrooms alike. As such, Pearson and its partner network exemplify how new sources and forms of data politics and non-human algorithmic power are coming to play a role in education governance as it seeks monopoly over educational data production and its empirical narration.

References

Anagnostopoulos, D., Rutledge, S. A., and Jacobsen, R. (eds). 2013. *The Infrastructure of Accountability: Data Use and the Transformation of American Education*, pp. 1–20. Cambridge, MA: Harvard Education Press.

Ball, S. J. 2016. 'Following policy: networks, network ethnography and education policy mobilities'. *Journal of Education Policy* 31 (5): 549–566.

Barber, M., and Ozga, J. 2014. 'Data work: Michael Barber in conversation with Jenny Ozga'. In T. Fenwick, E. Mangez, and J. Ozga (eds), *Governing Knowledge: Comparison, Knowledge-Based Technologies and Expertise in the Regulation of Education*, pp. 75–85. London: Routledge.

Beer, D. 2016. *Metric Power*. London: Palgrave Macmillan.

Behrens, J. 2013. Harnessing the Currents of the Digital Ocean. Paper presented at the Annual Meeting of the American Educational Research Association, San Francisco, CA, April 2013.

Cheney-Lippold, J. 2011. 'A new algorithmic identity: Soft biopolitics and the modulation of control'. *Theory, Culture & Society* 28 (6): 164–181.

Davies, W. 2017. 'Elite power under advanced neoliberalism'. *Theory, Culture & Society* 34 (5–6): 227–250.

Desrosieres, A. 2001. 'How real are statistics? Four possible attitudes.' *Social Research* 68 (2): 339–355.

DiCerbo, K. E., and Behrens, J. T. 2014. *Impacts of the Digital Ocean*. Austin, TX: Pearson.

Dunleavy, P., and Margetts, H. 2015. Design Principles for Essentially Digital Governance. Annual Meeting of the American Political Science Association, San Francisco, 3–6 September 2015.

Economist Intelligence Unit. 2012. *The Learning Curve: Lessons in Country Performance*. London: Pearson.

Foucault, M. 2007. *Security, Territory and Population: Lectures at the College de France 1977–1978*. Trans. G. Burchell. New York: Palgrave Macmillan.

Gulson, N. K., Lewis, S., Lingard, B., Lubienski, C., Takayama, K., and Webb, P. T. 2017. 'Policy mobilities and methodology: a proposition for inventive methods in education policy studies.' *Critical Studies in Education* 58 (2): 224–241.

Hartong, S. 2016. 'Between assessments, digital technologies and big data: The growing influence of "hidden" data mediators in education.' *European Educational Research Journal* 15 (5): 523–536.

Hill, P., and Barber, M. 2014. *Preparing for a Renaissance in Assessment*. London: Pearson.

Hogan, A. 2016. '# tellPearson: The activist "public education" network.' *Discourse: Studies in the Cultural Politics of Education* 39 (3): 377–392.

Hogan, A., Sellar, S., and Lingard, B. 2015. 'Network restructuring of global edu-business: The case of Pearson's *Efficacy Framework*'. In W. Au and J. J. Ferrare (eds), *Mapping Corporate Education Reform: Power and Policy Networks in the Neoliberal State*, pp. 43–64. London: Routledge.

Hogan, A., Sellar, S., and Lingard, B. 2016. 'Commercialising comparison: Pearson puts the TLC in soft capitalism.' *Journal of Education Policy*, http://dx.doi.org/10.1080/026 80939.2015.1112922

IBM. 2016. IBM Watson Education and Pearson to Drive Cognitive Learning Experiences for College Students. IBM Press. Accessed on 27 April 2018. Available at: http://www-03.ibm.com/press/us/en/pressrelease/50842.wss (last accessed: 23/04/18).

IBM Research. 2011. IBM's first cognitive computing chips mimic functions of the brain. IBM Research News, 18 August 2011. Accessed on 27 April 2018. Available at: http://ibmresearchnews.blogspot.co.uk/2011/08/this-cognitive-computing-chip-taught.html (last accessed: 23/04/18).

IBM Watson Education. 2016. Transform education with Watson. IBM Watson. Accessed on 27 April 2018. Available at: http://www.ibm.com/watson/education/ (last accessed: 23/04/18).

Ismael, N. 2016. 'Pearson's learning platform set to transform the education industry.' *Information Age*, 17 October. Accessed on 27 April 2018. Available at: http://www.information-age.com/pearsons-learning-platform-123462720/ (last accessed: 23/04/18).

Johnson, D. G., and Verdicchio, M. 2017. 'Reframing AI discourse'. *Minds & Machines*. Accessed on 27 April 2018. Available at: http://dx.doi.org/10.1007/s11023-017-9417-6 (last accessed: 23/04/18).

Junemann, C., and Ball, S. J. 2015. *Pearson and PALF: The Mutating Giant*. Brussels: Education International.

Kelly III, J. E. 2015. *Computing, Cognition and the Future of Knowing: How Humans and Machines Are Forging a New Age of Understanding*. Somers, NY: IBM Corporation.

King, M., Cave, R., Foden, M., and Stent, M. 2016. *Personalised Education: From Curriculum to Career with Cognitive Systems*. Portsmouth: IBM Corporation.

Kitchin, R., and Dodge, M. 2011. *Code/Space: Software and Everyday Life*. London: MIT Press.

Knewton. 2011. Pearson and Knewton partner to advance next generation of digital education. Knewton in the News, 1 November. Accessed on 27 April 2018. Available at: http://www.knewton.com/press-releases/pearson-partnership/ (last accessed: 23/04/18).

Knewton. 2013. Knewton Adaptive Learning: Building the world's most powerful education recommendation engine. Accessed on 27 April 2018. Available at: https://www.knewton.com/wp-content/uploads/knewton-adaptive-learning-whitepaper.pdf (last accessed: 23/04/18).

Lascoumes, P., and le Gales, P. 2007. 'Introduction: Understanding public policy through its instruments – From the nature of instruments to the sociology of public policy instrumentation'. *Governance* 20 (1): 1–21.

Lewis, S., and Hogan, A. 2016. 'Reform first and ask questions later? The implications of (fast) schooling policy and "silver bullet" solutions'. *Critical Studies in Education*. iFirst

Luckin, R., Holmes, W., Griffiths, M., and Forcier, L. B. 2016. *Intelligence Unleashed: An Argument for AI in Education*. London: Pearson.

Mackenzie, A. 2015. 'The production of prediction: What does machine learning want?' *European Journal of Cultural Studies* 18 (4–5): 429–445.

Mayer-Schönberger, V., and Cukier, K. 2014. *Learning from Big Data: The Future of Education*. New York: Houghton Mifflin Harcourt Publishing Co.

McCann, E., and Ward, K. 2012. 'Assembling urbanism: following policies and "studying through" the sites and situations of policy making'. *Environment and Planning A* 44: 42–51.

Ozga, J., Dahler-Larsen, P., Segerholm, C., and Simola, H. (eds). 2011. *Fabricating Quality in Education: Data and Governance in Europe*. London: Routledge.

Pearson. 2016. IBM Watson Education and Pearson to Drive Cognitive Learning Experiences for College Students. Pearson News. Accessed on 27 April 2018. Available at: https://www.pearson.com/news/media/news-announcements/2016/10/ibm-watson-education-and-pearson-to-drive-cognitive-learning-exp.html

Peck, J., and Theodore, N. 2015. *Fast Policy: Experimental Statecraft at the Thresholds of Neoliberalism*. London: University of Minnesota Press.

Rieder, G., and Simon, J. 2016. 'Datatrust: Or, the political quest for numerical evidence and the epistemologies of Big Data'. *Big Data and Society* 3 (1): 1–6.

Roberts-Mahoney, H., Means A. J., and Garrison, M. J. 2016. 'Netflixing human capital development: personalized learning technology and the corporatization of K-12 education'. *Journal of Education Policy* 31 (4): 405–420.

Rose, N. 1999. *Powers of Freedom: Reframing Political Thought*. Cambridge: Cambridge University Press.

Rouvroy, A., and Berns, T. 2013. 'Algorithmic governmentality and prospects of emancipation: Disparateness as a precondition for individuation through relationships?' *Reseaux* 177: 163–196.

Ruppert, E., Isin, E., and Bigo, D. 2017. 'Data politics'. *Big Data & Society*, July–December: 1–7.

Sellar, S. 2015. 'Data infrastructure: a review of expanding accountability systems and large-scale assessments in education'. *Discourse: Studies in the Cultural Politics of Education* 36 (5): 765–777.

Wan, T. 2017. 'Pearson, an Investor in Knewton, Is "Phasing Out" Partnership on Adaptive Products'. *EdSurge*, 12 May. Accessed on 27 April 2018. Available at: https://www.edsurge.com/news/2017-05-12-pearson-an-investor-in-knewton-is-phasing-out-partnership-on-adaptive-products (last accessed: 23/04/18).

Watters, A. 2017. Pearson: a timeline. Hack Education, 20 June. Accessed on 27 April 2018. Available at: http://network.hackeducation.com/2017/06/20/pearson (last accessed: 23/04/18).

Wilkins, A. 2017. 'Rescaling the local: multi-academy trusts, private monopoly and statecraft in England'. *Journal of Educational Administration and History* 49 (2): 171–185.

Williamson, B. 2016. 'Digital methodologies of education governance: Pearson plc and the remediation of methods'. *European Educational Research Journal* 15 (1): 34–53.

Wilson, K., and Nichols, Z. 2015. The Knewton Platform: A General-Purpose Adaptive Learning Infrastructure. Knewton. Accessed on 27 April 2018. Available at: https://www.knewton.com/wp-content/uploads/knewton-technical-white-paper-201501.pdf (last accessed: 23/04/18)

Young, J. R. 2017. 'Amid Struggles, Knewton Names Former Pearson Exec as New CEO'. *EdSurge*, 11 July. Accessed on 27 April 2018. Available at: https://www.edsurge.com/news/2017-07-11-amid-struggles-knewton-names-former-pearson-exec-as-new-ceo (last accessed: 23/04/18).

2

Learning Personalization: Technics, Disorientation and Governance

Greg Thompson

In the education technology industry there is a widely held belief that technical, or digital, personalization of learning is the next 'revolution'. This belief has translated into speculative investment. For example, in the United States, the Bill & Melinda Gates Foundation and the Chan Zuckerberg Initiative gave $12 million to New Profit, a venture philanthropy organization, to develop digital personalized learning solutions for classrooms (Herold 2017). The Bush Foundation, a US-based progressive charity, announced in 2017 that it would redirect all of its philanthropy to individualized learning programs that adopt 'technologies to help students learn at their own pace and manner' (Prather 2017). Pearson, one of the largest edu-businesses in the world, positioned itself in 2014 to take advantage of the emerging 'digital ocean' of Big Data, 'transforming' learning in schools and classrooms. Corporations, philanthropic organizations and not-for-profits are just some of the policy actors devoting significant energy and resources pursuing personalized learning in classrooms using adaptive technologies. Recent work has begun to engage with the problems, challenges and possibilities of these new forms of technological governance in education (Sellar and Thompson 2016; Selwyn 2015; Williamson 2015).

Advocates claim the aim of personalized learning is to revolutionize teaching, learning, assessment and the school itself. In the foreword to the EdSurge report on adaptive technology written for Pearson's Open Ideas platform, Michael Horn argued that 'adaptive learning is a powerful force to make those [learning] pursuits more effective and efficient' (p. 9). Horn further goes on to argue that adaptive technology accelerates 'our knowledge of what learning experiences work best, for which students, in which circumstances, so that educators can adapt to a reality in which they can help all children find their passions and reach their fullest potential' (p. 9). In the digital ocean, 'learning is personalised based on learners' knowledge states and trajectories, and the creators of the systems improve them over time as data helps them to understand the processes of learning' (DiCerbo et al. 2014: 2). This desire for personalized learning is often informed by a particular anxiety that traditional schooling isn't keeping up with a rapidly changing technological society, with jobs that don't exist yet requiring new skills and computational literacy in a globalized economy (Hughes 2017).

Deleuze (1995) coined the phrase 'control society' to explain this new flow of political, social, economic and technological forces. Control society is typified by the 'shift from mastery over visible space to the integrated management of information' (Bogard 2009: 19) whereby patterned digital data predict behaviour, curate potential stimulus and cultivate responses through the logics of algorithmic calculation. Rose (2000: 325) argues that in a control society, information networks that consist of fluid qualities of 'elements, capacities and potentialities' are plugged into multiple networks which use algorithms to predict, and respond in advance, to manage conduct. In this chapter I use Stiegler's work on technological systems (which he calls technics) and their relationship to memory and time to argue that digital technologies are a form of 'education governance' that require placing time and the temporal at the centre of inquiry because of the hyper-industrialized technological society that we move within. This chapter follows Deleuze's (1995: 181) argument that there is always 'correspondence between any society and some kind of machine, which isn't to say that their machines determine different kinds of society but that they express the social forms capable of producing them and making use of them'. The move towards personalized, digital technologies in schools is an expression of the social forms in which we find ourselves.

Alongside this anxiety about the various 'lacks' evident in education institutions is the opportunity for private interests to benefit from a restructured state. As governments have pursued new, networked forms of policy formulation (Rhodes 1996), new players have entered the global policy arena offering a variety of solutions. Ball (2009: 537) identified that in many nations there has been a shift from government to governance typified by four characteristics:

> One is in forms of government (structures and agencies), another in the form and nature of the participants in processes of governance, a third in the prevailing

discourses within governance, and a fourth in the governing of and production of new kinds of 'willing' subjects.

Much of what Ball names as the 'governance turn', the shift from government to governance that has emerged in sociology, policy studies and associated fields has focused its gaze on spatial aspects of that governance. This has extended to work on the decentred and devolved education systems (Lawn 2013), the role of data to assign status in educational rankings (Ozga 2009) and the rescaling of politics and policy in education systems (Lingard and Rawolle 2011). Of course, one of the problems of seeing governance as a spatial form is that it tends to stumble over how it is that these practices subjectify and subjectivate, how it is that these new kinds of willing subjects are formed self-regulate. As Hunter (1994: xviii) reminds us, there is a tightrope that must be walked in theorizing education governance, between giving the state too much power on the one hand and ignoring the technologies that work to elicit the self-governance required for these to be effective and sustained on the other. My argument is that studies of governance in education need to attend to the temporal as well as the spatial to provide compelling analyses as to how governance in general, and technology in particular, work in education contexts. In particular, one aspect of education governance concerns who sells the future, and how the vision of that future becomes compelling in constituting education subjects. This chapter uses reports generated by advocates for adaptive learning in educational institutions to consider how technics has become a pressing concern for education governance.

The problem of technology

The notion of technology as a problem is a very specific idea. It follows from Gilles Deleuze who argued that the value in theory is in the articulation of questions or problems, rather than solutions. Deleuze saw that it is through the framing of insightful problems we can challenge doxa or common sense, or what Deleuze calls our image of thought. How we think, what we perceive as usual, commonplace, reasonable and so forth are grounded within our times, are social and temporal formulations. Problems belong to thought, they 'are determined neither subjectively nor privatively, so that they would mark an insufficiency in knowledge, but that problems belong to thought as transformative moments in the act of learning' (Wasser 2017: 50). The point of the problem is not the solutions that are presented, and how these solutions determine the rightness or wrongness of the problem, but rather the ways that problems allow us to understand the constitution of our condition. A solution 'always has the truth it deserves according to the problem to which it is a response' (Deleuze 1994: 158–159). A problem, however, forces us into an encounter where something new emerges, new thinking, new possibilities, new understanding.

Technology is a problem because it is difficult to think about it outside the frames of reference long taken for granted. Technology is often presented as technical objects or tools which limits thought to concepts of effectiveness and efficiency in given circumstances. Another trope of technology is as a utopian promise where technology will solve 'wicked' social problems beyond the understanding of humans. Stiegler (2009) argues that these conceptualizations portray the weakness of their thought. From the very beginning of Western philosophy itself when the Greeks split episteme (knowledge) from technics (craft or art) so that episteme became the proper material for philosophical work, the utopia/tool binary became a rarely troubled belief. This split at least partly stems from hostility to the Sophists in ancient Athens because the skill of the Sophists in rhetoric, their craft or technics, 'was perceived as indifference to establishing truth or, worse, as an attempt to make truth instrumental to power' (Fabretti 2015: 4). One result of this was that truth became the object of epistêmê, which became a foundational presupposition of philosophy itself.

For example, Aristostle defined the category of 'technical being' as 'something that does not have an own end in itself and that is just a tool used by someone else for their ends' (Fabretti 2015: 4). Clark (2000: 238) argues that the 'Aristotelian view is that technology is extrinsic to human nature as a tool which is used to bring about certain ends. Technology is applied science, an instrument of knowledge'. If technics, and by extension technology itself, is viewed in instrumental terms, its value and meaning are essentially constrained by what it does and how its activity provides a solution to some pre-existing need. In the context of education, these arguments are usually framed in terms of efficiencies, and extend to the solving of problems such as time, speed and functionality. If digital technology improves the efficiency of learning processes, that in and of itself is necessarily a moral virtue.

The inverse of this morality of efficiency is another doxic position, that technology is corrupting humanity, forcing inauthentic experience or economic and social alienation. For example, one only has to read the various opinion pieces expressed in mainstream media cautioning about the dangers that social media presents for human intimacy and flourishing (Campbell 2017; Kendrick and Bodfrod 2014). However, there is another way of thinking about technology, as a temporal support, always co-constitutive of those who use it. This argument comes from the French philosopher Bernard Stiegler.

Technics and time

For Stiegler, the split of technics and episteme, and the subsequent dominance of the Aristotelian instrumental definition in Western thinking is problematic for a number of reasons. First, Stiegler argues that the history of Western philosophy is essentially a forgetting of technics. Second, this forgetting has the subsequent effect of limiting how technology is thought as tools or utilities rather than as 'a general economy of sense, meaning and purposeful, worldly engagement rooted in withdrawal of absence of origin' (James 2012: 64). Stiegler argues for 'the need, today, to forge another relation to technics, one that rethinks the bond originally formed by, and between, humanity, technics, language' (1998: 21). For Stiegler, technics is co-constitutive of humanity itself, 'A tool is before anything else, memory: if this were not the case, it could never function as a reference of significance' (1998: 254). Technics are traces of collective memory that the individual accesses through use or exposure. For Stiegler, what makes humans distinctive 'is their ability to conserve the past through the meaning sedimented in technical prosthesis' (James 2012: 67).

> Human beings disappear; their histories remain . . . Among the various traces humans leave behind, some are products with entirely different ends from any 'conversation with memory': a clay pot, for example, is not a tool made to transmit memory. But it does so, spontaneously, nonetheless, which is why archaeologists consult it in their research. (Stiegler 2011: 131)

This 'conversation with memory' or, perhaps better, the exteriorization of memory, relies on Stiegler's reading of the French evolutionary palaeontologist André Leroi-Gourhan and in particular his book *Le Geste et la Parole* (*Gesture and Meaning*). Levi-Gourhan argues that technology, in particular the tools that prehistoric humans used, are intimately co-creative of the characteristics that we use to define the human. Walking upright, using hands to hold tools and language as characteristics of the human species. For example, Levi-Gourhan argues that 'language is a characteristic of humans as are tools, but also that both are the expression of the same intrinsically human property' because the evolution of tools and the evolution of language are 'neurologically linked and cannot be dissociated within the social structures of humankind'

(Leroi-Gourhan 1993: 113–114). While this model of co-constitution of tools and humans is evolutionary, for Stiegler this reaches a point of particular importance with the technics of writing. Stiegler, influenced by Jacques Derrida who supervised his PhD, argues that writing was one of the significant tools that humans developed that crystallized tertiary memory, that is, the experience of others that becomes accessible to us through a medium of recording (technics). The human is an effect of three forms of memory: genetic memory such as that found in DNA, individual memory which stores all our experiences and 'the techno-logical ('epiphylogenetic') memory, which preserves the experiences of past generations in the tools and language we inherit from the past, and therefore is an 'externalized, shared memory' (Fabretti 2015: 14). For Stiegler, each tool contains the memories of past generations, a primitive stone axe is the memory of those who first conceived it, used it and passed it down to the next generation who may have improved the design and added to its uses before then passing it on again. This explains Stiegler's reference to the co-constitution of the who (the human) and the what (the technology).

> Technology carries with it memories of the past – not only of the individual past, but of the past generations. In this sense, it can be said that the 'who' (the human being) invents technology, but at the same time it is invented ('instructed') by it, by the memory of past experiences that technology carries. (Fabretti 2015: 14)

Thus, digital technologies are 'epiphylogenetic' in that they are co-constitutive of how sense is made of social systems and the values communicated within them. One benefit of Stiegler's approach to technics is that it allows us to think about the ways that different technological epochs impact how we understand time, remembering for Stiegler as for Heidegger, it is protention and retention, which constitutes experienced time mediated through the technological tools of a given epoch. If we return to Ball's notion of 'willing subjects', one way of affecting this willing is through mediating the image of the future that an individual accesses as common sense, their culture if you will.

In *Disorientation*, Stiegler outlines how culture is reprogrammed by new technological systems in any given epoch. He calls this 'epochal redoubling' (Stiegler 2009: 7). Epochal redoubling in French (*redoublement epochale*) 'carries the sense of doubling, beginning once again, overhauling or renewing' as well as 'meaning to double, repeat, accelerate or overtake' (James 2012: 69). Stiegler's argument is that due to the industrialization of technology during the twentieth century, the culture is no longer keeping up with, and therefore, renewing, technics. This, for Stiegler, is the kernel of disorientation: technology creates, rather than co-constitutes, human culture.

> Contemporary disorientation is the experience of incapacity to achieve epochal redoubling. It is linked to speed, to the industrialisation of memory resulting from the struggle for speed, and to the specifics of the technologies deployed in that struggle. (Stiegler 2009: 7)

The industrialization of memory refers to Stiegler's concern that memory (time consciousness) is essentially being created by digital technologies that we can never catch up with, or get a grip on. For Stiegler, this disorientation is particularly a product of digital technologies and media because they overturn the constitution of the historical past and 'event-ize' the present through those technologies that select content to construct memories such as news media, social media and technologies that work through engagement (Stiegler 2009: 100). James suggests that Stigler's concern is that when 'our dominant access to, or retention of, the past passes through the diverse media of digital communications and information technologies, then our relation to the perception of 'historical past' may be profoundly altered' (James 2012: 70).

At this stage, it appears that Stiegler is offering a pessimistic view of technology. However, I would argue that this is not the case. He is concerned about the absence of situatedness within global information flows and our ability to take charge of our information, our memories, our experiences and the ways that these can be so easily manipulated through these media platforms. Moreover, he argues, this synchronization of experience is necessary for mass consumption and markets: 'the current prosthetisation of consciousness, the systematic industrialisation of the entirety of retentional devices, is an obstacle to the very individuation process of which consciousness consists' (Stiegler 2011: 4). The challenge, then for Stiegler, is not to condemn these digital technologies (which would be contradictory because for Stiegler all consciousness is always mediated by technics) but rather to understand the ways that these technologies shape consciousness. 'Understanding the singular way in which temporal objects affect consciousness means beginning to understand what gives . . . specificity, its force, and its meaning of transforming life' (Stiegler 2011: 17). If we come to understand the relationship between technology, memory and experience and their potential to be both homogenizing and singular, we can begin to develop strategies to potentially transform our culture.

Digital disruption

Many education systems remain paradoxically torn between the problems of 'basic' skills such as literacy and numeracy and twenty-first-century skills such as creativity and computational proficiencies. It is not unusual to find policy texts extolling back to basics approaches sitting next to other policy texts claiming to want to future-proof students for the 'jobs that don't exist yet'. At the same time, classrooms, schools and school systems are opening themselves up to external forces in ways perhaps unseen in their relatively short history. Data, evidence, informed decision-making, target setting, value-added measures and school ranking are just some of the ways that technology is reshaping school practice and producing new kinds of willing subjects. For example, while notions of good teaching have always shaped teacher conduct, the introduction of standardized testing invariably alters the content of good teaching, such that good teaching is demonstrated by desirable data patterns (Thompson and Cook 2013). This is an example about how change is affected through the technologies at hand, of particular import with the emergence of the 'edtech' industry that sells technological solutions for assessment to schools and school systems. Digital providers are investing heavily in data solutions that aim to revolutionize how schools undertake assessment through digital personalization.

In 2014 the Education Technology Industry Network (ETIN) of the Software & Information Industry Association (SIIA) commissioned a report that looked at the education technology market in P-12 schools in the United States (Richards and Struminger 2014). The report estimated that in 2013 the industry was worth US$8.38 billion. The largest category was in assessment, which was estimated to have claimed US$2.5 billion in the period (Richards and Struminger 2014: 15). Within this, the report found that Personalized Learning Environments (PLEs) that 'included incorporating the use of blended learning environments, expanded use of digital learning platforms, and using adaptive instructional software' were one of the growth areas for profit in the sector in the coming years (Richards and Struminger 2014: 39). This emerging market included the growth of cloud-based services, app development for mobile devices, Big Data analytics and social networks customized for educators. To return to the analysis of Stiegler, this push towards adaptive tech solutions for schools is an example of the move towards an industrialization of memory, relying as it does on standardizing personal experience.

Teaching machines and personal learning –
the story of the analogue

Of course, those digital and adaptive technologies have an analogue antecedent. In the early part of the twentieth century there was much interest in the creation of teaching machines. While teaching machines may be difficult to define, given that there are many technologies or machines that exist in schools and classrooms that do not specifically teach, the standard definition is 'an automatic or self-controlling device that (a) presents a unit of information, (b) provides some means for the learner to respond to the information, and (c) provides feedback about the correctness of the learner's responses' (Benjamin 1988: 704).

The most well-known purveyor of teaching machines was B. F. Skinner, the behavioural psychologist, but the earliest patented teaching machine that satisfies the above requirements was developed and patented by Sidney Pressey in 1928. This machine – the Machine for Intelligence Tests – used a large rotating drum to expose written material in a small window (Benjamin 1988: 705). Students were presented with multiple choice questions with four alternative answers. Pressey's machine could operate in a testing or teaching mode. In the testing mode, the machine recorded student responses and recorded the correct answers on a counter on the back of the machines. In the teaching mode, a lever was raised on the back that prevented the drum rolling onto the next question in the viewing panel until the correct answer had been entered (Benjamin 1988: 705). In the teaching mode, students could attempt each question multiple times. The counter on the back recorded the number of attempts each student had made.

What is notable about Pressey's teaching machine is that it is predicated on behavioural psychology and contemporary views on what constitutes learning – a moral imprimatur to be both efficient and precise. The machine could, if desired, be set to a reward dial that determined how many correct responses a student would need to gain candy as a reward (Benjamin 1988: 706). The logic of Pressey's machine was that efficient machines operating on behaviourist principles could make learning more effective. However, most telling is what Pressey wrote in his 1933 book *Psychology and the New Education*:

> There must be an 'industrial revolution' in education, in which educational science and the ingenuity of educational technology combine to modernize the grossly inefficient and clumsy procedures of conventional education. Work in the schools of the future will be marvelously though simply organized, so as to adjust almost automatically to individual differences and the characteristics of

the learning process . . . for the freeing of teacher and pupil from educational drudgery and incompetence. (pp. 582–583)

The key logics here are individualism, efficiency and the 'freeing' of teachers and pupils from education drudgery. What it demonstrates is that teaching machines have long manifested the desires of their creators for solutions to education problems such as increased student engagement, forms of personalized instruction and learning and for more efficient learning as demonstrated through the precise and correct movement, or speed, that a student manifests in these machinic tasks. Of course, Pressey's machine (and those of his contemporaries) should be seen as analogue machines, in that they specified singular paths and patterns (i.e. spaces) through which a student progresses. The Pressey example shows that the desire for personal, efficient technologies to accelerate learning in ways that free the students from drudgery and, presumably, from the incompetence of the teacher, are neither new nor novel. It is almost as though these desires are hardwired into the problem of education and the history of solutionism in schools and other educational institutions.

Digital personalization – the story of adaptive technologies

If we move forward to the new millennium, advances in computational capacity, software design and the creation of networked infrastructure have created renewed interest in the possibilities of adaptive learning solutions. Personalized learning encompasses many digital promises in education, but its appeal stems largely from the seductive message of the uniqueness of each learner, the promise of learning experiences that will be able to adapt to these individuals with the promise of improved efficiency. Learning personalization is the modification of resources and environments using adaptive technologies 'with the goal that learners remain invested and continue to seek the highest level of knowledge possible for them in each specific field of knowledge' (Thompson and Cook 2017: 746). Adaptive learning systems are 'education technologies that can respond to a student's interactions in real-time by automatically providing the student with individual support' (EdSurge 2016: 15). Adaptive technologies, then, are responsive to the learner, with the promise that continually adapting and updating the content, human–computer interactions and the tasks that each learner confronts improve engagement and motivation. The promise is of improved, if not complete, learner investment, as the learning content, environment and tasks are continually updated and responsive to the profiles/patterns of the learner.

A particularly potent example of this is learning analytics and Big Data, built as it is on a logistics of engagement where 'educational resources and learning environments are continually modified with the goal that learners remain invested' as the 'learning content, environment and tasks are continually updated and responsive to the profiles/patterns of the learner' (Thompson and Cook 2017: 745). Examples include data dashboards that may integrate various surveillance and tracking technologies, digital learning management systems, interactive learning environments, adaptive curriculum, computer adaptive testing, administrative data and various log data. As schools produce, collect and digitize more data, the solutions proffered and the ways that they contribute to new forms of education governance require critical consideration.

> In the age of big data and formative assessment, companies working to help schools efficiently collect, analyze, and make actionable their student data have a tremendous opportunity. This opportunity includes support not only for basic testing, attendance, and grading information, but also for social networks (established and custom-built), new adaptive learning platforms, and relevant family and community information. (Richards and Struminger 2014: 41)

Nowhere is this more evident than in the appeal of digital technologies to solve the problem of standardization. As school systems have pursued strategies of standardization such as standardized tests in recent decades with the aim of improving student achievement, there has been much criticism of the ways that these technologies fail to cater for diverse students and their individual needs (Polesel et al. 2012). Concerns regarding these and other 'unintended consequences' have created fertile conditions for digital solutions that can adapt to individual students and provide feedback in real time.

One example of an adaptive learning system that has had a long involvement in education are Intelligent Tutoring Systems (ITS). ITS are 'computerized learning environments that incorporate computational models from the cognitive sciences, learning sciences, computational linguistics, artificial intelligence (AI), mathematics, and other fields' (Graesser et al. 2012: 451). According to Graesser et al. (2012: 451) ITS are characterized by:

- tracking the psychological states of learners in fine detail, a process called student modeling. These may include subject matter knowledge, skills, strategies, motivation, emotions, and other student attributes.
- adaptively responding with activities that are sensitive to these states and that advance its instructional agenda.

- interactions between student and computer evolve in a flexible fashion that caters to the constraints of both the student and the instructional agenda.

ITS are descendants of the behaviourist psychology that informed the early teaching machines. Technological advances, including the ability to make decisions, to analyse and to respond to learner dispositions, assess levels of motivation and competence and devise the next challenge effected in 'real time'. Many ITS aim to deliver personalized learning experiences to students.

ITS can take a number of different forms. These include Cognitive Tutors that utilize psychological modelling for problem solving where students are exposed to interactions that model either the correct steps to the solution or 'buggy' rules that require the student to have to deviate from the suggested solution path (Graesser et al. 2012: 459). Another example is Constraint-Based Tutors that work through the declarative structure of a solution as opposed to simply working through the procedural steps (Graesser et al. 2012: 462). Conversational Agents are another form of ITS that model human modes of communication such as having a conversation. They can perform different roles such as 'mentors, tutors, peers, players in multiparty games, or avatars' and use speech, gestures, expressions, postures and other forms of embodied interactions to communicate (Graesser et al. 2012: 465).

Computerized technologies that enable the collection and analysis of large data sets in short periods of time result in a surface where the continual modification of activities and objectives is designed to maximize engagement. This constant deformation, to induce the greatest and most effective effort on the part of that learner, a 'logistics of engagement', is crucial to the individuating path that unfolds before while also enfolding a learner. Each learning personalization technology is characterized by its representation of six domains: the field of knowledge, individual learning preferences, a learner's current state of knowledge, learning behaviour, a learner's disposition (level of motivation) and the technical presentation most effective in regard to a learner's profile developed from their preferences, behaviours and dispositions (Thompson and Cook 2017). Each of these must be datafied and patterned for learning personalization to function as a machine of constant engagement. This is an epiphylogenetic system at work: what is captured is always past fields of knowledge, past learning preferences, past behaviours and dispositions and so on that are then compared with external reference points, themselves points in past time, in order to make decisions about the 'real-time' future for the learner. Adaptive systems re-member each learner, and in that re-membering work to co-constitute a better version of the learner that was.

If learning personalization is to involve continual modification of learning environments, then various means of making that environment personal (and effective) for the learner must be available in the system. The learning personalization system must contain a variety of possibilities with respect to: presenting a learning environment, modifying the features of any learning agents that may be at work in that environment, altering the grammar of the written or spoken material involved and changing styles of presentation such as from verbal to visual. These modifications are not always aimed at overcoming a lack of student motivation; they can also intervene to induce even higher levels of motivation from those already motivated. An effective learning personalization process is designed to induce the highest levels of motivation possible for all learners. It must have the capacity to adapt in whatever ways are necessary to maintain the highest possible level of motivation as often as possible. This, then, is the promise of adaptive technologies, personalized learning that fosters high engagement and ongoing motivation. In Stiegler's (2009: 115) terms, motivation and engagement have become 'event-ized', understood as the 'preservation of memory, of the memorable'. This selection, it must be re-membered, is co-constitutive, with implications for how people think the future is mediated through constant engagement. This is the industrialization of memory, where the memory of each learner is constructed through collected data and future activities, tasks and incentive selections based on those patterns (Stiegler 2009).

In 2016 Pearson launched its *Intelligence Unleashed: An Argument for AI in Education* Report as part of its Open Ideas at Pearson blog. This report was a collaboration between Pearson staff and academics from University College, London's Knowledge Lab. This chapter addresses AI, which are

> computer systems that have been designed to interact with the world through capabilities (for example, visual perception and speech recognition) and intelligent behaviours (for example, assessing the available information and then taking the most sensible action to achieve a stated goal) that we would think of as essentially human. (Luckin et al. 2016: 14)

AI in education works through adopting models (the pedagogical model, the domain model and the learner model) which are then used to 'determine the next most appropriate interaction (learning materials or learning activities)' so that the learner continues to engage with the tasks (Luckin et al. 2016: 19). The AI also 'learns', in that 'the learner's activities are continually fed back into the learner model, making the model richer and more complete, and the system "smarter"' (Luckin et al. 2016: 19).

Intelligence Unleashed suggests that an advantage of AI is that 'they typically gather large amounts of data, which, in a virtuous circle, can then be computed to dynamically improve the pedagogy and domain models. This process helps inform new ways to provide more efficient, personalised, and contextualised support, while also testing and refining our understanding of the processes of teaching and learning' (Luckin et al. 2016: 20). AI has further developed models that represent the social, emotional and meta-cognitive aspects of learning enabling 'AIEd systems to accommodate the full range of factors that influence learning' (Luckin et al. 2016: 21). These include ITS 'delivering learning activities best matched to a learner's cognitive needs and providing targeted and timely feedback, all without an individual teacher having to be present' (Luckin et al. 2016: 24). The report concludes by suggesting that AI has the following benefits for education:

- Helps learners gain twenty-first-century skills
- Supports a Renaissance in Assessment
  - Provides just-in-time assessments to shape learning
  - Provides new insights into how learning is progressing
  - Helps us move beyond 'stop-and-test'
- Embodies new insights from the learning sciences
- Gives us lifelong learning partners

What this report shows is the belief that adaptive technologies will change instruction and learning in the future. To be clear, the report does not call for the replacement of teachers; rather, it sees AI as augmenting teaching to make it more efficient and effective. There is a moral need implied for efficiency because this will help to solve pressing problems such as the achievement gap and access to quality learning opportunities. Of course, within this logic of efficiency and effectiveness, a future problem may emerge when machine intelligence is able to do some aspects of a teacher's job as well, if not better, than what they can. As Graesser et al. (2012: 468) state in the context of human versus machine tutors, computers 'may do a better job in cracking the illusions of communication, in inducing student knowledge states, and in implementing complex intelligent-tutoring strategies'.

Implications for education governance

Edtech has long been seen as a key driver of how schools might change. This is big business. The edtech industry is adept at marketing solutions to education problems. The next suite of technologies being marketed to systems and institutions are adaptive and 'real-time', promising rapid feedback and predictive applications. If, as Rhodes (1996) suggests, a new governing structure has emerged in public policy, there is much to gain through examining those 'socio-cybernetic systems' at work. Further, there is much to be gained through understanding these systems in terms of Stiegler's 'the who' and 'the what', what is the technology, how it used, how does it augment memory, how is apperception event-ized? If all consciousness is mediated through technics, then adaptive technologies represent the latest iteration of co-constitution, and the real question concerns the ways that this mediation works. There is something of a double potential here. On the one hand, personalizing technologies in schools have the potential to merely reinforce the programmatic mass consumption that Stiegler sees as disastrous for culture and the human. In this model, personalizing technologies act to reinforce this system such as through a standardizable approach to personalization. Tech solutions are sold to schools and school systems, promising quicker, faster, more efficient tools that will adapt to learner's levels of motivation, to keep them moving, obedient, compliant so to speak. There are a number of dangers with this model. First, it may be that technicizing engagement in this manner forecloses possibilities to think, to be bored, to communicate that may be central to the actualization of learning itself. Second, there is the possibility that what we will get is not tools to help us think better, but a homogenizing technics that in effect standardizes a hyper-individualism when the problems that confront us require form of collective consideration and action. Third, these technologies may shut down possibilities to understand the future as it might be. The temporal beings co-constituted by this mode of technics will always harken to a past inscribed into the algorithms and code at the outset.

This essentially is the problem with the logistics of engagement as a new behaviourism. Keeping students moving is a new tactic of control that works through predictive analytics (Thompson and Cook 2017). However, as Stiegler argues, the double potential of technology is that it also has the potential to deliver what he terms 'singularization'. One of the ways of thinking about this is to consider how it is that culture can interrupt (or catch up) with the ultrarapid technological change that students, schools and school personnel are increasingly contending with. As Stiegler argues, what is needed is an engaged politics of technology:

> such a politics must be a politics of technics, a practical thought of becoming capable of furnishing it with an idea projecting into the future in which becoming

> is an agent . . . A politics of technics should be able to elaborate practical ideas
> capable of asking and regularizing the question as to what must be done within
> the practical domain. (Stiegler 2011: 198–199)

This does not mean that the speed at which this technology operates, its 'real-time' analysis and decision-making, and using engagement as a tool to keep people moving aren't problematic. However, it does suggest an interesting line of inquiry for studies in the socio-cybernetic systems of education governance. These systems are not external to the human or society; they are always and already social (Sellar and Thompson 2016). With that in mind, I thought I'd pose some points at which those interested in education governance might engage technological systems and 'what must be done'.

These include the problem created by the technical expertise required to understand, and therefore interrupt when necessary, these advanced adaptive systems. As these systems become more and more advanced, indeed as they learn strategies for optimization themselves, how can the teacher, parent or even the student make sense of how they work, how decisions are made, how meaning is formed on the basis of adaptive algorithms? The politics requires us to think about how might those so overtly constituted – the good student, the good teacher, the good school – through these systems understand and communicate their limitations, interrupt them, disagree with them and even redesign them.

Also, education is a field that is often regulated through legislation and policy. Historically, education systems change slowly, and to an extent this may be a protective strategy against fads and bad ideas. However, technological change proceeds quickly, much faster than the ability of traditional protective mechanisms to adequately operate. In particular, the nature and speed of technological development and expansion require the production of mass markets for mass consumption, and this necessarily involves large corporations in the design, administration, marketing and analysis of these technological systems. Corporations access public school data, including that produced by students, and use this to improve their products which they sell back to those systems. At the very least this blurs the line between public and private entities. Ongoing ethical dilemmas include how public systems guarantee data privacy, the ethics of seeking consent from these students and their parents for data to be used in these ways, and who ultimately benefits from these technological systems which rely on data produced for 'free'.

Perhaps a student, or a teacher, or a principal may come to own their data and decide who and how it is used.

Finally, a significant challenge confronting adaptive technological systems is their tendency towards a reconfigured morality of efficiency predicated upon an economic logic. The challenge, of course, is to discover how it is that these adaptive technologies could, in Stiegler's view, allow us to ask questions about how we should live, what we should do and how we should desire, which can only happen when they are uncoupled from the exigencies of economic production. Perhaps one strategy is that of Isabelle Stengers (2005), who advocates for systems that promote slowing down, a means for culture to catch up with technology to fully understand the limits of the epoch in which we find ourselves. Epochal redoubling, as Stiegler may suggest. At the very least, responding to ethical questions about data, regulation and the aims of these systems could be an example of culture beginning to grasp the challenge of these adaptive systems.

To return to the main argument in this chapter, as Wilkins and Olmedo argue in their introduction to this book, the governance turn in critical education scholarship has identified that a new policy strategy is at work in education. In this chapter, I have argued that much is to be gained by focusing attention on the effects of temporal politics, particularly in the context of the emergence of digital technologies in systems, schools and classrooms. This is particularly important for adaptive technologies that aim to personalize learning. There is an ongoing danger that education systems will roll out the worst aspect of these technical systems, a homogenizing, standardizing platform that perverts engagement in the name of profitability. Using the work of Stiegler, this chapter suggests that we need to understand technology as temporal machines, and pay attention to how subjectivity functions with the specifics of each technical assemblage.

References

Ball, S. 2009. 'The governance turn!' *Journal of Education Policy* 24 (5): 537–538.

Benjamin, L. 1988. 'A history of teaching machines'. *American Psychologist* 43 (9): 703–712.

Bogard, W. 2009. 'Deleuze and machines: A politics of technology?' In M. Poster and D. Savat (eds), *Deleuze and New Technology*, pp. 15–31. Edinburgh: Edinburgh University Press.

Campbell, D. 2017. 'Facebook and Twitter "harm young people's mental health"'. *The Guardian*, 19 May. Accessed on 27 April 2018. Available at: https://www.theguardian.com/society/2017/may/19/popular-social-media-sites-harm-young-peoples-mental-health (last accessed: 23/04/18).

Clark, T. 2000. 'Deconstruction and technology'. In N. Royle (ed.), *Deconstructions: A User's Guide*, pp. 238–257. Basingstoke: Palgrave Macmillan.

Deleuze, G. 1994. *Difference and Repetition*. New York: Columbia University Press.

Deleuze, G. 1995. 'Postscript on control societies'. In Gilles Deleuze (ed.), *Negotiations*, pp. 177–182. New York: Columbia University Press.

DiCerbo, K., Behrens, J., and Barber, M. 2014. *Impacts of the Digital Ocean on Education*. London: Pearson.

EdSurge. 2016. *Decoding Adaptive*. London: Pearson.

Fabretti, F. 2015. *Software Theory: A Cultural and Philosophical Study*. London: Rowman and Littlefield.

Graesser, A., Conley, M., and Olney, A. 2012. 'Intelligent tutoring systems'. In K. Harris, S. Graham, and T. Urdan (eds), *APA Educational Psychology Handbook: Vol. 3. Application to Learning and Teaching*, pp. 451–473. Washington, DC: American Psychological Association.

Herold, B. 2017. 'Gates, Zuckerberg teaming up on personalized learning'. *Education Week*, 20 June. Accessed on 27 April 2018. Available at: http://www.edweek.org/ew/articles/2017/06/21/gates-zuckerberg-teaming-up-on-personalized-learning.html (last accessed: 23/04/18).

Hughes, J. 2017. 'What is the job creation potential of new technologies?' In K. LaGrandeur, and J. Hughes (eds), *Surviving the Machine Age*, pp. 131–145. Basingstoke: Palgrave Macmillan.

Hunter, I. 1994. *Rethinking the School: Subjectivity, Bureaucracy, Criticism*. St Leonards, NSW: Allen and Unwin.

James, I. 2012. *The New French Philosophy*. Cambridge: Polity Press.

Kendrick, D., and Bodfrod, J. 2014. '7 ways Facebook is bad for your mental health'. *Psychology Today*, 11 April. Accessed on 27 April 2018. Available at: https://www.psychologytoday.com/blog/sex-murder-and-the-meaning-life/201404/7-ways-facebook-is-bad-your-mental-health (last accessed: 23/04/18).

Lawn, M. 2013. 'A systemless system: Designing the disarticulation of English state education'. *European Educational Research Journal* 12 (2): 231–241.

Leroi-Gourhan, A. 1993. *Gesture and Speech*. Cambridge, MA: MIT Press.

Lingard, B., and Rawolle, S. 2011. 'New scalar politics: Implications for education policy'. *Comparative Education* 47 (4): 489–502.

Luckin, R., Holmes, W., Griffiths, M., and Forcier, L. 2016. 'Intelligence unleashed: An argument for AI in education'. *Open Ideas: Thought Leadership from Pearson*. Accessed on 27 April 2018. Available at: https://www.pearson.com/corporate/about-pearson/innovation/open-ideas-at-pearson.html (last accessed: 23/04/18).

Ozga, J. 2009. 'Governing education through data in England: From regulation to self-evaluation'. *Journal of Education Policy* 24 (2): 149–162.

Polesel, J., Dulfer, N., and Turnbull, M. 2012. *The Experience of Education: The Impacts of High Stakes Testing on School Students and Their Families*. Sydney: Whitlam Institute.

Prather, S. 2017. 'Bush Foundation unveils plan to customize how students learn'. *Star Tribune*, 22 February. Accessed on 27 April 2018. Available at: http://www.startribune.com/bush-foundation-unveils-plan-to-customize-how-students-learn/414563723/

Rhodes, R. 1996. 'The new governance: Governing without government'. *Political Studies* 44 (4): 652–667.

Richards, J., and Struminger, R. 2014. *US Education Technology Industry Market: PreK-12*. Washington, DC: Software & Information Industry Association.

Rose, N. 2000. 'Government and control'. *British Journal of Criminology* 40 (2): 321–339.

Sellar, S., and Thompson, G. 2016. 'The becoming-statistic: Information ontologies and computerized adaptive testing in education'. *Cultural Studies<–>Critical Methodologies* 16 (5): 491–501.

Selwyn, N. 2015. 'Data entry: Towards the critical study of digital data and education'. *Learning, Media and Technology* 40 (1): 64–82.

Stengers, I. 2005. 'A cosmopolitical proposal'. In Bruno Latour and Peter Weibel (eds), *Making Things Public: Atmospheres of Democracy*, pp. 994–1003. Cambridge, MA: MIT Press.

Stiegler, B. 1998. *Technics and Time: The Fault of Epimetheus (Vol. 1)*. Stanford: Stanford University Press.

Stiegler, B. 2009. *Technics and Time: Disorientation (Vol. 2)*. Stanford: Stanford University Press.

Stiegler, B. 2011. *Technics and Time 3: Cinematic Time and the Question of Malaise*. Stanford: Stanford University Press.

Thompson, G., and Cook, I. 2013. 'The logics of good teaching in an audit culture: A Deleuzian analysis'. *Educational Philosophy and Theory* 45 (3): 243–258.

Thompson, G., and Cook, I. 2017. 'The logic of data-sense: Thinking through Learning Personalisation'. *Discourse: Studies in the Cultural Politics of Education* 38(5): 1–15.

Wasser, A. 2017. 'How do we recognise problems?' *Deleuze Studies* 11 (1): 48–67.

Williamson, B. 2015. 'Governing software: Networks, databases and algorithmic power in the digital governance of public education'. *Learning, Media and Technology* 40 (1): 83–105.

3

Dispositions and Situations of Education Governance: The Example of Data Infrastructure in Australian Schooling

Sam Sellar and Kalervo N. Gulson

Introduction

This chapter examines the role played in education governance by infrastructures that facilitate the generation, management, analysis and use of data. Following Rhodes (1997: 15), we understand governance to describe 'a change in the meaning of government referring to a *new* process of governing' through '*self-organising, interorganisational networks* characterised by interdependence, resource exchange, rules of the game and significant autonomy from the state' (original emphasis). Data play an important role within these networks. Ozga (2009) has argued, specifically in relation to education, that 'data production and management were and are essential to the new governance turn', and Lawn (2013: 237) has argued that in England 'all elements of education have been altered by the creation and flow of these data . . . The system is held together, and re-imagined, through data'. Our chapter begins from the premise that analysing contemporary education governance entails examining how data in schools and school systems arrange people and things, and shape thinking, values and beliefs.

Our specific focus is on *data infrastructures* (Sellar 2015): the information systems implemented by organizations involved in the governance of schooling that work across and connect multiple scales, from schools and local school boards to state and provincial education ministries, commercial providers of education products and services, national education departments and international organizations such as the Organisation for Economic Co-operation and Development (OECD). The field of infrastructure studies (Edwards et al. 2009) gathered momentum with the rise of the Internet and associated developments in computing and information systems during the 1990s (e.g. Hanseth et al. 1996; Star 1999; Star and Ruhleder 1996). This work can be seen as part of the broader field of science and technology studies, which has been concerned with the history and philosophy of science and the role that practices of classification, standardization and networking have played in the development of modern science. More recently scholars across a range of fields in the social sciences and humanities have used the concept of infrastructure to examine the cultural and technical underpinnings of contemporary life (e.g. Berlant 2016 Easterling 2014; Larkin 2013; Rossiter 2016. The concept of data infrastructure, as we define it here, builds on these studies and refers to information systems that have an explicit focus on making data usable for organizational purposes, including moving data use away 'from individual computers and local networks to more distributed grid or cloud paradigms dependent on ubiquitous links to and through the global Internet' (Edwards et al. 2009: 365). However, infrastructure exceeds its material instantiations in hardware and software; it is also constituted from, and constitutes, social relations, desires and beliefs.

In relation to schooling, Anagnostopoulos et al. (2013: 2) have examined the development of test-based accountability infrastructures in the United States, which they conceptualize as 'complex assemblages of technology, people, and policies that stretch across and beyond the boundaries of our formal educational system'. The development of these infrastructures enables multiple forms of power and new modes of governance. Drawing inspiration from Mukerji (2010), Anagnostopoulos et al. (2013) use the concept of *informatic power* to describe the political effects of large-scale data infrastructures.

Informatic power combines both strategic and logistical power as it ties systems of incentives and sanctions to measurement and computing technologies. Informatic power appears impersonal as its exercise depends on the knowledge, use, production of and control over measurement and computing technologies (ibid.: 11).

The concept of informatic power combines both sides of Mukerji's (2010) distinction between *strategics* – the use of rewards and punishments to control the behaviour of others – and *logistics* – 'the ability to mobilize the natural world for political affect' by 'affecting the environment (context, situation, location) in which human action and cognition take place' (ibid.: 402). The relation between these two elements of informatic power – impersonal logistical power and the desires that strategic power operates on and through – is central to our analysis and our conceptualization of education governance.

The chapter focuses on the empirical example of the Australian National Schools Interoperability Program (NSIP). As part of a larger multinational study of data infrastructure in schooling,[1] we conducted six interviews with government and commercial actors involved in the work of NSIP. We also conducted extensive documentary analysis of relevant websites, technical reports and promotional materials relating to NSIP, interoperability standards and other similar projects such as inBloom in the United States. These data sets inform our analysis of NSIP and the two stories about the project that we tell here.

We use this example to illustrate how a diverse set of conceptual tools drawn from critical social theories can help us to analyse the operation of informatic power in data-driven modes of education governance. We introduce and contrast two main concepts: dispositions and situations. *Dispositions* refer to the synthetic objects that critical macro-sociologies must fashion to explain networks of power relations that constitute social orders (e.g. social class or market society) (Boltanski 2011). *Situations* refer to contexts in which people act and interpret the meaning of their actions and contexts. As Boltanski (2011: 69) writes, a situation can be identified as:

> a certain context in which . . . action occurs and . . . the meaning given to this context by relating it to a determinate type of action. One and the same context can therefore be the site of different situations, at successive moments, but even, particularly in the case of disputes, at the same time for different actors.

We argue that analysing the role of data infrastructure in education governance requires both concepts in order to analyse macro-level dispositions, on the one hand, and what Bevir and Rhodes (2006: 3) call situated agency, on the other; recognizing that dispositions frame and constrain situations, but 'no practice or norm can fix the ways in which people will act, let alone how they will innovate when responding to new circumstances'. Our aim is not to focus once again on the problem of structure and agency, but rather to offer a view of infrastructure and governance as constituted from multiple dynamics across multiple scales.

The rest of our chapter is organized into four main sections. Next, we outline our theoretical framework, which emphasizes the importance of *stories* as a concept that helps to link our two levels of analysis. Stories, or narratives, explain 'actions and practices by reference to the beliefs and desires of actors' (Bevir 2006: 285) and provide a methodological vantage point from which to see dispositions framing, and being re-framed by, narratives woven from particular situations. We then offer two stories: one concerning the disposition of the data infrastructure developed by NSIP for Australian schooling and another that reflects the situated beliefs and interpretations of agents helping to build this infrastructure. We conclude by discussing how these two different stories provide us with a multifaceted understanding of education governance in this particular case.

Theoretical framework: between dispositions and situations

Given the diverse sets of networks that constitute infrastructures, and the diverse set of conceptual tools available to analysts of infrastructure, Larkin (2013: 330) argues 'that discussing an infrastructure is a categorical act. It is a moment of tearing into those heterogeneous networks to define which aspect of which network is to be discussed and which parts will be ignored'. Theorizing infrastructure with the aim to understand what it is – the ontology of infrastructure – is a project in pursuit of a general account. As Levinas (1987: 50) has shown, this is a pursuit that characterizes philosophy more broadly, which tends to reduce the singularity of exterior things by capturing them under a general concept: 'Cognition consists in grasping the individual, which alone exists, not in its singularity which does not count, but in its generality, of which alone there is science.' Here we set out to follow a different path. We assume that infrastructures are large and complex systems that exceed comprehension from a single vantage point. Stories told about infrastructures reflect the multiple and disparate situations from which infrastructures are experienced and the multiple and disparate things and events from which infrastructures are constituted. We seek to avoid the traps for critical explanation that arise when the social theorist assumes a special right to narrate the actions and beliefs of others (Latour 2004. Rather than tearing into infrastructure to make sense of it, we add our narrative to those told by others involved in this particular infrastructure-in-the-making.

The concept of disposition, which we draw from the work of Easterling (2014), is the first of two concepts around which our critical-theoretical story will be told. Easterling (2014: 15) has shown how infrastructure creates spaces of extrastatecraft: 'often undisclosed activities outside of, or in addition to, and sometimes even in partnership with statecraft'. Extrastatecraft is another way to conceive of how governance operates through interorganizational networks and a range of actors that include, but also exceed, the state. Easterling (2014: 21) introduces disposition, defined as 'the character or propensity of an organization that results from all its activity', as a tool for analysing how infrastructures enable extrastatecraft. She argues that, as '[a]n important diagnostic in the fluid politics of extrastatecraft, disposition uncovers accidental, covert, or stubborn forms of power – political temperaments of aggression, submission, or violence – hiding in the folds of infrastructure space' (ibid.: 73). In a classical critical theory move, Easterling argues that reading disposition involves seeking out the hidden by distinguishing between 'what the organization is saying and what it is doing . . . the difference between a declared intent and an underlying disposition' (ibid.: 21).

Disposition is what Boltanski (2011: 1) would characterize as a synthetic object, 'in the sense that it cannot give rise to direct observation, so that revealing it is necessarily the result of a reconstruction on the part of the analyst'. Boltanski argues that critical theories focus on structural asymmetries that produce dominant and dominated groups and he argues that '[d]omination must be unmasked. It does not speak of itself and is concealed in *systems* whose patent forms of power are merely their most superficial dimension' (ibid.: 2). Reading disposition means speaking of the domination concealed in what systems are doing, by attending not only to the social orders that produce domination, but also to how material orders, or logistics, can 'act as an independent form of power in contest with strategies of social domination' (Mukerji 2010: 421). Of course, logistics may also operate in ways that complement such strategies. Analysing disposition, then, is a matter of fabricating something through speaking about what cannot be observed. Critical-theoretical narratives, like other forms of storytelling, involve an imaginative construction (Bevir 2006).

Easterling's concept of disposition can be traced back to the work of Francois Jullien (1995). As Janet Lloyd explains in her translator's introduction, Jullien employs the French term *dispositif strategique* to refer to 'how things are disposed strategically so as to be effective' (ibid.: 9). This notion is present in other philosophical developments of the term, of which Foucault's work is perhaps the most prominent example. Foucault (1980) describes a dispositif as a system of relations established between heterogeneous elements. A dispositif is primarily strategic and, as Agamben (2009) argues, realizes the activity of governance by producing the governed subject. A dispositif is 'a set of practices, bodies of knowledge, measures, and institutions that aim to manage, govern, control, and orient – in a way that purports to be useful – the behaviors, gestures, and thoughts of human beings' (ibid.: 12). However, a dispositif also involves '*functional overdetermination*', or logistical power, which produces effects that resonate with one another to rework the system in ways that generate new strategic capacities (Foucault 1980). Bailey (2013: 814) has applied this concept to the analysis of education policy, showing how 'policy refers not only to formal codes and directives from a central authority, but also to a multiplicity of "material" and "technical" forms'. Strategics and logistics, once again. With this genealogy of the concept in mind, we can say that disposition produces the subjects that find themselves situated within infrastructures, understood as particular arrangements of things and capacities for thought and action. Disposition affords a perspective on how the social traditions and material environments from which infrastructure is constituted act as substrates for, and modes of, governance.

The subjects produced by dispositions interpret and act upon the situations in which they find themselves, narrating their activities in ways that influence disposition in turn. Easterling (2014: 88) suggests that 'the stories that a culture tells about infrastructure space can script the use of that space . . . some social stories play an additional, powerful role in the ongoing process of shaping disposition'. Larkin (2013: 329) argues for the importance of 'being alive to the formal dimensions of infrastructures, understanding what sort of semiotic objects they are, and determining how they address and constitute subjects, as well as their technical operations'. While there has been a tendency in infrastructure studies to focus on logistical power produced through impersonal technical operations, which are often hidden or 'black boxed', the importance of analysing how infrastructure is represented and interpreted in stories, and as situations, cannot be overlooked.

Bevir and Rhodes (2006) argue for an interpretivist approach to studying governance that focuses on situated agency. While recognizing the importance of analysing synthetic objects such as disposition, Bevir and Rhodes draw attention to the situations and beliefs of individuals from which political and social structures emerge. This is a bottom-up approach that foregrounds the contingency of governance. For Bevir and Rhodes (2006), political phenomena must be analysed from their basis in intersubjective beliefs. Stories are situated interpretations that play an important role in this approach, as both objects of study and modes of representation.

Our theoretical framework seeks to combine attention to dispositions *and* situations as both part of infrastructure and governance, without subsuming the latter under the former. We heed Bevir and Rhodes (2006: 5) point about the need for this dual focus in the analysis of governance:

> Explanatory concepts must suggest . . . how social influences permeate beliefs and actions even when actors do not recognize such influence [disposition]. To accept agency is, however, to imply people have the capacity to adopt beliefs and actions, even novel ones, for reasons of their own [situations].

Therefore, we do not aim to provide one general view of governance. Instead, we begin from the view that studies of governance should analyse how it emerges, functions and is narrated in specific cases. We turn to one such case now, that of NSIP, to analyse the interplay between disposition and situation in this particular infrastructure of governance.

Context: the Australian National Schools Interoperability Program

The Australian National Schools Interoperability Program, or NSIP, was established to implement the Schools Interoperability Framework (SIF) in Australia. SIF is an interoperability standard that specifies common data formats and enables data to be exchanged between systems. Interoperability is a particular requirement of increasingly networked information systems (Gruber 1993). SIF was originally developed in the United States and Australian Ministers of Education agreed to adopt and develop an Australian specification in 2009.

The NSIP was formally established in 2010 to use SIF to make interoperable the information systems used by government and non-government schools and school systems across Australia. It is a joint initiative of Federal, State and Territory Ministers for Education and is supported by State and Territory school systems, the Australian Government, and the Catholic and Independent school sectors. Chief Information Officers (CIOs) from each State and Territory education system direct the programme through a steering group and a relatively small team undertake the day-to-day technical work.

An early NSIP pilot project deployed SIF to develop a system for sharing data between schools in Western Australia, South Australia and Northern Territory (SIF AU, n.d.). This project used a unique student identifier and a central application to aggregate student data from three jurisdictions and to update it on a near real-time basis. Two key findings were that to 'continue to serve the needs of the Australian education sector, the SIF AU specification requires ongoing development, including regular engagement with local industry and SIF vendors' and '[v]endors need access to infrastructure within jurisdictions' (SIF AU, n.d.). From its first stages, then, building this infrastructure has involved public–private partnerships between government and education technology companies.

Given its mission, NSIP is closely aligned with the Australian SIF Association (SIF AU), which currently has around forty members, including governments and government bodies, Catholic and independent school bodies, and commercial vendors. The main product categories offered by the vendors are information management systems, including student information systems and other school administration software, but there is a diverse array of companies involved, including app developers and providers of medical simulation software. These companies range in size and their level of participation.

Australian State and Territory education departments have agreed to purchase SIF-compliant student information systems when replacing their current systems. NSIP has also overseen the development of a Student Information System Baseline Profile (SPB) that uses the SIF data model to specify common data definitions. The Australian SIF Association explains that '[i]t will facilitate the next generation of online services being linked securely into a school's systems – by reducing the complexity, cost for schools and increasing the ease for vendors' (SIF AU, n.d.; emphasis added). The SPB was developed in collaboration with a group of nine SIF vendors and illustrates the potential commercial benefits of interoperability standards.

NSIP has created the conditions for new relationships between governments, schools and commercial providers, based on data sharing arrangements. The aim is to enable vendors to discover information that supports their business operations by accessing relevant data about schools and students. The NSIP website explains that:

> in the next 3–5 years the CIOs of all education jurisdictions see a significant shift in their role in the market. This shift will be for education jurisdictions to act as information hubs, exposing student, staff and school data to trusted third party developers, with the expectation that the market will provide products of value to schools that make use of that information. (http://www.nsip.edu.au/ hits-hub-integration-testing-service)

This is a model where school systems provide access to data for vendors to use as a resource for product development and maintenance. For example, testing to ensure that a particular software package is interoperable can be undertaken before tendering for a project or to develop commercial off-the-shelf products or services that can be marketed to a broader customer base.

NSIP has now established a national Learning Services Architecture (LSA) for integrating information systems across schools, school systems and commercial vendors. These systems are central to the interorganizational networks through which schooling is now governed (Lawn 2013). The LSA maps out a trajectory towards the establishment of data hubs for all Australian school systems. This model has the potential to enfranchise students and schools in relation to data privacy and management through a Student Data Entitlement and smart contracts that could provide schools and students with control over what data can be used, by whom and for what purposes (http://www.nsip.edu.au/lsa-2017-roadmap).

NSIP is an exemplary case of what is now one of the most well-established data infrastructures in education. In 2015, the Access 4 Learning (A4L) community was launched as an overarching organization bringing together SIF associations that had emerged in North America, the United Kingdom and Australia over the previous 15 years. The A4L community identifies itself as 'non-profit collaboration composed of schools, districts, local authorities, states, US and International Ministries of Education, software vendors and consultants who collectively address all aspects of learning information management and access to support learning' (www.a4l.org). A4L argues that SIF now constitutes 'the most comprehensive data model and mature infrastructure interoperability framework in use globally in education' (A4L 2015).

Story 1: making markets

Our first story about NSIP is a critical-theoretical reading of disposition (see Sellar 2017 for a fuller account) that shows how this particular data infrastructure is making markets for education products and services and thereby increasing the role of commercial actors within governance networks. SIF has its genesis in the software industry as the brainchild of Bill Gates, who launched the concept at the US School Administrator's Annual Conference in 1999 (SIF Association 2012). Gates described the need for school districts to develop 'digital nervous systems' built on data standards that would constitute 'a big step forward for both the educational software industry and schools' (Microsoft Corp. 1999). This initiative was led by Microsoft and was supported by 18 other software companies and the Software and Information Industry Association (SIIA). As described earlier, the development of an Australian SIF specification has involved a community of education technology vendors in Australia.

Standardization makes markets possible (Busch 2011) because it helps to disentangle and identify the various goods and agents involved in market exchanges (Callon 1998). In some cases, commercial actors seek to impose their own proprietary standards (e.g. Microsoft Windows Media Audio, or WMA, as an alternative to MP3), but SIF is an open standard that has been developed by a community of vendors. As Callon (1998) argues, standardization often begins with a more open process that enables markets to emerge. While some actors may seek to impose proprietary standards to 'lock-in' customers, jumpstarting the work of standardization is a necessary precursor and in the initial stages of market making it can be advantageous to participate in open standards-setting forums.

Education technology markets are currently in the early stages of being standardized and made profitable at scale, and these are network markets in which the value of a product depends on how widely it is used. Shapiro and Varian (1999: 13) explain that:

> technologies subject to strong network effects tend to exhibit long lead times followed by explosive growth. The pattern results from positive feedback: as the installed base of users grows, more and more users find adoption worthwhile. Eventually, the product achieves critical mass and takes over the market.

The long lead time for the market for information management systems in education stretches back to when SIF was initially specified in 1999. In these circumstances, the development of open standards is a good strategy for growing the total value of the market and potentially sparking explosive growth of positive externalities as the network of users reaches a critical point. From this perspective, the work of NSIP, and the development of data infrastructure in Australian schooling, can be understood as a strategy to make network markets for data-driven products and services, with benefits for both customers and suppliers.

As Pollock and Williams (2008) argue, managing the relationship between users and suppliers is an important element of growing markets for software packages. NSIP constitutes an example of 'management by community', which enables a transition from providing particular solutions for individual customers to developing standardized generic technologies for a wider customer base whose requirements are shaped by vendors. The forum provided by NSIP enables 'suppliers and users of software packages [to] constantly work towards a pragmatic solution of the tension between the generic and the particular' (Pollock and Williams 2008: 175).

The data infrastructure being created by NSIP is creating new conditions for education technology vendors to work with schools, school systems and governments to specify and design an architecture for data management and use in Australian schooling. By agreeing to purchase SIF-compliant information systems, Australian governments and their school systems have exercised strategic power to incentivize vendors to engage in the work of standardization because it promises to create larger markets. In turn, vendor participation in this work involves the exercise of logistical power as their commercial interests shape the technical systems through which schooling is represented and understood. While reading the surface of this infrastructure presents us with a mundane technical story about more efficient data exchange, a critical-theoretical analysis of disposition draws attention to informatic power operating across interorganizational networks and suggests that this infrastructure enables a form of extrastatecraft driven by commercial interests that the state has encouraged.

Story 2: moralizing markets

Our second story also begins with Bill Gates. InBloom is another data interoperability initiative that Gates sponsored, through the Bill and Melinda Gates Foundation, and it was launched in the United States in 2013. As Bulger et al. (2017: 3) explain, inBloom was 'intended to address the challenge of siloed data storage that prevented the interoperability of existing school data sets by introducing shared standards [SIF], an open source platform that would allow local iteration, and district-level user authentication to improve security'. However, it generated a powerful backlash of concern about student data privacy and was drawn to a close after one year. InBloom shared similar aspirations to NSIP and its spectacular failure has served as a warning to those involved in similar initiatives elsewhere. There has also been growing public concern and political opposition in response to the level of influence that large and powerful educational publishers, such as Pearson, are gaining in schooling through new data-driven education technologies and associated modes of digital governance (Hogan et al. 2016; Williamson 2016). These developments are creating a new tradition against which some education technology companies are narrating their business objectives and ethos. We present one such narrative, or story of infrastructure, here.

The Australian education technology market is relatively modest and is populated by many small- to medium-sized companies that have tended to mainly serve one jurisdiction; that is, one state or territory school system, or private schools rather than government schools. As NSIP gains momentum it may reconfigure this market by opening up growth possibilities for these companies if they can more easily sell their products into other jurisdictions. However, the value to commercial vendors has yet to be fully realized and those involved in the development of NSIP have not been motivated by short-term profits. We spoke to two staff members – Luke and Ryan (both pseudonyms) – who work at a medium-sized company that has been active in the development of NSIP. Both spoke about the motivations for this involvement in ways that trouble simplistic narratives about commercial interests.

Luke is a software developer who has worked on the technical advisory board for NSIP. He explained that, up until now, there has been 'no commercial reason to [participate in NSIP], so why go and invest ten, twenty, thirty thousand dollars developing this stuff if you can't plug into it'? While the platform may now provide significant opportunities to 'scale up', this reinforces the point made earlier that the market is still in the lead time during which network effects emerge. However, Luke explained that despite initially high barriers to entry his company has contributed to pilot projects and participated in technical working groups to help establish the standard. In the process, Luke has attempted to represent the views of smaller companies that cannot afford to participate in this work, as well as defending the design intent of the standard against attempts to modify it in ways that make it less elegant and functional. He also described how he helped other group members, often from school systems, to understand better how the standard operates and how to configure their information systems.

Ryan, another more senior staff member from the same company, explained to us that their business objectives were different from those of larger multinational companies, such as Pearson or IBM, which have been actively pursuing data-driven technologies that aim to optimize learning and may potentially displace the teacher in the classroom. Ryan explained that his company sought to stand 'out of the way of teachers as much as we can and provide them with the data that they need . . . so that it is complementary to their delivery'. In contrast to other prominent corporate visions of artificial intelligence in the classroom (Luckin et al. 2016), Ryan indicated that he 'sincerely hopes that doesn't happen. I think teachers are such a big part of the learning life, I hope that we find a complementary mechanism for teachers . . . to do what they do better'. He continued:

> I think the relationship that people have with teachers . . . growing up through an education system you always find . . . people that you look up to not only for the academic thing but for their human qualities and I think that replacing

that teaching by a purely automated thing would mean that people miss out on something that is important . . . a lot of it is about learning how to be a person.

During this interview, we were presented with an unexpected vision of data infrastructure as a complement to liberal education, and this vision provides a striking counterpoint to much of the rhetoric about big data in education.

Across both of these interviews, we heard stories about working closely with a range of partners to undertake careful and collaborative technical work and to develop tools that help teachers do a good job of work. Luke's story is framed by a commitment to his profession and its craft, while Ryan's is framed by the tradition of liberal education. Neither understand their work in relation to governance and both invoke values and desires beyond commercial interests to explain their actions. These values and desires are also part of this infrastructure-in-the-making.

Discussion and conclusion

Our story about the disposition of NSIP draws attention to the interests that ostensibly give this infrastructure a particular propensity. Emerging from the business strategy of Microsoft in the 1990s, SIF and its various implementations can be understood as a long game of standardization that will make school systems more open to commercial activity as education technology markets develop. Moreover, this story provides a frame through which the actions of Australian education technology companies, and the staff who work for them, can be read. There is no hiding the fact that these companies exist to make a profit and the actions of software developers and CIOs in these companies could be explained in these terms.

From the perspective of the first story, we can read the second as one about interests linked to (a) early adoption of a standard and active participation in standards setting and (b) using social values to carve out a market niche that is distinct from that of larger companies experiencing public criticism. Set against the backdrop of inBloom's failure and the outcry about Pearson, the narrative provided by Ryan could be interpreted in terms of Shamir's (2008: 3) arguments about the moralization of the economy and corporate social responsibility:

The moralization of the market . . . has a critical potential in that the demand for socially responsible market actors – typically exerted through social struggles in the form of consumer boycotts and public shaming campaigns – may somewhat restrain their drive for financial gains.

Ryan's privileging of the values of liberal education may be a response to the moralization of the market, but at the same time this 'entails the economization of morality; a process which is compatible with the general neo-liberal drive to ground social relations in the economic rationality of markets' (Shamir 2008: 3). In other words, social responsibility becomes a new, profitable and potentially necessary market niche as large educational publishing and technology companies face public backlashes. While this theorization surely offers some insight into this situation, to assume that it provides a sufficient account would be to miss something important about this infrastructure and, especially, to foreclose on possibilities for change in relation to values that can be easily ignored in analyses of large-scale, technologically advanced systems. Ryan's narrative offers insight into how the *context* of datafication in education could give rise to different *situations*.

Interoperability standards in Australian schooling provide an important substrate for new governance functions by further embedding market logics and behaviours in public education systems, by moralizing the market and economizing morality, and by enabling the further spread and development of data-driven practices of audit and accountability. These forms of education governance emerge from particular traditions (e.g. neo-liberalism), but are also being reworked in relation to situated agencies. We argue that the case of NSIP is both a commercially interested market-making process and includes situations where the moralization of the market (Shamir 2008) is helping to generate imaginaries of education technology that vary from what has been the standard script.

The people who are helping to build this infrastructure interpret their work in relation to their commitment to professional communities and performing their craft well. The values and beliefs that frame their narratives are also part of this infrastructure and this troubles the notion that that infrastructure space has a single disposition hiding in its folds. While we could explain these situated interpretations in economic terms, we have sought to avoid that strategy here, because this would make us complicit in excluding these values from the analysis by claiming that they cynically dissimulate or misrecognize more fundamental interests. Resisting the interpretation of the second story in terms of the first can feel uncomfortable to critical minds, but critical theory itself is also part of an infrastructure, with all that entails in terms of governance and the production of subjects. We have instead tried to offer both stories on a level footing. We argue that this approach to presenting multiple situated narratives about governing dispositions provides a better story about what this particular infrastructure is, what it does, where it might be open to change and how new traditions of digital education governance might emerge.

Note

1   The project is titled *Data infrastructure, mobilities and network governance in education* and is funded by the Australian Research Council Discovery Project scheme (DP150102098). The Chief Investigators are Bob Lingard, Kalervo N. Gulson, Sam Sellar and Keita Takayama. The Partner Investigators are Christopher Lubienski and P. Taylor Webb.

References

A4L. 2015. Introducing the Access 4 Learning Community – The SIF Association Matures to Address Not Only Data Management but Data Usage for Learning. Accessed on 27 April 2018. Retrieved from: https://web.archive.org/web/20160304072743/https://www.sifassociation.org/NewsRoom/Press%20Releases/Introducing%20the%20Access%204%20Learning%20Community.pdf (last accessed: 23/04/18).

Agamben, G. 2009. *What Is an Apparatus? And Other Essays*. Stanford: Stanford University Press.

Anagnostopolous, D., Rutledge, S. A., and Jacobsen, R. (eds). 2013. *The Infrastructure of Accountability: Data Use and the Transformation of American Education*. Cambridge, MA: Harvard Education Press.

Bailey, P. L. 2013. 'The policy dispositif: historical formation and method'. *Journal of Education Policy* 28 (6): 807–827.

Berlant, L. 2016. 'The commons: Infrastructures for troubling times'. *Environment and Planning D: Society and Space* 34 (3): 393–419.

Bevir, M. 2006. 'How narratives explain'. In D. Yanow and P. Schwartz-Shea (eds), *Interpretation and Method: Empirical Research Methods and the Interpretive Turn*, pp. 281–290. London and New York: M. E. Sharpe.

Bevir, M., and Rhodes, R. 2006. *Governance Stories*. London: Routledge.

Boltanski, L. 2011. *On Critique: A Sociology of Emancipation*. Cambridge, UK and Malden, MA: Polity.

Bulger, M., McCormick, P., and Pitcan, M. 2017. *The Legacy of InBloom: Working Paper*. New York: Data & Society Research Institute.

Busch, L. 2011. *Standards: Recipes for Reality*. Cambridge, MA and London: The MIT Press.

Callon, M. 1998. 'Introduction: The embeddedness of economic markets in economics'. *The Sociological Review* 46 (S1): 1–57.

Easterling, K. 2014. *Extrastatecraft: The Power of Infrastructure Space*. London and New York: Verso.

Edwards, P. N., Bowker, G. C., Jackson, S. J., and Williams, R. 2009. 'Introduction: An agenda for infrastructure studies'. *Journal of the Association for Information Systems* 10 (5): 6.

Foucault, M. 1980. *Power/knowledge: Selected Interviews and Other Writings, 1972–1977*. New York: Pantheon Books.

Gruber, T. 1993. 'A translation approach to portable ontology specifications'. *Knowledge Acquisition* 5: 199–220.

Hanseth, O., Monteiro, E., and Hatling, M. 1996. 'Developing information infrastructure: The tension between standardization and flexibility'. *Science, Technology, & Human Values* 21 (4): 407–426.

Hogan, A., Sellar, S., and Lingard, B. 2016. 'Commercialising comparison: Pearson puts the TLC in soft capitalism'. *Journal of Education Policy* 31 (3): 243–258.

Jullien, F. 1995. *The Propensity of Things: Toward a History of Efficacy in China*. New York: Zone Books.

Larkin, B. 2013. 'The politics and poetics of infrastructure'. *Annual Review of Anthropology* 42: 327–343.

Latour, B. 2004. 'Why has critique run out of steam? From matters of fact to matters of concern'. *Critical Inquiry* 30(2): 225–248.

Lawn, M. 2013. 'A systemless system: Designing the disarticulation of English state education'. *European Educational Research Journal* 12 (2): 231–241.

Levinas, E. 1987. *Collected Philosophical Essays*. Pittsburgh, PA: Duquesne University Press.

Luckin, R., Holmes, W., Griffiths, M., and Forcier, L. 2016. Intelligence unleashed: An argument for AI in education. Accessed on 27 April 2018. Retrieved from Open Ideas: Thought Leadership from Pearson: https://www.pearson.com/corporate/about-pearson/innovation/open-ideas-at-pearson.html (last accessed: 23/04/18).

Microsoft Corp. 1999. Schools Interoperability Framework Initiative Releases First Working Specification Following Successful School Pilots. Accessed on 27 April 2018. Retrieved from https://news.microsoft.com/1999/11/10/schools-interoperability-framework-initiative-releases-first-working-specification-following-successful-school-pilots/#sm.0000yj2my0lc0dswwc41t8rob1yxg (last accessed: 23/04/18).

Mukerji, C. 2010. 'The territorial state as a figured world of power: Strategics, logistics, and impersonal rule'. *Sociological Theory* 28 (4): 402–424.

Ozga, J. 2009. 'Governing education through data in England: From regulation to self-evaluation'. *Journal of Education Policy* 24 (2): 149–162.

Pollock, N., and Williams, R. 2008. *Software and Organisations: The Biography of the Enterprise-Wide System or How SAP Conquered the World*. London and New York: Routledge.

Rhodes, R. A. 1997. *Understanding Governance: Policy Networks, Governance, Reflexivity and Accountability*. Buckingham: Open University Press.

Rossiter, N. 2016. *Software, Infrastructure, Labor: A Media Theory of Logistical Nightmares*. London: Routledge.

Sellar, S. 2015. 'Data infrastructure: A review of expanding accountability systems and large-scale assessments in education'. *Discourse: Studies in the Cultural Politics of Education* 36 (5): 765–777.

Sellar, S. 2017. 'Making network markets in education: The development of data infrastructure in Australian schooling'. *Globalisation, Societies and Education* 15 (3): 341–351.

Shamir, R. (2008). 'The age of responsibilization: On market-embedded morality'. *Economy and Society* 37 (1): 1–19.

Shapiro, C., and Varian, H. 1999. *Information Rules: A Strategic Guide to the Network Economy*. Boston, MA: Harvard Business School Press.

SIF Association. 2012. The SIF Association celebrates 15 years! Accessed on 27 April 2018. Retrieved from https://www.sifassociation.org/NewsRoom/Press%20Releases/SIF%20Association%20Celebrates%2015%20Years.pdf (last accessed: 23/04/18).

SIF Association Australia. n.d. Tri-Borders: Supporting students across SA, NT and WA. Accessed on 27 April 2018. Retrieved from http://www.nsip.edu.au/sites/nsip.edu.au/files/Pilot%202.1%20Tri-Borders.pdf (last accessed: 23/04/18).

Star, S. L. 1999. 'The ethnography of infrastructure'. *American Behavioural Scientist* 43 (3): 377–391.

Star, S., and Ruhleder, K. 1996. 'Steps toward an ecology of infrastructure: Design and access for large information spaces'. *Information Systems Research* 7 (1): 111–134.

Williamson, B. 2016. 'Digital methodologies of education governance: Pearson plc and the remediation of methods'. *European Educational Research Journal* 15 (1): 34–53.

Part Two

Evaluation Regimes

Exploring the Role of School Inspectors in Implementing and Shaping Policy: A Narrative Approach

Jacqueline Baxter

Introduction and context

School inspection, the inspection of standards and quality of education, has gained enormous credence throughout the OECD (Organisation for Economic Co-operation and Development) over the last twenty years. There are a number of reasons for its rise in popularity among governments within Western democracies. The first is the rising tide of neo-liberal ideas in education emanating from the Chicago School of Economics, leading to dominant narratives of education as an economic driver and to a 'governing by numbers' approach to quality control (Ozga et al. 2011: 205). This approach relies upon statistical evaluations of pupil results, league tables and bilateral country comparisons of student performance such as PISA (The Programme for International Student Assessment) (Bieber and Martens 2011; Grek 2009). Such cross-national comparators have become highly influential in convincing governments that their education systems are performing well or otherwise (Clarke and Baxter 2014). The media have amplified this effect by relying heavily upon these regular reports which appear to simplify rationale for failure while lionizing examples of successful systems – for example, Finland (Baxter and Rönnberg 2014).

Inspection systems, however, are not homogenous but operate in a variety of different ways according to whether they favour a 'hard regulatory' approach or one that is no less powerful but rather relies upon professional conversations to drive school improvement – often termed the 'soft' approach (Grek et al. 2013). For example, in Scotland the school's inspectorate places great emphasis on the ability of inspectors to evaluate schools and through narrative and dialogue, convince the schools of the need to improve. Their training and development programmes include elements such as influencing skills (e.g. see Ozga et al. 2014). Other countries such as the Republic of Eire rely heavily on school self-evaluation, believing that school improvement should be driven by the schools themselves (for further information see Brown et al. 2017).

In England, the system of inspection has changed radically since its inception as Her Majesty's Inspectorate (HMI) in 1839, and reinvention as Ofsted (The Office for Standards in Education, Children's Services and Skills) in 1992. As Lawton and Gordon (1987: 1) proudly announce in their book HMI, 'Her Majesty's Inspectorate of Schools (HMI) is unique. No other country possesses a group of professional educational advisers who operate independently from the controlling central authority – The Department of Education and Science (DES)'. However, since then the impartiality of Ofsted has frequently been questioned and the agency has frequently been the subject of numerous media stories alleging that it has become too 'cosy' with its political masters (Baxter and Rönnberg 2014).

The role of the school inspector is a complex one and differs widely from country to country. Yet even close scrutiny of the job description fails to give a good account of the work of inspectors as it is operationalized; the political aspects of the work and of the identities and motivation of those who seek to perform this work as my recent research reports (Baxter 2016). Inspectors play a unique role in the policy implementation process, but also feeding into and strongly influencing its creation, as accounts from a number of OECD (Organisation for Economic Co-operation and Development) countries into the work of inspector's reports reveal. The publication *School Inspectors: Policy Implementers, Policy Shapers in National Policy* Contexts (Baxter 2016) includes qualitative studies from several OECD member states and explores the ways in which inspectors carry out policy and, in turn, their role in the evolution of new policies and new inspection systems.

Investigating such phenomena involves exploration of both the macro context (the national and international policy contexts in which such systems are situated) while also calling for a focused investigation of the quotidian activities of inspectors as they go about their work and practices. This chapter offers an account of such work introducing narrative as a method of exploring stories of inspection.

This chapter adds to the work on education governance by exploring how a quasi-autonomous non-government organization (QUANGO) is used by government not only to evaluate standards in education but, through the act of inspection, to govern it (Ozga and Segerholm 2014). It illustrates how the outsourcing of inspection to this quango constitutes an instrument of governmentality (Foucault 1980) in which the state essentially outsources the responsibility for ensuring the 'well-being' of education to an external body. This phenomenon is illustrative of Foucault's definition of governmentality, highlighting on the one hand the centrality of the state, and on the other the need to govern at arm's-length (Baxter and Clarke 2013). The inspectorate, with its perpetual reinvention of what a good education looks like (Baxter 2014) via shifting sets of criteria, is essentially understood by this study as one of the tactics of government to make possible 'the continual definition and re definition of what is within the competence of the state and what is not' (Foucault 1994: 221). The inspectorate was set up as a prism through which the public would be able to view the so-called secret garden of education (Maclure 2000). This was achieved by the creation of rolling sets of criteria and the recruitment of inspectors whose role it is to judge schools according to those criteria (Ozga et al. 2013). The inspectorate's power to effectively shut down schools whose performance does not match up to expectations articulated within the criteria renders it one of the hybrid forms of governance established between old bureau-professional and new managerial regimes (Clarke and Newman 1997). As such it is a core element within the state's ability to 'discipline' managers into maximizing the value of this vital public service (Power 1997).

The approach used in this study, the narrative approach, has been employed in order to explore the ways in which inspectors view their role and purpose. This approach was chosen for its ability to reveal not only what inspectors do, but the ways in which they think about their role and purpose, illustrated through other studies of this nature (Patterson 2002; Snow and Anderson 1987). The chapter adds to knowledge in this area through demonstrating the power of this approach in investigating some of the challenges and tensions around the state's approach to governing education.

The chapter begins with an account of the research questions and how they arose. This is followed by explanation of the narrative approach and rationale for its use. The chapter then goes on to explore the findings of the study and concludes with an exploration of the advantages and drawbacks of this approach within qualitative research.

Background

As already mentioned, school inspection has formed part of many OECD member states' approaches to governing education for some time now (Maclure

2000; Segerholm 2009). International comparisons such as PISA (Programme of International Student Assessment) have combined with a neo-liberal hegemony emanating from the Chicago School of Economics and impacting on public services worldwide. This has resulted in 'developed' countries placing a strong emphasis on education as an economic driver (Ozga et al. 2013). Given its resultant importance to governments, political leaders have turned to inspection as a form of quality controlling and governing education (Baxter et al. 2015). These inspectorates are far from homogenous, differing in their modus operandi and also their approaches to using inspection to drive improvement (Ehren and Swanborn 2012; Ehren et al. 2013). They are also far from static, modifying their inspection frameworks depending upon the prevailing political climate in which they are situated (Baxter and Hult 2017).

In England, the inception of the Coalition administration in 2010 continued a pattern that had begun in 1988 with the Education Reform Act (Parliament 1988), an act which introduced local management of schools (LMS), concomitantly offering state-funded schools control of their own budgets. The Conservative-Liberal Democrat Coalition which came to power in 2010 sought to extend these freedoms by ensuring that far greater numbers of schools converted to academy status. Academy status for schools was first introduced by Labour under Prime Minister Tony Blair. Originally intended to improve inner city failing schools, the project had delivered some outstanding successes in its first iteration (see Woods and Brighouse 2014) but was also prone to criticisms, namely whether academy status in itself accounted for success, and stressing that some academies had serious shortcomings. There were also considerable concerns about the influence of sponsors, and about the apparent lack of accountability of these organizations (HOC 2015). The Coalition built on the idea of academies – state-funded schools with curricular and financial freedoms – in a drive to create a more competitive education system, one in which poor schools would be shut down or forcibly converted to academy status or sponsored by other organizations, often from the world of commercial business (HCEC 2014–15). The inspectorate would play a pivotal part in this by ensuring that inspections were regularly carried out and the results of these inspections would determine a school's future (Ofsted 2012). Although the inspectorate since 1992 had been central in benchmarking quality in education, they had not so far operated in a fully marketized environment such as that proposed by the Coalition Government.

But, in common with other areas of the public service undergoing similar disaggregation, new levels of school autonomy have demanded new systems of inspection and inspection frameworks that are able to monitor and control newly autonomous institutions, while also retaining credibility with government and public (Baxter and Hult 2017). Several white papers and acts had also made it clear that in order for inspection to be cost-effective at a time of so many cuts to public services, a far greater link must be made between inspection and school improvement. In order to effect this the government not only demanded a change in inspection frameworks, but also aimed at creating an inspectorate that was 'much closer to the ground and much nearer to schools' (Parliament 2011a: section 44). This change was combined with a drive to re-model the inspectorate workforce which had been criticized in the past for being out of touch with the schools it inspects (Baxter 2013; Paton 2012).

The research explored in this chapter, carried out at a time when the inspectorate was in transition, explores the inspector's role as a policy implementer as well as some of the challenges of the role and the underlying drive. In so doing it explores whether inspectors see themselves as policy shapers or as policy implementers. This chapter also reports in some depth the use of a constructionist narrative approach and what this lent to the evidence gathering process and findings.

Background to the project and caveat

The data explored in this chapter were collected for the project Governing by inspection: School Inspection and Education Governance in Scotland, England and Sweden (RES-062-23-2241). This chapter has as its focus the English case study. This particular case study was carried out in England at a time when the inspectorate was facing new pressures from government to effect school improvement. At this time, Ofsted employed three principal contractors to carry out 75 per cent of its work (Education Development Trust, then CfBT, SERCO and TRIBAL). These agencies were contracted using a bid system in 2009, replacing numerous smaller agencies that had held tenders since then. Inspections in England are organized according to inspection frameworks. These inspection frameworks change and evolve depending upon government policy and what is required from each framework, as the government report into the role and performance of Ofsted (2011) illustrates:

> There is quite a regular phrase around Ofsted's walls that if you put it in the criteria, it will get inspected and people will do it. It depends whether you think that is perverse or not. If there is something you particularly want to happen in

the education system in this country, put it in the inspection framework because it will happen.

But the bids to get in the framework are very lengthy. It is almost a weekly task – I don't know if this was your experience, Mike – to bat off people who want this or that in the framework. What you put in the Ofsted framework will get inspected and will improve, in my experience, but the bids to get in there are lengthy. (Parliament 2011b: Question 11)

This research reported in this chapter involved a mix of documentary evidence including parliamentary reports, Ofsted reports, Ofsted website material, inspection frameworks (listed in bibliography) along with twenty-five qualitative interviews with inspectors based across England. A central aim of the research was to investigate how inspectors perceive their role as policy implementers and whether they also perceive themselves to be policy shapers. The terms 'policy implementer' and 'policy shaper' derive from the literature on policy implementation (see, e.g. Hogwood and Gunn 1984) in which policy implementers are tasked with implementation of policy while policy shapers exert influence on how the implementation is effected, the effects of which are fed back into the policy making cycle and help to shape future policies (for further information see Baxter 2017).

The following section begins with a summary of the narrative approach, why it was adopted for this research and how useful it is in conceptualizing education governance. This is followed by a section featuring the findings. The concluding section of the chapter investigates the merits and drawbacks of the method in relation to the findings.

Narrative approach

It is impossible to attribute the narrative approach to a single theorist, just as is the case for many methodologies. Not only theorists but myriad disciplines have contributed to the narrative approach over a considerable period of time. Jane Elliot (2005: 7), in her book 'Using Narrative in Social Research' (a good place to start if you are new to the approach), offers a useful definition of the method: 'Perhaps the simplest definition of narrative, and one that has been traced back to Aristotle in his Poetics, is that narrative is a story with a beginning, middle and an end.' Narrative, just like any story, has the capacity to capture the diachronic elements of an individual story; that is to say, rather than asking a series of questions with, presumably, a set of responses, the narrative

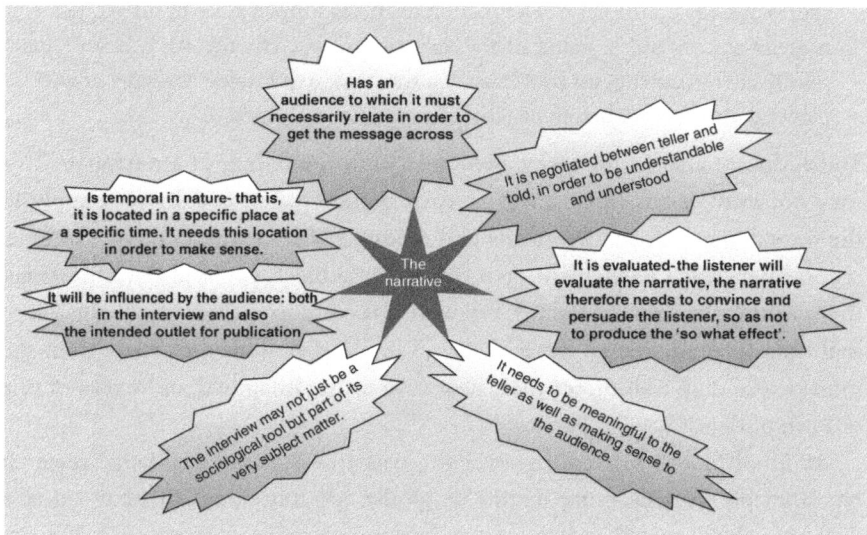

Figure 1 Characteristics of narrative

interviewer solicits the respondent's story, looking for the beginning, middle and end of the story, thus engendering elements of past, present and future. This is not the only way of looking at narrative as many narrative researchers argue that rather than having a conventional beginning, middle and end, breaks in a narrative can signify changes in practice or approach (Mishler 2000). These breaks are thought of as highly significant to researchers as they often represent the imposition of new policies or changes in the way that individuals define their identities and practices (McAdams et al. 2006). Indeed, narrative has a number of characteristics, as illustrated in Figure 1.

As Ricoeur (2010: 3 in McAdams 1997) states, 'Time becomes a human time to the extent it is organized after the manner of narrative; narrative in turn is meaningful to the extent it portrays the features of temporal existence.' In order to have a sense of the narrative and the meaning within it, the narrative needs to offer a sense of temporality: a past, present and future. This shapes the story giving it a sense of flow and coherence for both teller and told. Coherence is vital in order to create a unity of experience for the teller. As Taylor (1989: 24) reports: 'Successful adaptation to a stressful event involves creating a mastery over the event.' In order to achieve this 'mastery' the narrative must attain a measure of coherence. Erikson (1993: 111–112) too described this vital element:

> To be adult means among other things to see one's life in continuous perspective, both in retrospect and prospect. By accepting some definition as to who he [or

> she] is, usually on the basis of a function in an economy, a place in the sequence
> of generations, and a status in the structure of society, the adult is able to
> selectively reconstruct his past in such a way that, step by step, it seems to have
> planned him [her] or better, he [she] seems to have planned it.

The audience also forms a key element within the telling of a narrative. This may not only be the interviewer or co-respondent, but equally may apply to the intended audience; the means and medium of transmission. For example, if you interview a participant on a particular subject, you will have informed them of the purposes of the interview. If this were to include the inclusion of that data in academic works and, for example, a newspaper article then the interviewee may well direct their narrative to the imagined audiences of one or both outlets.

As Elliot (2005: 18) reports, over the past two decades qualitative research has 'arguably become more methodologically self-conscious'. This has led to a distinction between researchers who understand narrative interviews as a resource and those who see the interview itself as a topic for inquiry. These two approaches are known as (a) the naturalist approach to interviewing and (b) the constructionist approach to interviewing. A clear distinction between the two approaches is made by Harris (2003) in his work on equality/inequality in marriage. He describes the approaches as considerably divergent. In Harris' (2003: 203) view, naturalists aim to document lived realities, 'beliefs, behaviors, dilemmas, strategies, and so on – without questioning the facticity of the world. Firsthand observation and in-depth interviewing are viewed as procedures that can be used to try and capture the real experiences of individuals and groups'. A key distinction between the naturalist approach and the constructionist approach is to be found in the role of the researcher. In the naturalist approach, 'when interpretive differences are noticed, it is the researcher's task to resolve discrepancies and incorporate the informants' divergent stories into some larger explanatory and descriptive scheme' (Gubrium and Holstein 1999: 303 in Harris 2003).

In contrast with this approach, constructionists take less for granted and treat the meanings of things as indeterminate, essentially relying more on the interpretations of the respondents on the given phenomena. This approach sees the research project in part as an active constituent of the field and the interview as a site of production of meaning. The approach is closely linked to the phenomenological approaches of Husserl (1997) and Heidegger (1962). This includes the belief that it is possible for the interviewer to 'bracket' out all subjectivity and to see the interview purely in isolation as a sense-making activity. This extreme approach is not the one taken for this work, which instead views the interview as a site of productivity and views the researcher as part of the audience. It also assumes that it is the interviewer's considerable knowledge of the field of education that shapes and colors the interaction. This creates a sense of conversation in the narrative, more of a two-way conversation in which the interviewer fulfils the role of both interlocutor and audience.

A key element of the constructionist approach to narrative inquiry is founded on the premise that narrative is a process that is at once 'dialectical, flexible and conditioned' (Harris 2003: 205). It is up to the teller to decide which anecdotes, metaphors and language will best convince the listener. This element of 'being convincing' is a key part of the narration – if the narrative lacks conviction it will assumedly be of little interest to the listener. This means too that the narrator must be sensitive to the wider culture within which the interview is situated (Berger 1992, 1997). The role of metaphor is central in the narrative, linking to dominant discourses which reflect the cultural location of the teller while also offering some indication of where, in the teller's view, power lies (Ricoeur 2003). This links to important ideas proposed by both Ricoeur (2010) and Foucault (2007) on discourse, power and knowledge. An important element within the approach taken by constructionists is the lack of assumption on what the particular phenomenon means – so, for example, rather than assuming that inspectors would understand their role in both policy implementing and policy shaping, the constructionist interviewer would explore respondent's understanding of what is meant by policy implementation and policy shaping, before launching into the rest of the interview. For this reason, constructionists often return to the same respondent for a follow-up interview (having first established understandings of key terms in the research).

The constructionist approach to narrative interviewing is to seek out the expert practitioner rather than the expert informant. This is to say that anyone practising in the area under scrutiny (any inspectors in this case) will be able to produce a narration of the phenomenon. This in contrast to the naturalist approach in which the researcher will be looking for the *expert informant*: inspectors who will be able to produce informed accounts of the inspector's role in policy implementation and formation, namely inspectors who may have already considered this aspect of their work. For this reason, inspectors chosen for this research were self-selecting – many were approached through the online group LinkedIn. They were identified by the fact that they had included the word inspector in their job titles.

Findings

The findings of this project produced several broad themes which are explored in the section that follows:

(a) Inspectors as policy implementers – constrained by actual rules and discourses of inspection which colour and condition their everyday work.
(b) Inspectors' sense of mission, combined with the view that their work is difficult, multifaceted and involves a strong sense of duty and 'doing their best for the pupil'. This also combined with a strong sense of 'doing things by the book'.
(c) Little sense of their power as policy shapers – awareness of making a difference at a local but not national level.

Inspectors as policy implementers

On the surface, the research revealed that inspectors appeared to think of their work more in terms of policy implementation, but applying narrative analysis revealed a more complex and nuanced picture. It appeared that initial conceptualizations of being an inspector changed once appointed, as this inspector reported:

> I used to drive away from the training [to be an inspector] thinking, you know any of my staff could do this, whether it is the most highflying senior teacher that you've got or the newly qualified teaching assistant with no experience. Cos surely it's a case of applying a set of criteria to a given situation? In my naivety, I underestimated the interpersonal element and as I inspected more it came very vividly to me that actually it's 98% interpersonal. (Lead Head Teacher Inspector, England)

The 'tick box' approach that had characterized this head teacher's knowledge of inspection as an inspectee was dramatically altered when they trained as an inspector themselves. Suddenly inspection took on a far more nuanced quality and this inspector realized the considerable interpersonal skills involved in inspecting and feeding back to schools: that the process resembled a conversation rather than a didactic one-way exercise. This presents a tension inherent within the governance process, inasmuch as far from being a rational objective process as imagined by the inspectorate, the process is infinitely more nuanced. The reductionist view of the process as taken by this head teacher is concerning in its capacity to highlight how misunderstood this process can be by schools.

Inherent within this was a strong sense of information exchange – of inspection as a professional development and learning exercise in which exegis of conclusions would be expected by schools. Perhaps understandable given that around this time there was a very strong steer to change inspection systems and ensure that they provided much more of a driver for school improvement as this statement from parliament reflects:

> Within our system, the team inspectors are themselves current serving practitioners. We deploy around a thousand of these a year to go into and inspect other schools. The exchange of information and the opportunity to see the most effective practice and to take it back into their particular institutions is phenomenal. The inspectors themselves frequently comment that it is the best professional development that they get, as well as the benefit to the sector as a whole. (Parliament 2011b)

Although the inspectors did show evidence of mission, there were also strong indications that there was a particular discourse of inspection – facets of inspection that were 'expected' but yet not actually articulated in any written documentation as this inspector explains:

> They [the lead inspectors] are responsible for putting it all together in one report and at the same time they will Quality Assure [QA] the sections that come in from other inspectors. If HMI say they are not signing it off then it becomes a key performance indicator failure for the provider, so they are paranoid about this because they get slapped, you get contract action notices that will say that unless you improve this will happen, but . . . so you get tied up in these knots and in the end what inspectors are doing is saying ok well I have to follow this rule . . There isn't a rule but I have to follow I. (Contract inspector, September 2011).

The idea of 'coming up to scratch' was mentioned frequently in the narratives, although what this actually meant was less clear. There appeared to be a great deal of effort expended in writing and quality assuring reports as this lead inspector maintained:

> We have about 20 or 30 readers and between us we read everything, maybe 25, so every report is read by somebody, and checked, sometimes 2 or three times, it's really heavily controlled. We check to see if it's up to scratch. (Lead inspector – contract)

Yet in spite of this, there was often little sense of who inspectors were writing for and what the multi-tiered quality assurance procedures were actually for, as the same inspector reported:

> Everything, clarity, compliance, a lot of it's compliance, and then there is a huge long checklist in terms of compliance, you check it for all of these things but you also check for clarity. No jargon, it's meant to be for parents . . . supposedly for parents and in some areas, well middle-class ones that's fine but I'm not sure that with all the compliance requirements you could ever make it easy for parents with lower levels of literacy to understand what these reports are saying. (Lead inspector – contract)

The rather vague feeling about the audience for reports was amplified by the fact that at the time, reports would be featured in headline fashion by the press, as this excerpt from The Role and Performance of Ofsted illustrates:

> The press will be the press, and they perform a very important function, because parents want to know. But every report, every set of statistics and every league table should carry a health warning – 'this assesses x, but not y'. The Ofsted report, however, is in a particularly important category, because it is meant to be written in digestible prose. There is a problem there. We worked hard on it for 18 to 20 years, but it was hard going, not least because of how prose can be misused, which is the problem. I do not know what the answer is, because there is a clash of interests and, almost, of power bases. The press will publish-they will get a good story if they think it is a good story, which sometimes it is. (Parliament 2011b: section 17)

As I argue elsewhere (Baxter and Rönnberg 2014), the media play a considerable part in the governance process and the mediatization of instruments of governance is core to their ability to function (for more information see Baxter 2016, chapter 3). The quote above illustrates how on one hand the media play a vital part in exposing both good and poor practices in education, yet on the other can exert a profound influence in just how reports are interpreted by the public. As certain stories 'sell' better than others, good news about school standards is less palpably marketable than the converse (see also Baxter, 2016, chapter 3: 55).

There was certainly evidence that the reports would be read by any number of people and that inspectors themselves were unlikely to be able to craft narratives that would appeal to such an eclectic mix of audience. This in many senses led to feelings of disempowerment and constraint in the way that they approached report writing. Their anxiety about writing reports was evident from the outset – what effect this had on the reports and what resemblance original reports bear to final report is less clear. It is however a pertinent question which arises from the study.

Difficulties over audience were not the only factors that made report writing tricky. Inspectors came under considerable pressure to produce 'the appropriate' results as this inspector reported:

> And they had made a real difference in very difficult circumstances, but trying to use the Ofsted framework to that is really difficult, my report went backwards and forwards with inspectors, and my report was really difficult to write. Because it had satisfactory in the last one and they are saying well you can't have 2 satisfactory cos that means they haven't made sufficient progress since last time, but hold on, if you are raising the bar all the time, raising expectations all the time you have to make progress just to stay satisfactory. (Lead inspector – Contract)

The overall impression that inspectors gave with regard to report writing was one of relative disempowerment: they were disempowered because they were unaware of how to write for the numerous (and unknown) audiences because they were under pressure from HMI (Her Majesty's Inspectors: individuals employed full time and directly by Ofsted in an inspection and quality control role) to tell a story of school improvement. So the writing of reports was not just a quality assurance issue; it was far more complex than that. The layers of quality assurance in this case appeared to obfuscate rather than clarify findings and often final reports looked nothing like their earlier predecessors as this inspector told me:

> I looked at it and I thought, did I write that? (Lead inspector – contract)

A sense of mission versus doing things 'by the book'

The word cloud (see Figure 2) was run on all raw transcripts within the sample. As it reveals, there is a firm focus on trust which occurred throughout the narratives. The idea of trust between the inspectors and schools was pertinent, yet also of the lack of trust between agencies in schools. This appears throughout several of the narratives, not only in relation to report writing (as above) but also in terms of the relationship between full-time HMI and agency inspectors. Aligned with this was the sense of challenge – that inspectors worked in challenging circumstances, that their work was highly nuanced and complex and that their own performance as well as that of schools was constantly on the line.

Figure 2 Word cloud of inspector transcripts

Yet alongside these issues around trust and evaluation, there was also a strong sense of duty, namely a duty to improve the lives of children but also to 'do a good job' for the schools concerned. But the sense of duty was sometimes troublesome for inspector trainers who found it a blessing and a curse as this lead inspector and inspector trainer advised:

> We do interviews and assessment and part of that interview and it's quite a crucial part is to try and look at the nature of the person: we are looking for people who can apply the criteria fairly and err, leave behind their baggage. That is actual quite difficult; it's one of the issues that we face above anything else; even throughout the training, we often encounter people that say, 'that's not the way I would do it' and the emphasis is not only what they would do but what a school or other institution is doing and whether it works. (Lead inspector, England)

This sense of duty and dedication to the causes of students was also troublesome in terms of what the inspectorate set out to do, as this individual points out:

> Where people do well, and we give them a very clear formulate of writing an evidence form and you can see, the more intuitive inspectors have taken on board the formula and have looked at it and thought, yes I can do that and they

are producing highly evaluative non narrative objective evidence forms and yet they find it almost impossible not to advise. And inspectors don't advise, they make judgements, they make evaluations and so we still get some trainees who will say, if the teacher had done this then progress would have been better, but there is no evidence for that and teachers justifiably when an inspector says to them I think you should have done it like this cos it would have been better, people will say, well how do you know. And it doesn't do Ofsted any favors when people give that type of feedback so we are very clear we don't give that type of feedback that crystal ball act. (Inspector trainer – agency)

The above quote illustrates the complexity of the governance process and the ability of inspectors, as policy implementers, to also shape and form policy as policy actors (see also Baxter 2017). This phenomenon is core not only to understandings of power within the governance process, but also how differing power relations play out in practice, forming and shaping governance practices (Hult and Segerholm 2012).

Relationship building was seen as a key element of the role featuring in many of the discussions on trust and how to facilitate development. This was seen in direct opposition to a discourse relating to clinical and 'impartial' evidence as this inspector reported:

It's a very, very difficult role; because you've got all of that responsibility at the start of inspection: to prepare; you've got to build a relationship with the head teacher and the senior team and I think that's a crucial part of a successful inspection: if they feel they've been listened to and you've gone to look at the stuff they suggested: lesson plans etc. But one of the criticisms made [recently] about our evidence forms was that they weren't clinical enough, judgmental enough or explicit enough. (Inspector trainer and lead inspector, England)

According to the data, inspectors – even those in leading positions – did not see themselves as policy shapers but as implementers. Yet probing a little deeper into their narratives produced metaphors relating to mission and duty that portrayed inspectors as professionals with a mission to change schools and practices and make things better for students (and teachers). This is an interesting phenomenon which illustrates the power of narrative to reveal hidden tensions not only within roles and practices, but equally in terms of identities. There was a strong sense of the need to build trust and that inspectors were the conduit linking inspection findings to the harder task of convincing staff to act upon them. This element along with findings (a) and (b) will be discussed in terms of the narrative approach in the concluding section of this chapter.

Use and insights from a narrative approach

The narrative approach proved to be very effective in revealing the hidden discourses of inspection: the qualities required of inspectors and the ways in which they were expected to go about their work. Metaphors and anecdotes provided by respondents illustrated the often conflicted nature of their work and the struggle to reconcile the need to 'inspect without fear or favour' combined with the need to build relationships with the schools in order to convince them of the need for change. This dual challenge illustrates only too well the challenges inherent within the governance processes: the hybridity described by Rhodes (1997) in terms of the interaction and conflicting demands made by decision-makers and staff. The constructionist nature of the interviews created a space in which inspector stories could be told and the narrative tools that inspectors used to convince were revelatory in the sense that they indicated how inspectors set out to convince me of what they imagined to be their core purpose, while also revealing how they saw themselves and their work. The analysis also offered key insights into discourses that permeated their work and while not being formalized in any sense had evolved into powerful myths that dominated their working lives. This finding is consistent with the work of Barthes (1972) in its capacity to expose the hidden within the normative praxis of individuals, while also giving some insight into the rationale behind normative approaches to tasks. This was also revelatory in exposing the creation of a lingua franca among inspectors, a common understanding of what was required without actually acknowledging where this understanding came from.

Yet the narratives also often revealed a perceived lack of power within the role and job satisfaction which was countered by their ability to take pleasure in 'small wins', such as the capacity to convince individuals of the need to change certain practices. This appeared to be far more engaging for them than the perceived impact of their final reports which gave the impression of being so altered by the quality control systems as to be unrecognizable in some cases. Within this created sense of job satisfaction lay the somewhat quixotic ideal of 'improving schools'. Yet how this would link to future education policy was completely negated within the narratives. The diachronic facet of the research revealed how inspectors crafted their sense of identity within their work and how this linked to their sense of power or salience within their praxis. Adopting a constructionist approach to the interviews permitted a study of ways in which inspectors sought to convince the audience; both present and perceived, of the value of their work, while this also linked to personal codes and values that permeated their working lives. This methodology and the insights it produces is clearly effective in tapping into the normative practices that are revelatory in examining the micro processes of inspection as a form of education governance, while also offering insights into how this contributes to the bigger picture of inspection in England and how it operates in practice.

Postscript

In September 2015 Ofsted reversed its policy of contracting out inspection and brought all recruitment of inspectors in-house (https://www.theguardian.com/education/2014/may/29/ofsted-end-third-party-contracts-employ-school-inspectors-directly).

Acknowledgements

The author is grateful for the support of the ESRC who funded this research: http://www.researchcatalogue.esrc.ac.uk/grants/RES-062-23-2241/read Grant number RES-062-23-2241

References

Barthes, R. 1972. *Mythologies. 1957*, pp. 302–306. Trans. Annette Lavers. New York: Hill and Wang.

Baxter, J. 2013. 'Professional inspector or inspecting professional? Teachers as inspectors in the new regulatory regime in England'. *Cambridge Review of Education* 43 (4): 467–487.

Baxter, J. 2014. 'Working knowledge: Shifting criteria in inspection'. Paper presented at *Governing by Inspection: Insights from International Studies*, 28 March The Open University UK. Accessed 27 April 2018. Available at: http://www.open.ac.uk/ccig/events/governing-by-inspection-insights-from-international-studies

Baxter, J. (ed.). 2016. *School Inspectors: Policy Implementers, Policy Shapers in National Policy Contexts*. In Ehren, M. C. M, and Merkei Maag, K., *Educational Accountablity*. London: Springer.

Baxter, J. (ed.). 2017. *School Inspectors: Policy Implementers, Policy Shapers in National Policy Contexts* (2 ed. Vol. 1). London: Springer

Baxter, J., and Clarke, J. 2013. 'Farewell to the tickbox inspector? Ofsted and the changing regime of school inspection in Enland'. *Oxford Review of Education* 39 (5): 702–718.

Baxter, J., and Hult, A. 2017. 'Different systems, different identities: The work of inspectors in Sweden and England'. In J. Baxer (ed.), *School Inspectors: Policy Implementers, Policy Shapers in National Policy Contexts*, pp. 45–781. Switzerland: Springer.

Baxter, J., and Rönnberg, L. 2014. 'Inspection in the media: The media in inspection'. In S. Grek and J. Lindengren (eds), *Governing by Inspection*, pp. 160–171. London: Routledge.

Baxter, J., Grek, S., and Segerholm, C. 2015. 'Regulatory frameworks: Shifting frameworks, shifting criteria'. In S. Grek and J. Lindgren (eds), *Governing by Inspection*, pp. 74–95. London: Routledge.

Berger, A. A. 1992. *Popular Culture Genres: Theories and Texts*, Vol. 2. New York: Sage Publications, Inc.

Berger, A. A. 1997. *Narratives in Popular Culture, Media, and Everyday Life*. London: Sage.

Bieber, T., and Martens, K. 2011. 'The OECD PISA study as a soft power in education? Lessons from Switzerland and the US'. *European Journal of Education* 46 (1): 101–116. doi: 10.1111/j.1465-3435.2010.01462.x.

Brown, M., McNamara, G., O'Hara, J., and O'Brian, S. 2017. 'Inspectors and the process of self-evaluation in Ireland'. In J. Baxter (ed.), *School Inspectors: Policy Implementers, Policy Shapers in National Policy Contexts*, pp. 71–97. Switzerland: Springer.

Clarke, J., and Baxter, J. 2014. 'Satisfactory progress? keywords in English school inspection'. *Education Inquiry* 5 (4): 481–496 .

Clarke, J., and Newman, J. 1997. *The Managerial State: Power, Politics and Ideology in the Remaking of Social Welfare*. London: Sage Publications, Ltd.

Ehren, M. C. M., and Swanborn, M. S. L. 2012. 'Strategic data use of schools in accountability systems'. *School Effectiveness and School Improvement* 23 (2): 257–280.

Ehren, M. C. M., Altrichter, H., McNamara, G., and O'Hara, J. 2013. 'Impact of school inspections on improvement of schools-describing assumptions on causal mechanisms in six European countries'. In K. Edge (ed.), *Educational Assessment, Evaluation and Accountability*, pp. 3–43. London: Springer.

Elliot, J. 2005. *Using Narrative in Social Research*. London: Sage.

Erikson, E. H. 1993. *Young Man Luther: A Study in Psychoanalysis and History*. New York: WW Norton & Company.

Foucault, M. 1980. *Power and Knowledge*. Brighton: Harvester Press.

Foucault, M. 1994. 'Governmentality'. In J. D. Faubion (ed.), *Michel Foucault Power: Essential Works of Foucault 1954–1984*, pp. 201–223. London: Penguin.

Foucault, M. 2007. *Archaeology of Knowledge*. London: Routledge.

Grek, S. 2009. 'Governing by numbers: The PISA "effect" in Europe'. *Journal of Education Policy* 24 (1): 23–37.

Grek, S., Lawn, M., Ozga, J., and Segerholm, C. 2013. 'Governing by inspection: European inspectorates and the creation of a European education policy space'. *Comparative Education* 49 (4): 486–502.

Gubrium, J. F., and Holstein, J. A. 1999. 'The new language of qualitative method'. *Symbolic Interaction* 2 (22): 185–186.

Harris, S. R. 2003. 'Studying equality/inequality: Naturalist and constructionist approaches to equality in marriage'. *Journal of Contemporary Ethnography* 32 (2): 200–232.

HCEC. 2014–15. *House of Commons Education Committee: Academies and Free Schools.* London: House of Commons Education Committee.

Heidegger, M. 1962. *Being and Time*, trans. J. Macquarrie and E. Robinson. New York: Harper & Row.

HOC. 2015. *Academies under the Labour Government.* London: The House of Commons.

Hogwood, B. W., and Gunn, L. A. 1984. *Policy Analysis for the Real World.* Oxford: Oxford University Press.

Hult, A., and Segerholm, C. 2012. 'Inspection effects through the eyes of the inspectors: Swedish notions'. Paper presented at the European Conference for Educational Research, Network 23 Symposium 'Governing by Inspection (ii): National Developments', Cádiz, September 17–20, 2012, Cadiz, Spain.

Husserl, E. 1997. *Collected Works: Psychological and Transcendental Phenomenology and the Confrontation with Heidegger (1927–1931)*, Vol. 6. Dordrech: Kluwer Academic Publishers.

Lawton, D., and Gordon, P. 1987. *HMI.* London: Routledge and Kegan Paul.

Maclure, S. 2000. *The Inspectors' Calling.* Oxford: Hodder and Stoughton.

McAdams, D. P. 1997. *Stories We Live by; Personal Myths and the Making of the Self.* Guildford: Guildford Press.

McAdams, D. P., Josselson, R., and Lieblich, A. 2006. *Identity and Story; Create Self in Narrative.* Washington, DC: American Psychological Association.

Mishler, E. 2000. *Storylines: Craft Narratives of Identity.* Cambridge, MA: Harvard University Press.

Ofsted. 2012. *Conducting School Inspections: Guidance for the Inspection of Schools in England under Section 5 of the Education Act 2005 from January 2012.* Edited by Ofsted. London: Ofsted.

Ozga, J., and Segerholm, C. 2014. 'Neoliberal agendas in education'. In S. Grek and J. Lindengren (eds), *Governing by Inspection*, pp. 27–37. London: Routledge.

Ozga, J., Segerholm, C., and Lawn, M. 2014. 'The history and development of the inspectorates in England, Sweden and Scotland'. In S. Grek and J. Lindengren (eds), *Governing by Inspection*, pp. 58–73. London: Routledge.

Ozga J., Dahler-Larsen, P., Segerholm, C., and Simola, H. 2011. *Fabricating quality in education: Data and governance in Europe.* London: Routledge.

Ozga, J., Baxter, J., Clarke, J., Grek, S., and Lawn, M. 2013. 'The politics of educational change: Governance and school inspection in England and Scotland'. *Swiss Journal of Sociology* 39 (2): 37–55.

Parliament. 1988. *Education Reform Act 1988*. London: HM Stationary Office.

Parliament. 2011a. *The Education Act 2011*. Edited by Department for Education. London: HM Stationary Office.

Parliament. 2011b. *The Role and Performance of Ofsted*. London: The House of Commons Education Committee.

Paton, G. 2012. 'Ofsted "taking the soul out of school", adviser warns'. Accessed 27 April 2018. Available at: https://www.telegraph.co.uk/education/educationnews/9640875/Ofsted-taking-the-soul-out-of-school-adviser-warns.html (last accessed: 24/04/18).

Patterson, W. 2002. *Strategic Narrative. New Perspectives in the Power of Personal and Cultural Stories*. Oxford: Lexington.

Power, M. 1997. *The Audit Society*. Oxford: Oxford University Press.

Rhodes, R. A. W. 1997. *Understanding Governance: Policy Networks, Governance, Reflexivity and Accountability*. Buckingham: Open University Press.

Ricoeur, P. 2003. *The Rule of Metaphor: The Creation of Meaning in Language*. Psychology Press.

Ricoeur, P. 2010. *Time and Narrative*, Vol. 3. Chicago, IL: University of Chicago Press.

Snow, D., and Anderson, L. 1987. 'Identity work among the homeless: The verbal construction and avowal of personal identities'. *AJS* 92 (6): 1336–1371.

Taylor, S. E. 1989. *Positive Illusions: Creative Self-Deception and the Healthy Mind*. New York: Basic Books.

Woods, D., and Brighouse, T. 2014. *The Story of the London Challenge*. London: The London Leadership Strategy.

How Can Transnational Connection Hold? An Actor Network Theory Approach to the Materiality of Transnational Education Governance

Nelli Piattoeva

Introduction

In October of 2008, the World Bank and the Russian government signed a cooperation agreement with regard to the Russia Education Aid for Development Trust Fund (READ), settling on a six-year period with a budget of $32 million USD (Piattoeva and Takala 2015). READ was established to provide 'dedicated support for education quality, and in particular, for student learning assessment aimed at improving learning outcomes' (READ 2010: 8). The activities undertaken in the course of the joint project targeted eight developing countries (Angola, Armenia, Ethiopia, the Kyrgyz Republic, Mozambique, Tajikistan, Vietnam and Zambia), though it also aimed at improving Russia's own policies and practices with regard to educational assessment, as well as building the country's capacity as a re-emerging aid donor country. In addition, a large proportion of READ funding was relocated to the World Bank for the development of its 'global products' in educational assessment, in particular, the student assessment component of the Systems Approach to Better Education Results (SABER).

This chapter mobilizes the concept of education governance to refer to the governance of education that transcends national borders. I draw on aspects of Actor-Network Theory (ANT) and understand such a transnational form of governance as an establishment and extension of governance networks that seek to exert influence on what education systems prioritize and how they operate. If global governance is understood as a transnational, networked structure that builds on allies and connections to spread particular policy messages, then questions concerning how that structure is held in place, how it expands and how it wields influence become crucial. I posit that such questions can be productively answered with the help of ANT's methodological sensibilities, particularly its emphasis on the heterogeneity of actors in networked relations (Fenwick and Edwards 2011). The concept of heterogeneity foregrounds the materiality of social connections and the role of non-humans in forging associations between actors located across vast distances. In this manner, the overall approach helps to grasp how transnational governance relies on the affordances of non-humans to form and sustain relationships across space and time, demonstrating how humans and non-humans intersect and co-evolve.

The term 'non-human' may refer to a range of actors including animals, plants, environments or technologies. In this chapter, non-humans concern exclusively the tests of learning outcomes. ANT emphasizes that humans and non-humans are closely intertwined and therefore actors could often be examined as hybrids (Michael 2017). This is an important perspective to keep in mind when focusing on measurement techniques that incorporate human and non-human capacities. Numbers produced through the tests of learning outcomes rely on expert knowledge and technical skills as well as machinery. They represent sociological phenomena in the sense of having an impact on some of the most significant societal organizations, and they exercise political power when provoking discussions and directing policy actions (Gorur 2017). Following ANT, this chapter argues that if we want to understand the nature of transnational, long-distance governance in education, it is imperative to consider the role of people and non-humans in the same analytical terms (see Law 1986).

In the following, READ provides a window into the role of learning metrics as important non-humans that help to assemble transnational networks of global education governance to distribute what has been termed by different authors as a global education reform movement (e.g. Sahlberg 2011), an international education reform agenda (Valverde 2014) and a globalized education policy discourse (Rizvi and Lingard 2010). This global agenda contains a set of more or less settled assumptions as to how to improve education (Lingard et al. 2013; Resnik 2006). One of these principles concerns the idea of standards- and outcomes-based education and the related notion of test-based accountability as important tools for improving learning outcomes (Sahlberg 2011). In this manner, the global policy of educational assessment is centrally focused on metrics of learning outcomes, with most if not all discussions revolving around the question of how to measure learning, as opposed to what learning entails, how children learn or to what purpose learning should be directed. Debates on the nature of education and learning thus appear to have been bypassed in favour of more technical questions concerning the measuring of learning outcomes (Valverde 2014; Verger et al. 2014). The focus of global education policy on the outcomes of learning can be traced to particular authoritative agents, such as (and most commonly) the Organisation for Economic Co-operation and Development (OECD), United Nations Educational, Scientific and Cultural Organization (UNESCO) and the World Bank (Lingard et al. 2013; Meyer and Benavot 2013).

The chapter is organized as follows: first, I discuss the methodological and theoretical aspects of ANT employed in the analysis. I then briefly describe the data of this study and READ as an empirical window into the connecting affordances of assessment metrics. In the rest of the chapter, I demonstrate via READ how an ANT-inspired approach helps to understand the role of non-humans to supporting the construction of global governance networks. In particular, I focus on how the deployment of assessment metrics contributes to the emergence of diverse human and non-human actors connected through the practical labour of developing and disseminating assessment tools.

The heterogeneity of actors in networked relations

ANT builds on an understanding of power as decentred and distributed. In the ANT literature, this ontology of power is called relational or translational (e.g. Latour 1986; Piattoeva 2015a) as opposed to power as resource-perspectives, and postulates that no actor can become powerful unless supported by others. Thus, while disparate actors share thinking that gives rise to policies and measurement tools with a similar functioning logic, actors, such as the World Bank and others, play an active role in bringing such states of affairs into existence. The latter mobilize, align and assemble actors, including non-humans, to support a particular view of education and methods of assessment required for its realization. Thus, as intergovernmental organizations (co-)produce a particular global education agenda, they exercise power not as single actors but through multiple alignments and translations that rely on the will of others (Fenwick and Edwards 2010; Resnik 2006).

Convergence or consent, whenever present, do not result from a form of pre-existent top-down authority, but arise through the hard work of assembling connections between human and non-human actors. For instance, despite the fact that intergovernmental organizations have unquestionably become authoritative centres of global knowledge and discourse production related to education (Rizvi and Lingard 2010), their knowledge repositories are not self-sufficient. Rather, they re-assemble knowledge supplied from multiple sources. Research on the Programme for International Assessment (PISA) has shown how the construction of PISA relies on the work of multiple actors outside the OECD, even though this work is packaged within OECD headquarters (Morgan and Shahjahan 2014; von Bogdandy and Goldmann 2012).

This particular understanding of power, which is foundational to all ANT research, relates to ANT's interest in encouraging reasoning beyond forms of dualistic thinking that are common to social theory and studies of transnational governance. ANT particularly helps to problematize two sets of binaries: one being the binary of 'local' and 'global' and the other binary postulating the agency of humans and the lack of non-human actors.

The problematization of the first binary contributes to the ongoing discussions in education policy and comparative education research on methodological nationalism and methodological globalism, highlighting the heterogeneous and multi-scalar nature of networks that move education policies across different geographical locations. The complex entanglement of categories such as national and global, public and private ('edu-businesses'), for example, means that global governance of education is hard to disentangle into neat levels of governance (Ball 2012; Lingard et al. 2013; Resnik 2008). Indeed, actors with varying degrees of institutional leverage are loosely connected via policy discourses and material means. They are located in multiple sites that are not necessarily geographically fixed (Wedel et al. 2005). Thus, policy networks proliferate 'somewhere in between multilateral agencies, national governments, NGOs, think tanks, and advocacy groups, consultants, social entrepreneurs and international business, in and beyond the traditional sites and circulations of policy-making' (Ball 2012: 10).

Ball's (2016) approach to the study of global education governance seeks to capture this complexity by shifting focus from a rigid global/local binary to the mutual interpenetration of these scales. This involves examination of interdependencies and contingencies as well as deep sociality among human actors that construct and distribute policies through networks. Ball (2016) also emphasizes the incompleteness and the consequent need for unceasing labour to reassemble and sustain the global governance of education via a myriad of actors and chains of ongoing effort (see also Fenwick and Edwards 2010). The global is thus not an added level to the already existing national and local levels (Lendvai and Stubbs 2009) and does not operate independently from either. The global is always emerging through dynamic and productive relations between individual actors, organizations, discourses and objects within a transnational or multi-scalar arena of activity (Ball 2016; Larsen and Beech 2014; Lingard and Rawolle 2011). Transnational actors are thus – in 'ANTish' terms and bearing in mind ANT's take on power – micro actors that have either grown or are growing in size (Law 2004a). Consequently, actors are not easily delineated from one another in their entanglements as actor-networks.

Problematizing the second binary – the privileged agency of human actors – ANT helps to move beyond an understanding that centres on the sociality of human actors in governance networks to probe the role of non-humans as resources required to constitute and make transnational networks durable. In postulating the agentic qualities of assessment metrics, I follow ANT's call to question the human-centricity within the social sciences and the field's lack of attention to the role of non-human actors. As Porter (2012: 553) writes:

> Often global governance is seen as consisting of large forces without sufficient consideration of the specific humans, objects and networks that are needed if these forces are to be transmitted. Alone, humans have great difficulty in transmitting actions across the distances that global governance involves, and they therefore rely heavily on objects such as written texts, electronic networks, weapons systems, transportation systems, and meeting rooms and offices.

Indeed, as Radhika Gorur (2015: 90) recently summarized, 'non-humans may participate as delegates of humans . . . [assisting] humans in gaining the ability to act at a distance. Non-humans are thus deeply implicated in technologies of governance'.

ANT represents a response to the messy nature of the relationality and materiality of the world (Law 2009). It does not assume phenomena, systems and objects to be big or small a priori, but rather focuses on how the networks that constitute them can grow in size, become stabilized and gain power (Gorur 2015). Developing the idea that education policy is held together not merely by ideologies and discourses but numerous material objects, I experiment with a method of 'following metrics', described in the next section, that focuses on tracing some of the activities and actors facilitated by assessments of learning outcomes.

Following metrics through READ

The idea of READ was born in the context of the Education for All Fast-Track Initiative (FTI, which was later renamed the Global Partnership for Education, GPE), which Russia joined in 2006.[1] The FTI Annual Report of 2008 noted that 'within the FTI partnership, an implicit agreement has emerged that all FTI countries should track progress in children's reading (and, over time, mathematics and other content areas)' (FTI 2008: 18). Initiated in 2008 and operating until 2015, the READ Trust Fund, administered by the World Bank, manifested Russia's efforts to reinstate itself as an aid donor by way of funding initiatives that monitor educational evaluation policies and promoting evaluation practices in eight developing countries: Angola, Armenia, Ethiopia, the Kyrgyz Republic, Mozambique, Tajikistan, Vietnam and Zambia. While it is not clear why these particular countries were selected, it is notable that the African countries and Vietnam are former recipients of Soviet assistance to educational development, whereas the remaining three countries are former Soviet republics. The READ countries were also recipients of other forms of assistance from Russia, such as debt relief in Ethiopia, Mozambique and Zambia, and Russian food aid through the World Food Programme in the three CIS countries, Angola and Ethiopia (Piattoeva and Takala 2015).

The primary data sources utilized in this chapter consist of different documents (project plans and reports, agreements and leaflets), research interviews and informal conversations, representing various organizations that I came to know in studying READ. A total of nineteen interviews were conducted with individuals involved with the READ programme as representatives of the Russian government, the World Bank, READ beneficiary countries, other IGOs and research groups, or individual consultants. Three trips to Russia in 2012–2014 allowed for interviews to be conducted and observation data to be collected at a number of READ-related conferences and learning events.

Analytical work with the research material focused on extracting information on different assessment metrics and references made in the READ-affiliated publications to the work of different organizations and individual experts focused on developing and distributing assessment tools. I also analysed various activities (e.g. seminars, workshops and conferences) reported in the documents or witnessed during fieldwork, paying attention to the concrete actions, responses and responsibilities of all those who were implicated in the events. I qualitatively examined the actors that took part in the activities in terms of who or what they are and how they relate to educational assessment policies and assessment tools. Equally, I explored the types of work that were subcontracted at different stages of the project, and to whom.

In working this way, I aimed to map and understand the connecting role of assessment metrics, working my way out of the particularity of READ. On the one hand, I was interested in understanding which actors are joined together through assessment metrics, and on the other hand, I sought to explore how these actors, too, are constituted by heterogeneous actor-networks. *Following metrics* (Piattoeva 2015b) presented a methodological means to capture the circulation of assessment metrics among assessment experts, commercial players, officials and intergovernmental organizations, using metrics as a research focus and a compass to guide my analytical journey. Building on Actor-Network Theory's sensibilities, I considered metrics as both an actor-network that unfolds in and through the relations that constitute it, and an actor that enters and acts in its own right in and through other actor networks. In ANT's methodology the macro appears inside the micro, entailing that extensive relations constitute the most defined and local practices and actors. This means that research that starts from the concrete actually unravels broader relations and contexts, and changes therein, shedding light on the emerging spatialities and temporalities of governance (Law 2004b; Law and Singleton 2013).

The role of assessment metrics in assembling governance networks

Using metrics as a research focus and a compass to guide my analytical journey, this section illustrates how assessment tools contribute to the emergence of diverse human and non-human actors and particular actor relations over vast distances through the practical labour of developing and disseminating assessment tools. In order to illustrate the profusion of assessment metrics and their interrelatedness, the measurements in Table 1, encountered through READ, will be referred to in the ensuing text.

The World Bank's Education Strategy (Learning for All 2020, 2011) emphasizes the need to collect data on learning outcomes for use in the policy-making process. In response to the proclaimed need for data on learning outcomes, the World Bank's SABER stipulated an ideal set of different components for assessment systems across countries (READ 2012). In particular, SABER posited

Table 1 Assessment tools applied under READ

EGRA	Early Grade Reading Assessment
DIBELS	Dynamic Indicators of Basic Early Literacy Skills
ICT Literacy Test SABER	Test of ICT skills Systems Approach to Better Education Results
PISA, new reading component	Programme for International Student Assessment: amendment to the literacy part of PISA for lower performing countries
PISA for Development	PISA assessment for middle- and low-income countries
Provinha	Standardized reading test
SAM	Student Achievement Monitoring
TIMSS	Trends in International Mathematics and Science Study

that a well-functioning national assessment of learning would consist of three intertwined assessment levels and tools: classroom assessments, high-stakes national examinations and large-scale, system-level assessments, that is, regional or international comparative large-scale assessments.

SABER was developed at the World Bank, with background work outsourced to American Institutes for Research (READ 2012). READ's support for SABER began in 2010; and SABER has subsequently underpinned the work completed under the READ programme, which eventually led to re-naming the earlier 'READ diagnoses' and other READ activities as SABER activities (READ 2012; 2013). By the end of 2013, baseline studies following the SABER model were completed in all READ beneficiary countries and training in the use of the SABER student assessment tool had been provided to over 2000 professionals in more than 50 countries (READ 2014). These activities promoted the use of SABER in very diverse contexts, supporting the implementation of the World Bank's Education Strategy 2020 (READ 2012). The SABER country reports ranked and labelled a country's assessment structures as latent, emerging or established, employing vivid visualizations, such as tables, to signal ranking positions, and visual aids, such as arrows of different sizes, to prescribe where future action should be directed.

The development of certain learning metrics funded and transmitted by READ relied on and encouraged different forms of transnational cooperation from early on, while certain tools were clearly developed to become relevant beyond their original national contexts at a later stage in their usage. An example of the tool that emerged in transnational cooperation is *Provinha*, which was developed in Mozambique to diagnose the reading skills of grade 3 pupils, necessitating a study visit of Mozambican officials and experts to Brazil. In this manner *Provinha* acknowledged Brazil's expertise in assessment metrics, while fostering a connection between two former Portuguese colonies that are now entangled through the logic of South–South cooperation. Examples of the metrics that emerged in a particular national context to be transported to multiple locales are SAM (Student Achievements' Monitoring) and the Information and Communication Technology (ICT) Literacy Test, developed by Russian assessment experts and piloted during the implementation of READ to be later utilized beyond Russia, mostly in the post-Soviet region.

In this manner, SAM and ICT aspired to create a particular kind of transnational dependency and hierarchy between spaces, illustrating Russia's attempt to gain a more prominent role in the post-Soviet region, which it considers as its natural sphere of geopolitical and cultural influence. In this endeavour, Russia capitalized on both the attractiveness of global education agenda and the affordances of assessment metrics to materialize connections across distances. An agent of the global quality-of-outcomes policy on the one hand and an aspiring regional model on the other hand, Russia's actions recall the unidirectional and hierarchical knowledge transfers that prevailed in the Soviet times. In that period, Russia functioned as an imperial centre that spread norms and models to the peripheries. However, we can also witness how emerging assessment metrics, developed in cooperation between Russia, the World Bank and other Western agents, co-construct the authority of Western development agencies and the continuous peripheral status of post-Soviet states as knowledge producers (Silova et al. 2017).

Generating a transnational connectedness of numerical assessments, SAM's documents made numerous references to the PISA study. SAM's developers marketed it as a better version of PISA in its ability to provide pedagogical feedback for teachers, while PISA was said to only serve the interests of policy-makers (SAM 2011). Nevertheless, for SAM to become a credible tool in the international arena, it needed to secure positive appraisal from international testing experts both selected by and representing consultants of the World Bank, thus contributing to a particular order of how (or by whom) legitimate knowledge is validated.

Moreover, concomitant READ activities prepared a number of READ countries for the implementation of existing international assessment tools. For instance, Angolan staff were trained for and implemented the EGRA (Early

Grade Reading Assessment). EGRA is based on the Dynamic Indicators of Basic Early Literacy Skills (DIBELS) assessment, which is a tool developed in and for classrooms in the USA. In 2006, the United States Agency for International Development (USAID) contracted Research Triangle Institute to modify DIBELS to different languages, resulting in a suite of short, adaptable, timed tests that measure 'words correct per minute' (Bartlett et al. 2015). Subsequently, EGRA was made freely available online for potential users. With support from USAID and other organizations, already by 2011, it had been adapted and applied in fifty countries and seventy languages (ibid.).

READ prompted the Kyrgyz Republic to analyse its 'devastating' PISA results from 2006 and 2009 and make policy adjustments. Vietnam undertook a modified version of PISA in 2012 to prepare for participation in the 2015 PISA cycle. Zambia was selected as one of the pilot countries for 'PISA for Development', which aims to improve the relevance of PISA among developing countries by introducing a more nuanced way to present the learning outcomes of countries at the 'lower end of the scale' while still placing these countries on the same scale as all other participating countries (OECD 2013: 6). Finally, after taking part in READ, Armenia was expected to participate in the 2015 cycle of the TIMSS (Trends in International Mathematics and Science Study).

The fact that READ played a role in utilizing international large-scale assessments and adjusting them to local contexts demonstrates the ways in which the purposeful circulation of assessment metrics enabled partnerships with other global contributors to educational assessment and particularly generated support to the World Bank's own agenda. READ can be considered as both exposing and actively constructing connections between actors in this effort. Indeed, activities focused on the development and dissemination of assessment tools and data, identified in the examined project documents, specifically targeted key players, one of them being the OECD. Mundy (2007) and Lockheed (2013) have already noted the increasing tendency of the World Bank to quote PISA results in its publications, which has helped to spread an international testing culture to the developing world (Mundy 2007).

As shown above, within READ, the link between the World Bank and the OECD enabled by international assessments is obvious. Andreas Schleicher, Director of the Directorate of Education and Skills at the OECD, was a regular speaker at READ events, and since 2009, READ and the World Bank have contributed to adjusting PISA metrics in order to spread PISA throughout developing countries (READ 2010). For the World Bank, such strategic alignments are a means to 'ensure greater efficiency and complementarity of effort and better division of labour' (READ 2010: 31). Cooperation between these two players also relies upon and creates spaces for commercial interests to step in, extending actor-networks in new directions, while being enabled and mediated by the necessity to develop and make use of assessment metrics. With READ Trust Fund support, a new reading component skills assessment was subcontracted to the Education Testing Services that preceded ongoing work on PISA for Development and was made available for low-income countries already in the 2012 PISA cycle.

Finally, the tests of learning outcomes contributed to developing organizational structures and securing personnel within existing national governmental organizations and on a regional level to safeguard the use and circulation of learning metrics. In Tajikistan, for instance, READ funds complemented those from the national government of Tajikistan, the Open Society Institute and the World Bank education project in the planning, building and equipping of a new testing centre to develop items for and administer national standardized exams. In Ethiopia, READ enabled the new autonomous agency for large-scale assessments and examinations and a directorate for school inspection at the Federal Ministry of Education (READ 2012).

The work on the aforementioned SAM and ICT facilitated the establishment of at least three distinct though interrelated regional organizations. Being closely entangled with READ, The Eurasian Association for Educational Assessment (EAOKO), rooted in Russia, emerged in 2012 to create a Eurasian community of education assessment specialists while bringing global 'best practices' into the region. One of the aims of EAOKO was described as follows:

> to serve as a liaison between the region's expert community and international organizations; to provide region-specific analysis on international education quality assessment data, and to represent the region's know-how in the international arena. (http://eaoko.org/en/)

The CICED (the Center for International Cooperation in Education Development, http://www.ciced.org/), also based in Moscow, facilitated capacity-building in assessment, particularly in Russian-speaking countries, by focusing on both SAM and the ICT Literacy Test in many of its activities, such as workshops, seminars, short-term grants and conferences organized under the international umbrella of READ. These seminars and webinars were often implemented by yet another new organization – the RTC (Russian Training Center) – established to promote the training of experts and administration in the spheres of education reform, quality assessment and management in Eastern Europe and Central

Asia in order to disseminate the best international and Russian practices (http://www.rtc-edu.ru/about/rtc).

Regional actors, such as the new organizations described earlier, play a central role as mediators who serve to draw linkages 'in the flow of ideas and expertise between world-level professional and scientific groups and local groups at the country level' (Kamens and McNeely 2009: 17). They also act as 'intermediaries and buffers that help tailor tools, such as assessments, to the needs of countries in a common region, making such instruments of reform more acceptable or relevant to national and local policy-making elites' (ibid.: 17).

Conclusion

Global governance manifests a transnationally networked structure that builds on allies and connections to spread particular policy messages. ANT's methodological sensibilities, particularly its emphasis on the heterogeneity of actors in networked relations (Fenwick and Edwards 2011), help to understand how that structure is held in place, how it expands and how it wields influence. Following this interest, the chapter experimented with a method of 'following metrics' to map, using READ as a case study, how numerical assessments circulate and help to assemble extended and dense networks that wield influence over education systems across vast distances.

In examining the contingency, interpenetration and complex entanglements of different actors in global education policy, I emphasized the role of non-humans in connecting different actors in expanding networks of global governance, consequently carrying global policies around. However, this chapter showed that numerical assessments of learning are important not only because they are the circulating messages of the global education agenda. Assessment tools join and co-produce transnational policy networks, which extend across and draw together broad spaces, distances and times. In other words, numerical assessments of education are not only the consequences and manifestations of transnational governance, but constitute the very glue that holds it together. Global education governance and numerical assessments co-evolve and co-produce relationally.

The perspective that builds on the heterogeneity of networked actors and the role of non-humans represent an important contribution to the literature on global governance, which has predominantly given prevalence to the discursive and social at the expense of understating the role of the material and non-human (see Porter 2012). Thus, in contrast to research on governance operating from a Foucauldian governmentality perspective, this chapter focused not on the mentality or rationality underlying these metrical tools (see Porter 2012), but on the connections and the rise of diverse actors that these tools engender. These mutually developed/financed and/or jointly utilized measurement tools are fruitful for different human and non-human actors to emerge and gain credibility while simultaneously serving as the vital material of the organizational structure of a transnational educational assessment regime. Tracing the development and distribution of such tools of assessment helps bring to light the practical labour required for and contributing to global education governance.

ANT focuses particularly on local and concrete practices and the non-human elements they involve rather than treating the latter as secondary to larger mentalities or rationalities. These non-human elements can be understood as absolutely necessary for large transnational networks to hold because social and discursive ties are not sufficient for the task on their own. In this manner, ANT allows for an empirical sociological analysis of global assessment regimes (c.f. Lingard et al. 2013) that shows how assessment of learning outcomes is part of a mobile and distributed idea that is not constituted in a single identifiable centre of thought or power. Rather, such outcomes are facilitated by many variously interlinked players whose number, as research has shown, has increased rapidly over time (Benavot and Tanner 2007; Kamens and McNeely 2009; Lockheed 2013) and who are not easily classifiable into a global/local binary (c.f. Beech and Artopoulos 2015). It is precisely the blurred scalar identification of these human and non-human actors that can give them credibility and increase the speed at which they spread the agenda of assessmentization.

While the global governance structures may seem flat at first sight, the analysis above showed how particular hierarchical power relations are produced through the labour of developing and circulating assessment metrics. These hierarchical relations are enabled by the dynamics of who can produce legitimate assessment tools, who is the 'mover' of such tools and who is constituted as their primary user. In addition, the circulation of metrics generates interesting temporalities of governance. In the analysis above I described how Russia's Soviet past is revived and instrumentalized through the dissemination of assessment metrics in the post-Soviet region.

The analysis presented in this chapter privileged the demonstration of multiple connections and network expansion enabled through and consolidated by assessment metrics at the expense of focusing on the heterogeneous tensions and non-coherence that the practices aimed at forging and securing networks inevitably encounter and have to come to terms with. Another extension of the method might include a focus on the multiple roles of non-human actors, such as assessment metrics, and the multiplicity of scripts that they carry as well as the diversity of roles that they can be put to, and take, sometimes contrary to the initially ascribed functions. These ANT-inspired perspectives, among others, may offer additional valuable insight into the analysis documented in this chapter and to studies of education governance more generally.

Acknowledgements

I would like to acknowledge the contribution of Tuomas Takala to the research that is reflected in this chapter. I am grateful to the editors of the volume, as well as Susanne Ress and participants of the research colloquium at the Centre for Comparative and International Education, Humboldt University, Berlin, for their meticulous review of the first draft. This chapter was finalized during my visiting scholarship at Humboldt University, made possible by the Academy of Finland and the Finnish Cultural Foundation.

Note

1   After negotiations, the decision to implement a second phase of READ was finally made in 2016 with essentially the same objective as READ 1. This phase, which is to run through to 2019, includes countries selected from among seventeen submitted proposals. The chosen participants include four countries that were already part of READ 1 (Armenia, the Kyrgyz Republic, Tajikistan, Vietnam) and four newcomers (Cambodia, India, Mongolia, Nepal). (https://norrag.wordpress.com/2017/05/23/russia-and-education-assistance-searching-for-its-role-as-a-returning-donor/)

References

Ball, S. J. 2012. *Global Education Inc.* London: Routledge.

Ball, S. J. 2016. 'Following policy: networks, network ethnography and education policy mobilities'. *Journal of Education Policy* 31 (5): 549–566.

Bartlett, L., Dowd, A. J., and Jonason, C. 2015. 'Problematizing early grade reading: Should the post-2015 agenda treasure what is measured?' *International Journal of Educational Development* 40: 308–314.

Beech, J., and Artopoulos, A. 2015. 'Interpreting the circulation of educational discourse across space: searching for new vocabularies'. *Globalisation, Societies and Education* 14 (2): 251–271.

Benavot, A., and Tanner, E. 2007. *The Growth of National Learning Assessment in the World, 1995–2006*. Paris: UNESCO. http://unesdoc.unesco.org/images/0015/001555/155507e.pdf (accessed May 23, 2013).

Fenwick, T., and Edwards, R. 2010. *Actor-Network Theory in Education*. Abingdon: Routledge.

Fenwick, T., and Edwards, R. 2011. 'Considering materiality in education policy: Messy objects and multiple reals'. *Educational Theory* 61 (6): 709–726.

FTI. 2008. *The Road to 2015: Reaching the Education Goals*. Annual Report 2008. http://documents.worldbank.org/curated/en/2008/01/10358390/road-2015-reaching-education-goals-annual-report-2008 (accessed 5 September 2009).

Gorur, R. 2015. 'Situated, relational and practice-oriented: the actor-network theory approach'. In K. N. Gulson, M. Clarke, and E. Bendix Petersen (eds), *Education Policy and Contemporary Theory: Implications for Research*, pp. 123–143. London: Routledge.

Gorur, R. 2017. 'Towards productive critique of large-scale comparisons in education'. *Critical Studies in Education* 58 (3): 341–355.

Kamens, D. H., and McNeely, C. L. 2009. 'Globalization and the growth of international educational testing and national assessment'. *Comparative Education Review* 54 (1): 5–25.

Larsen, M. A., and Beech, J. 2014. 'Spatial theorizing in comparative and international education'. *Comparative Education Review* 58 (2): 191–214.

Latour, B. 1986. 'The powers of association'. In J. Law (ed.), *Power, Action and Belief: A New Sociology of Knowledge?*, pp. 264–280. London: Routledge & Kegan Paul.

Law, J. 1986. 'On the methods of long distance control: Vessels, navigation, and the Portuguese route to India'. In J. Law (ed.), *Power, Action and Belief: A New Sociology of Knowledge?*, pp. 234–263. London: Routledge & Kegan Paul.

Law, J. 2004a. 'And if the global were small and noncoherent? Method, complexity, and the baroque'. *Environment and Planning D: Society and Space* 22: 13–26.

Law, J. 2004b. *After Method: Mess in Social Science Research*. London, New York: Routledge.

Law, J. 2009. 'Actor network theory and material semiotics'. In B. S. Turner (ed.), *The New Blackwell Companion to Social Theory*, pp. 141–158. Oxford, UK: Blackwell-Wiley.

Law, J., and Singleton, V. 2013. 'ANT and politics: Working in and on the world'. *Qualitative Sociology* 36 (4): 485–502.

Learning for All 2020 (2011). *World Bank Group Education Strategy*. Washington, DC: World Bank.

Lendvai, N. and Stubbs, P. 2009. 'Assemblages, translation and intermediaries in South East Europe'. *European Societies* 11 (5): 673–695.

Lingard, B., and Rawolle, S. 2011. 'New scalar politics: Implications for education policy'. *Comparative Education* 47 (4): 489–502.

Lingard, B., Martino, W., and Rezai-Rashti, G. 2013. 'Testing regimes, accountabilities and education policy: Commensurate global and national developments'. *Journal of Education Policy* 28 (5): 539–556.

Lockheed, M. 2013. 'Causes and consequences of international assessments in developing countries'. In H. Meyer and A. Benavot (eds), *PISA, Power and Policy: The Emergence of Global Educational Governance*, pp. 163–183. Oxford: Symposium Books.

Meyer, H., and Benavot, A. (eds). 2013. *PISA, Power and Policy: The Emergence of Global Educational Governance*. Oxford: Symposium Books.

Michael, M. 2017. *Actor-Network Theory. Trials, Trails and Translations*. London: SAGE.

Morgan, C., and Shahjahan, R. A. 2014. 'The legitimation of OECD's global educational governance: Examining PISA and AHELO test production'. *Comparative Education* 50 (2): 192–205.

Mundy, K. 2007. 'Global governance, educational change'. *Comparative Education* 43 (3): 339–357.

OECD. 2013. *OECD → Post -2015. OECD and Post-2015 Reflections. The OECD's Contribution on Education to the Post-2015 Framework: PISA for Development*. Paris: OECD.

Piattoeva, N. 2015a. 'Power as translation in the global governance of education'. In M. Lawn and R. Normand (eds), *Shaping of European Education. Interdisciplinary Approaches*, pp. 66–80. Oxon: Routledge.

Piattoeva, N. 2015b. 'Elastic numbers – National examinations data as a technology of government'. *Journal of Education Policy* 30 (3): 316–334.

Piattoeva, N., and Takala, T. 2015. 'Russia as a returning donor – Four roles in development assistance to education'. *Globalisation, Societies and Education* 13 (3): 388–410.

Porter, T. 2012. 'Making serious measures: Numerical indices, peer review, and transnational actor-networks'. *Journal of International Relations and Development* 15: 532–557.

READ. 2010. *READ Annual Report 2009*. http://siteresources.worldbank.org/ INTREAD/Resources/READ_AnnualReport_2009_web.pdf (accessed 15 November 2012).

READ. 2012. *READ Annual Report 2011*. http://siteresources.worldbank.org/ INTREAD/Resources/7526469-1321484244216/READ_AR2011_CRA_62512.pdf (accessed 18 January 2013).

READ. 2013. *Annual Report 2012*. http://documents.worldbank.org/curated/ en/2013/02/18256898/russia-education-aid-development-read-trust-fund-annual-report-2012 (accessed 10 January 2013).

READ. 2014. *READ Annual Report 2013*. http://documents.worldbank.org/curated/en/2014/01/19796247/russia-education-aid-development-read-trust-fund-annual-report-2013 (accessed 15 June 2014).

Resnik, J. 2006. 'International organizations, the "education-economic" growth black box, and the development of world education culture'. *Comparative Education Review* 50 (2): 173–195.

Resnik, J. 2008. 'Understanding educational policies in the global era: A neo-Weberian perspective and knowledge producers as status groups'. In J. Resnik (ed.), *The Production of Educational Knowledge in the Global Era*, pp. 33–52. Rotterdam: Sense Publishers.

Rizvi, F., and Lingard, B. 2010. *Globalizing Education Policy*. Abingdon: Routledge.

Sahlberg, P. 2011. *Finnish Lessons*. New York: Teachers College Press.

SAM. 2011. *Student Achievements' Monitoring* [In Russian]. http://ciced.ru/conference2012/SAM_Framework_rus.pdf (accessed 20 October 2014).

Silova, I., Millei, Z., and Piattoeva, N. 2017. 'Interrupting the coloniality of knowledge production in comparative education: Post-socialist and post-colonial dialogues after the Cold War'. *Comparative Education Review* 61 (S1): 74–102.

Valverde, G. 2014. 'Educational quality: Global politics, comparative inquiry, and opportunities to learn'. *Comparative Education Review* 58 (4): 575–589.

Verger, A., Edwards, D. B. Jr., and Kosar Altinyelken, H. 2014. 'Learning from all? The World Bank. Aid agencies and the construction of hegemony in education for development'. *Comparative Education* 50 (4): 381–399.

von Bogdandy, A., and Goldmann, M. 2012. 'Taming and framing indicators. A legal reconstruction of the OECD's Programme for International Student Assessment (PISA)'. In K. E. Davis, A. Fisher, B. Kingsbury, and S. E. Merry (eds), Governance by Indicators, pp. 52–85. Oxford: Oxford University Press.

Wedel, J. R., Shore, C., Feldman, G., and Lathrop, S. 2005. 'Toward an anthropology of public policy'. *The ANNALS of the American Academy of Political and Social Science* 600 (1): 30–51. doi: 10.1177/0002716205276734.

Part Three

Knowledge Regimes

Revealing Market Hegemony through a Critical Logics Approach: The Case of England's Academy Schools Policy

Natalie Papanastasiou

Introduction: education governance and market discourse

It is widely acknowledged that the study of education needs to be placed within the wider context of the shift from 'government' to 'governance' (Rhodes 1997). The implication of this shift is that state hierarchy and bureaucratic administration are no longer the single most important shapers of education. Instead, education needs to be understood as a field of interactions between a multitude of policy communities which draw actors, knowledge and resources from both public and private spheres (Ball 2009; Jessop 2002). These complex and polycentric networks of governance produce powerful discourses which have profound effects on the nature of education policies and practices. A central aim of education governance studies is to reveal the constantly changing meanings and practices which are shaping education and to highlight their political implications. This chapter focuses on exploring the discourse of the market, which influences education governance across the globe (Ball 2012; Robertson et al. 2012; Simons et al. 2013) and conceptualizes the market as a hegemonic discourse which promotes particular visions of education governance while suppressing others. Among the most powerful principles of the market are an emphasis on the importance of competition, the pursuit of individual interests, the exercise of individual choice and the creation of consumer–producer relations.

In the governing of school systems, market principles have manifested themselves in diverse ways, such as schools competing with each other (e.g. over their position in ranking tables, or over their access to limited finances), prioritizing their individual interests to retain their competitive advantage, and parents and students being increasingly understood as customers (Chitty 2009; Gorard 1999). Importantly, these principles are interrelated; for example, the existence of competition relies on education being understood as a field consisting of customers and producers. While the reach of marketization has meant it is understood as a powerful shaper of education governance, its manifestations need to be understood as complex, contingent and inconsistent, due to the diverse local and national contexts with which its principles intersect (Verger et al. 2016). This chapter presents one way we might go about exploring this by showing how the conceptual tools of political discourse theory, in particular the 'critical logics approach', are highly valuable for exposing the ways market logics shape the meanings and practices of education policy.

The chapter is structured as follows: section one presents the principles of political discourse theory and fleshes out the conceptualization of the market as a 'hegemonic discourse'; section two presents the policy context of England's schooling system and outlines how its academy schools policy is shaped by powerful market discourses; section three presents the design of an empirical study exploring the implementation of academy schools in a local authority (LA) case study; section four is the main analysis section and identifies the social, political and fantasmatic logics featuring in the policy practices of school and local authority actors; and section five concludes by reflecting on how political discourse analysis helps to identify the possibilities for counter-hegemonic movements which resist narrowly defining education according to market logics.

Conceptualizing the market as a hegemonic discourse in education governance

This chapter argues that political discourse theory provides a powerful theoretical lens for exploring the politics of marketization in education governance. Political discourse theory is a subset of poststructuralist theory influenced by the work of Laclau and Mouffe (1985). By arguing that discourses are systems of signification that do 'not just consist of an abstract cognitive system of beliefs and words' but are also 'a constitutive dimension of social relations' (Griggs and Howarth 2011: 219), Laclau and Mouffe (1985) made significant advances in theorizing the relationship between discourses and social practices. This conceptualization underpins political discourse theory, which is based on a social ontology that 'stresses the *radical contingency* and *structural incompleteness* of all systems of social relations' (Glynos and Howarth 2007: 11, emphasis in original). Thus, discourses are always emergent, unstable and never fully formed, meaning they are subject to constant change and modification (Howarth 2000).

A central focus of political discourse theory is understanding the establishment, maintenance or transformation of hegemonic orders and practices. Hegemony refers to a discourse which has achieved the status of being taken-for-granted and whose meanings override those of competing discourses (Torfing 2005). Discourses gain hegemonic status by concealing the radical contingency of social relations and in this way become the 'commonsensical' way of understanding the world (Howarth 2010). A key part of this theorization is that the stable image of a hegemonic discourse will always be superficial due to the radical contingency of the social world, meaning it will be involved in constant struggles to maintain its hegemonic status in relation to challenges from competing, counter-hegemonic discourses.

This chapter utilizes a specific theoretical development from political discourse theory: Glynos and Howarth's (2007) 'logics of critical explanation approach'. This approach takes 'logics' as a key unit of critical explanation. Logics are defined as 'the rules that govern a practice or regime of practices, as well as the conditions that make such rules possible and impossible' (Griggs and Howarth 2011: 222). Glynos and Howarth emphasize that exploring the logic of a discourse is not just a descriptive exercise but it is also about coming to grips with how the discourse 'works'. Three types of logic – reflecting different aspects of social reality – constitute this conceptual approach. *Social logics* characterize 'the overall pattern or coherence of a discursive practice' (Glynos and Howarth 2007: 139) and enable analysis to understand the guiding rules through which practices emerge in particular contexts. *Political logics* help to reveal how social logics become established and maintained but also where their vulnerability lies. Two types of political practice are expressed through logics of *equivalence* and *difference* (Laclau and Mouffe 1985). The logic of equivalence involves attributing chains of meanings or identities to an overarching discourse, whereas the logic of difference fragments meaning and increases complexity through rupturing equivalential chains. Finally, *fantasmatic logics* describe how a discourse creates a sense of fullness or certainty of meaning to disguise the radical contingency of social relations. Fantasmatic narratives construct a desirable version of social reality and in this way they 'furnish us with the means to account for the grip of an existing or anticipated social practice or regime' (Glynos and Howarth 2007: 107). Fantasmatic logics mobilize both beatific, desirable scenarios and horrific, unwanted scenarios in order to, respectively, evoke positive and negative affective reactions that reinforce the grip of a hegemonic discourse. By drawing on the critical logics approach, this chapter conceptualizes 'the market' as a hegemonic discourse that has become a powerful shaper of education governance. The chapter now turns to outlining its empirical focus: the marketization of England's school system and how the 'academies policy' has been a key driver of market discourses in this context.

England's school system, the academies policy and the market

This chapter uses England's school system as a lens through which to explore the political dynamics of the market in education governance. England's schooling landscape is understood as one in which market principles have become firmly rooted. The most popular characterization of marketization in England's school system is one which describes the emergence of a 'quasi-market' (Walford 2014; West and Bailey 2013). It is a 'quasi', or limited, market because schools do not operate on a for-profit basis (Le Grand and Bartlett 1993), yet the system is guided by a distinct market logic. Since the 1988 Education Reform Act, a raft of policies have led to the slow creation of a school market which includes parental choice over which school to send their child, diversifying school types and the establishment of national 'school league tables' through the publication of examination results (Chitty 2009).

A major process through which market principles have become central to the governing of England's school system has been to 'pass the responsibility for the quality of education to the consumer' (Gorard 1999: 26). An assumption underpinning the system is that because parents can exercise their choice over which school to send their children by consulting examination league tables, this will result in increased demand for 'high-performing' schools. The argument that follows is that poor schools will either 'change or perish' due to pupil funds following pupils as they move between schools. Research has widely documented the profound effect of the quasi-market on actors working in the system, particularly how schools and senior managers make their choices 'based upon ensuring that their institutions thrive, or at least survive, in the marketplace' (Gewirtz et al. 1995: 2). Thus, market principles of competition, individual interests, individual choice, and consumer–producer relations are key governing principles shaping England's school system.

Since 2000, a major driver of marketization in England's school system has been the highly controversial 'academy schools policy'. In many ways, the academies policy itself embodies the fragmentation that it seeks to create in the schooling system – continuous reforms have resulted in the policy today referring to a wide range of school types (Courtney 2015). Academies were launched by the New Labour government in 2000 whose education rhetoric reflected a dedication to market principles from the outset by its commitment to introducing diversity in the comprehensive school system to give parents greater choice (DfEE 1997). The New Labour model of academies focused on the policy as a solution to 'educational failure' whereby a failing school would be closed down and reopened as an academy that was run by an external (usually private) sponsor (see Hatcher 2006; Papanastasiou 2013).

The academies policy attracted a great deal of controversy not only due to its private sponsor arrangements, but also because of its implications for local authorities. When a school converts to academy status it severs the accountability link with its local authority. Local authorities are therefore stripped of their powers to intervene if an academy's performance is considered 'problematic' (according to the school's inspectorate, Ofsted). Academies are instead centrally accountable and receive their funding directly from the central government, rather than through their local authority. The 203 sponsored academies set up during New Labour's time in government (House of Commons Library 2010) were therefore regarded as creating 'a "break" from roles and structures and relationships of accountability of a state education system' (Ball 2007: 177).

The academies policy was to become radically extended in its reach and effect on England's school system with the change to a Conservative-Liberal Democrat Coalition government in 2010. Two months after coming to power, the Conservative-Liberal Democrat government introduced the Academies Act 2010 so that all schools became eligible for conversion to academy status, subject to approval by the Secretary of State. This reform created two categories of academies: sponsored and converter. The former related to 'low-performing' schools which required an external sponsor (New Labour's academies were included in this), and the latter was a new type of academy relating to 'high-performing' schools that did not require external sponsorship. There was a very rapid, mass uptake of the converter academy status by eligible schools who overwhelmingly cited the substantial financial rewards resulting from funding formula calculations in the first nineteen months following the Academies Act (see Downes 2011). Today, academies account for 63 per cent of England's secondary schools, and 70 per cent of these are converter academies (DfE 2017).

The dominance of academies in England's schooling landscape has had massive implications for the role of local authorities. Their role in school governance has been significantly hollowed out, with converter academies and multi-academy trusts (MATs) – academy trusts which oversee multiple schools – being framed as 'system leaders' who can drive up school performance levels through the spread of best practices (DfE 2016). These changes have been the focus of an emerging critical education literature which highlights how academies are contributing to the primacy of market principles in the governance of England's school system (see Wilkins 2015). This literature also emphasizes the need for further research to understand the 'uneven and unpredictable' ways market discourses are influencing the implementation of academies (Chapman 2013: 345). This chapter contributes to this literature by focusing on how the hegemonic discourse of the market features in the implementation of academies, and its role in the governance of England's school system. By using a critical logics approach taken from political discourse theory, the chapter adopts an explicit commitment to understanding how the market exerts a hegemonic grip in shaping assumptions about how a school system ought to be governed, which includes the role played by central and local government, and what responsibilities should lie with individual schools. Furthermore, analysis aims to expose the contingencies and opportunities to resist market hegemony. Analysis is guided by the following questions:

> *Social logics:* How do actors tasked with implementing the academies policy interpret and experience the guiding principles of the market in their work?
> *Political logics:* What equivalential and differential logics does the market promote and what do these logics reveal about dominant understandings of how the school system should be governed?
> *Fantasmatic logics*: What beatific and horrific scenarios intersect with market discourses, and how do these promote particular understandings about the governing of the school system?

Exploring the implementation of the academies policy

This chapter draws on empirical research which explored how the academies policy was implemented in a specific local authority. Fieldwork was conducted between September 2012 and April 2013 and was part of a wider study of the academies policy (Papanastasiou 2015), but this chapter specifically focuses on converter academies. Converter academies exercise choice over whether to convert to academy status and are encouraged to behave as 'system leaders' in national policy narratives (DfE 2016). In this way, examining how schools come to the decision to convert to academy status, as well as the local authority's interpretation of this decision, makes converter academies a particularly fascinating focus for understanding the market as a powerful shaper of England's school system.

The local authority case study was selected according to Stake's (1994: 237) 'instrumental case study' design where the case is chosen 'to provide insight into an issue or refinement of theory'. A county in the East of England – given the pseudonym 'Eastshire' – was selected on the grounds that it was one of the local authorities with the most rapid converter academy growth following the Academies Act 2010 due to the majority of its schools performing above national averages. Eastshire covers a large, mostly rural geographical landscape with its largest city having a population of around 12,000. As a result, many of its schools are relatively isolated from each other. Eastshire is home to a unique type of secondary school institution called 'Area Colleges' (a pseudonym). Area Colleges developed during the 1930s and were schools in rural areas set up with the aim of reducing migration from rural to urban areas. They attempted to do so by having a philosophy which argued that schools should have a wider community function and not just focus on serving their students. Eastshire also has a high proportion of Community Colleges – a type of secondary school that emerged in the 1960s. Community Colleges have a similar aim to Area Colleges, which is to enhance the quality of life for the wider school area and offer activities and resources whose benefits are enjoyed outside their student population (Marks 1980). While Area Colleges and Community Colleges in Eastshire have now all been affected by reforms that have changed their official institutional status, these schools continue to describe themselves according to their founding identity.

The political leadership of Eastshire County Council has varied over time. However, the Conservative party had overall control when the Academies Act 2010 passed and during the fieldwork period. The County Council's response to the Academies Act 2010 was that it was 'neutral' towards the policy and that it would not intervene in an issue that related to individual school choice. Schools interpreted this as an indirect way of supporting the academies policy by not attempting to dissuade them from converting.

Fieldwork involved conducting fifteen semi-structured interviews with local authority officers, academy principals and academy chairs of governors. Local authority officers are non-party-affiliated civil servants who are tasked with developing detailed plans from the general policy direction given to them by councillors. Officers were selected for interviews because they were the actors who created strategies around responding to academies and who dealt directly with any issues relating to academy implementation. Principals and chairs of governors from four academies were also selected to be interviewed because, in England, the school principal and chair of governors are the two individuals who jointly decide whether their school should convert to academy status. Interviews explored actors' responses to the academies policy, the conversion process and actors' interpretations of the policy's consequences. The section which follows presents the empirical analysis of these interviews, drawing on the critical logics approach.

Revealing market hegemony

Social logics

Local authority and school actors' understandings of the academies policy in Eastshire demonstrated social logics which exposed that their policy choices were guided by rules of the market. The three dominant social logics – the 'guiding rules' of the school system – in Eastshire discussed in this section are: (i) schools should exercise individual choice; (ii) schools should pursue their individual interests; and (iii) schools are operating in a competitive marketplace.

Local authority officers consistently discussed their reaction to the academies policy as a 'neutral' stance whereby academy conversion was described as an issue related entirely to individual school choice. Statements such as '[schools] are in the best position to make their own choices' (LA officer 1) and 'we feel it's a school's *choice* about whether to become an academy or not' (LA officer 3, emphasis added) were typical. These quotations reveal social logics underpinned by a commitment to the market principles of pursuing individual interests and the exercise of individual choice. Furthermore, officers' argument that this was a 'neutral' stance is highly significant: it serves to underline the hegemonic status of the market by its underlying principles being normalized and considered empty of politics.

Principals and chairs of governors of newly converted academies described their decision to convert as overwhelmingly relating to financial incentives and reputational risk. As mentioned previously, in the nineteen-month period which followed the Academies Act 2010 the national funding formula calculation meant there were substantial financial gains associated with becoming a converter.

Every interviewee emphasized that this translated to a major incentive to convert. As one chair of governors bluntly put it, 'it's hard to argue with nearly £1 million going into your school's infrastructure' (Governor 3). Schools being guided by financial incentives exposes a social logic which places the pursuit of individual interests above all else. There was also a sense of inevitability expressed by school actors in their accounts about financial incentives. The governor in the previous quotation phrased incentives as being 'hard to argue with'. Other interviewees described this sense of inevitability in the following ways:

> You know, the government *set it up* this way, they *set it up* so that every individual school had pretty strong incentive [. . .] to become an academy [. . .] If you set up the playing field in a particular way we'll all rush like lemmings towards the corn. (Governor 2, emphasis added)
>
> when it became apparent, that there was some financial advantage in the way budget allocations would work in becoming an academy, we decided that we couldn't afford not to join the bandwagon. (Governor 4)

This sense of inevitability, of schools 'rushing like lemmings' towards finances made available by the academies policy, exemplifies the dominance of the social logic that schools operate in a marketplace. This dimension of the hegemonic discourse of the market also exposes how the market diminishes the agency of social actors; actors' decisions are instead guided by the 'invisible hand' of market incentives and risks.

Finally, the issue of reputational risk was a key issue cited by school actors when describing their decision to convert to academy status. This reputational risk related to how academy status is associated with being a 'good school'. One governor perceived an 'opportunity cost of *not* becoming an academy in marketing terms' (Governor 4, emphasis added). Similarly, one principal described how 'there is a kind of . . . unwritten *pecking order* of schools nationally [. . .] you know, we're a marketplace' and that 'reputations grow on the basis of these things [perceptions of academy status]' (Principal 1, emphasis added). These quotations show how school actors associated their decision to convert to academy status with the management of their institutional 'brand'. The social logic that schools are part of a competitive marketplace once again emerges, this time, in how reputational risk has shaped school actors' decision to convert to academy status.

This section demonstrates how social logics guiding the implementation of academies in Eastshire are dominated by the hegemonic discourse of the market. The discussion illustrates three powerful social logics framing the way local authority and school actors understand the 'rules of the game' when deciding how to respond to the academies policy. By identifying the social logics that schools should exercise individual choice, pursue their individual interests and their need to operate in a competitive marketplace, analysis has helped to expose the hegemonic grip of market discourse.

Political logics

Identifying social logics has enabled analysis to reveal the governing practices through which the individualization of schools is being deepened by the academies policy. Turning to examine the related political logics serves to expose further implications of how market discourses are shaping the school system.

The policy response to academies in Eastshire is dominated by a logic of difference. This logic of difference operates along two axes: one emphasizing difference between schools and another distancing schools from the local authority. Principals and chairs of governors mobilized a logic of difference which fragments the school landscape and justifies responding to the academies policy by exclusively considering their individual interests. This was especially apparent when these actors explained their decision to convert to academy status. Despite the financial benefits of converting being cited as the most important reason to convert, it was consistently discussed in relation to a wider dilemma. This dilemma related to the financial consequences caused by a school converting to academy status which triggered the change in its funding no longer being distributed via the local authority, with these funds instead being sent directly to the academy. This contrasts to the distribution of school funding via the local authority whereby schools that are perceived to have a greater need for funds are given a greater proportion relative to schools considered to be facing less challenges. In light of the 'high-performing' status of converter academies in Eastshire, their choice to convert and the diversion of their funding away from the local authority 'pool' had the knock-on effect of negatively impacting the funds available to 'low-performing' schools in the local authority area. Examples of how academy principals and governors justified their decisions include:

> we got over that morally and said: well actually it [academy status] gives us the right amount of money that *we* should be spending on children in *this* school. (Principal 1, emphasis added)

> at the larger policy level, is that [new financial arrangement] a *good* thing? To direct it towards academies rather than other schools? I don't know. [pause] But

that's my, my role in *this* is, as chair of governors [laughs slightly] there's just no argument. [. . .] I couldn't make my school a sort of sacrificial victim for some kind of policy statement. (Governor 2, emphasis added)

A political logic of difference can be clearly identified in the above quotations. They show how principals and governors overcame the 'moral dilemma' of their academy diverting funds away from other schools by focusing on the individual needs of their students and schools above all else. The second quotation in particular demonstrates how market logic makes the prospect of considering any other option beyond what was in the school's individual interests to be completely unreasonable. In this way, the Eastshire school landscape is not understood holistically; rather, it is made sense of through mobilizing a differential logic whereby the main focus is on individual schools operating according to their interests.

Not only does this issue highlight a differential logic emphasizing difference between schools, it also reveals a logic which creates a distance between schools and the local authority. Schools distance themselves from the local authority-wide consequences of their actions, and as a result disengage schools from the local authority. Indeed, throughout schools' discussions there was little reference to 'Eastshire', reflecting how the local authority did not constitute a meaningful institution or identity for considering issues related to the governance of the school system.

Identifying the political logics of difference and how these reinforce the hegemony of market discourse help to bring into focus the implications for governing dynamics shaping the school system. Most importantly, the logic of difference exposes the sidelining of local authorities. By emphasizing how schools and the local authority are distinct and distant from each other, political logics in Eastshire reveal how market principles are serving to erode the role of the local authority in terms of its participation in the governing of the school system.

Fantasmatic logics

Turning to fantasmatic logics, analysis now focuses on the kinds of imaginaries and affective dimensions which reinforce hegemonic market discourses. Two beatific scenarios dominated the response to academies in Eastshire. The first is the notion of a unique community existing around individual schools. Principals and chairs of governors consistently asserted that their schools' institutional identity was centred around their historic Area College or Community College status, and that converting to academy status was part of continuing to work in the best interests of their unique institutions. One principal articulated this by saying their Area College identity is 'a 75 year-old brand, it means more than "academy"' I think to people in this area. It's a very *local* [pause] particular thing' (Principal 1, emphasis). While the identity of Area and Community Colleges is seemingly unrelated to market discourses, the beatific scenario of individual school communities nonetheless supports the hegemonic status of the market. The beatific narrative mobilized by school actors focuses on preserving the unique identity of their schools which translates to their policy practices complementing market principles of pursuing individual interests and exercising individual school choice. In other words, an educational vision that is deeply historical, institutionalized and embedded in place has intersected with marketization in a complementary manner.

The second fantasmatic logic circulating in Eastshire related to the idea of a 'self-improving school system'. At the time of fieldwork this was being promoted by the Coalition government as a new system of school support that was a solution to the decreased capacity of local authorities and a schooling landscape increasingly being dominated by academies. The basic principle of a self-improving school system is that schools improve by engaging in school-to-school partnerships and collaborations (Hargreaves 2010). The idea has clear fantasmatic traits in the way it conveys an idealized situation of schools supporting each other in a collaborative and mutually beneficial manner. However, local authority and school actors in Eastshire were highly sceptical of the beatific scenario promoted by this policy idea. The following quotation is a particularly striking example:

> Does Apple get on the phone to whoever its leading competitor is and say, d' you know what, we're having difficulties with this little iPad we're kind of working on, you know, can you come and give us sort of support and . . .? Well *that* doesn't happen, does it? You know, *that's* the problem with, in a sense we've got *tensions* within a system. (Principal 2, emphasis added)

The fantasmatic logic of a self-improving school system has clearly failed to become established in Eastshire because actors perceive it to be incompatible with the hegemony of market principles. The quotation above is one illustration of widespread scepticism around the beatific principles of a self-improving school system and how this directly relates to the dominance of the market as the key organizing principle of the school system. The sense of competition and constant pursuit of self-interest has made meaningful collaboration or support between schools an unattainable prospect for actors in Eastshire.

By examining fantasmatic logics, analysis reveals the affective dimensions of the hegemonic discourse of the market. Analysis also shows how in the case of Eastshire, historic, institutionalized fantasmatic logics intersected with hegemonic discourses in such a way that unintentionally reinforced the latter. This underlines the value of the critical logics approach: by dissecting how a discourse 'works', analysis can develop a fine-grained understanding of how and why hegemonic discourses are established, embedded or destabilized in situated contexts.

Market hegemony and counter-hegemonic possibilities in education governance

By analysing how local authority and school actors have interpreted the academy school's policy in the context of Eastshire through the theoretical lens of the critical logics approach, this chapter has demonstrated how the hegemonic power of the market is expressed in the policy practices and governance dynamics of education. Analysis has shown how market discourses shape the social logics through which policy actors interpret education policies so that they accept individual choice, competition and the creation of producer–consumer relations as the central guiding principles which govern the school system. Furthermore, these social logics are reinforced by the market's political logic of difference, which fragments school landscapes by emphasizing the importance of individual interests and competition. Finally, analysis has shown how the hegemonic grip of the market is strengthened by fantasmatic visions of education which emphasize unique school identities, and how these are particularly powerful when they intersect with contexts that have historically diverse school landscapes.

Having used the tools of political discourse theory to expose the way in which the hegemonic discourse of the market has so effectively exerted its grip in the governing of England's school system, this chapter ends with a final normative reflection on what this implies for efforts to *resist* market hegemony. Perhaps the greatest potential for counter-hegemonic discourses lies in resisting the market's differential logic which is the cornerstone for fragmenting alternative educational visions and enabling the primacy of individual interests. Resisting market hegemony could involve mobilizing equivalential logics that call into question the differential logic of competition and individual interest. Equivalential logics could instead draw on broader notions of collaboration across local authorities or local areas, and promote ideas of school education as a collective endeavour rather than schools exclusively serving a specific catchment area. These reflections are by necessity broad, as their details will need to be shaped according to the specific historical, institutional and geographical context in which market hegemonies are expressed. While resisting market hegemonies in education governance presents a huge political challenge, doing so opens up possibilities for resisting the ever-narrowing definition of education as an issue relating to individual choice and competitiveness, and calling for education governance to include more prominent debates on wider issues of social justice and equality.

Funding information

This chapter draws on empirical material from a research project funded by the Economic and Social Research Council (2010–2014) (grant number: ESI01943X/1) and was written while the author was supported by funding from the Leverhulme Trust (grant number: SAS-2016–048).

References

Ball, S. J. 2007. *Education Plc: Understanding Private Sector Participation in Public Sector Education.* London and New York: Routledge.

Ball, S. J. 2009. 'Academies in context: Politics, business and philanthropy and heterarchical governance'. *Management in Education* 23: 100–103. doi:10.1177/0892020609105801.

Ball, S. J. 2012. *Global Education Inc.: New Policy Networks and the Neo-Liberal Imaginary.* London: Routledge.

Chapman, C. 2013. 'Academy federations, chains, and teaching schools in England: Reflections on leadership, policy, and practice'. *Journal of School Choice* 7: 334–352. doi:10.1080/15582159.2013.808936.

Chitty, C. 2009. *Education Policy in Britain*, 2nd ed. Basingstoke: Palgrave Macmillan.

Courtney, S. J. 2015. 'Mapping school types in England'. *Oxford Review of Education* 41: 799–818. doi:10.1080/03054985.2015.1121141.

DfE (Department for Education). 2016. *Educational Excellence Everywhere.* London: HMSO.

DfE (Department for Education). 2017. Open academies and academy projects in development. Accessed 27 April 2018. Available on https://www.gov.uk/government/publications/open-academies-and-academy-projects-in-development (last accessed: 24/04/18).

DfEE (Department for Education and Employment). 1997. *Excellence in Schools.* London: HMSO.

Downes, P. 2011. 'I can't believe what is happening to the English education system'. *Forum (Genova)* 53: 357. doi:10.2304/forum.2011.53.3.357.

Gewirtz, S., Ball, S. J., and Bowe, R. 1995. *Markets, Choice and Equity in Education.* Buckingham: Open University Press.

Glynos, J., and Howarth, D. R. 2007. *Logics of Critical Explanation in Social and Political Theory.* London: Routledge.

Gorard, S. 1999. ' "Well. That about wraps it up for school choice research": A state of the art review'. *School Leadership & Management* 19: 25–47. doi:10.1080/13632439969320.

Griggs, S., and Howarth, D. 2011. 'Discourse and practice: Using the power of well being'. *Evidence & Policy: A Journal of Research, Debate and Practice* 7: 213–226. doi:10.1332/174426411X579234.

Hargreaves, D. H. 2010. *Creating a Self-Improving School System.* Nottingham: National College for Leadership of Schools and Children's Services.

Hatcher, R. 2006. 'Privatization and sponsorship: The re-agenting of the school system in England'. *Journal of Education Policy* 21: 599–619. doi:10.1080/02680930600866199.

House of Commons Library. 2010. *Academies: An Overview.* London: House of Commons Library.

Howarth, D. 2000. *Discourse.* Maidenhead: Open University Press.

Howarth, D. 2010. 'Power, discourse, and policy: Articulating a hegemony approach to critical policy studies'. *Critical Policy Studies* 3: 309–335. doi:10.1080/19460171003619725.

Jessop, B. 2002. *The Future of the Capitalist State.* Cambridge: Polity Press.

Laclau, E., and Mouffe, C. 1985. *Hegemony and Socialist Strategy: Towards a Radical Democratic Politics.* London and New York: Verso.

Le Grand, J., and Bartlett, W. (eds). 1993. *Quasi-Markets and Social Policy.* Houndmills, Basingstoke, Hampshire: Macmillan Press.

Marks, H. (1980) 'The Roots of the Community College in England and Wales'. In B. Jennings (ed.). *Community Colleges in England and Wales*, pp. 15–21. Leicester: National Institute of Adult Education.

Papanastasiou, N. 2013. 'Commercial actors and the governing of education: The case of academy school sponsors in England'. *Eropean Educational Research Journal* 12: 447–462. doi:10.2304/eerj.2013.12.4.447.

Papanastasiou, N. 2015. *Scalecraft: Policy and Practice in England's Academy Schools.* PhD Thesis. Edinburgh: University of Edinburgh.

Rhodes, R. A. W. 1997. *Understanding Governance: Policy Networks, Governance, Reflexivity and Accountability.* Buckingham: Open University Press.

Robertson, S., Mundy, K., Verger, A., and Menashy, F. (eds). 2012. *Public Private Partnerships in Education: New Actors and Modes of Governance in a Globalizing World.* Cheltenham: Edward Elgar Publishing.

Simons, M., Lundahl, L., and Serpieri, R. 2013. 'The governing of education in Europe: Commercial actors, partnerships and strategies'. *European Educational Research Journal* 12: 416–424. doi:10.2304/eerj.2013.12.4.416.

Stake, R. 1994. 'Case study'. In N. Denzin and Y. Lincoln (eds), *Handbook of Qualitative Research*, pp. 236–247. London: SAGE Publications.

Torfing, J. 2005. 'Discourse theory: Achievements, arguments, and challenges'. In D. Howarth and J. Torfing. *Discourse Theory in European Politics*, pp. 1–32. Basingstoke: Palgrave Macmillan.

Verger, A., Fontdevila, C., and Zancajo, A. 2016. *The Privatisation of Education: A Political Economy of Global Education Reform*. New York: Teachers College Press.

Walford, G. 2014. 'From city technology colleges to free schools: Sponsoring new schools in England'. *Research Papers in Education* 29 (3): 315–329. doi:10.1080/0267 1522.2014.885731.

West, A., and Bailey, E. 2013. 'The development of the academies programme: "Privatising" school-based education in England 1986–2013'. *British Journal of Educational Studies* 61: 137–159. doi:10.1080/00071005.2013.789480.

Wilkins, A. 2015. 'Professionalizing school governance: The disciplinary effects of school autonomy and inspection on the changing role of school governors'. *Journal of Education Policy* 30: 182–200. doi:10.1080/02680939.2014.941414.

Test-Based Accountability and the Rise of Regulatory Governance in Education: A Review of Global Drivers

Antoni Verger and Lluís Parcerisa

Introduction: Regulatory governance and test-based accountability

Governance represents a shift in the style of governing public services that moves away from direct state provision towards the oversight of services delivered by a broader range of increasingly autonomous providers (Scott 2000). The governance shift also implies profound changes in how services are regulated and by whom, with the introduction of more independent regulatory agencies in the supervision of public services and with transparency and accountability gaining centrality in public administration (Lodge 2004).

The emergence of new forms of regulatory governance does not necessarily weaken the power and authority of the state but it implies that the state needs to readjust its functions and adopt new technologies that allow it to retain its regulatory powers and to 'steer at a distance' (Osborne and Gaebler 1993). Within the regulatory governance regime, accountability is one of the key mechanisms that allows the state to retain control over service providers' goals and outcomes without having to be directly involved in education provision.

Accountability can be broadly defined as a 'relationship between an actor and a forum, in which the actor has an obligation to explain and to justify his or her conduct, the forum can pose questions and pass judgement, and the actor may face consequences' (Bovens 2007: 450). While accountability is a multidimensional concept with multiple policy translations (see Maroy and Voisin, 2013; Verger and Parcerisa 2017), the form of accountability that is spreading more intensively in the governance of education has a managerial and outcomes-based nature and conceives teachers and schools as the actors that should mainly give the account to both public administration and society. This is an accountability approach that focuses on students' learning outcomes and involves the generation of data through large-scale standardized evaluation instruments. This model of accountability is also known as test-based accountability or TBA (Hamilton et al. 2002).

TBA is deeply involved in the alteration of power relations within educational systems. Through external evaluations (and the incentives distributed according to the results obtained in these evaluations) the state has the potential to gain control over the agents that configure the educational system, its constituent parts and the behaviour of those tasked with running it. As part of the TBA trend, school-level educational actors, including teachers and principals, are pressured to explain their decisions and actions to education authorities (including government-run education departments and their inspection services, external evaluation agencies, etc.) and to families further, and need to be more open and responsive to external judgment about their work and results (Olmedo and Wilkins 2017). To a great extent, TBA challenges the self-regulatory dynamics that have prevailed in the education profession, especially in those countries with more advanced welfare states such as Scandinavian countries, and strengthens the presence and regulatory powers of external agents.

As a tool for regulating schools and securing compliance with governmental priorities and goals in education, TBA can be considered a globalizing phenomenon (Smith 2016). Recent literature shows how TBA has penetrated a broad range of education systems in different countries and regions such as the United Kingdom and continental Europe (Barroso 2009; Grek et al. 2009; Ozga 2013; Verger and Curran 2014; Vesely 2012), the so-called Nordic countries (Elstad et al. 2009; Møller and Skedsmo 2013; Moos 2013), the United States (Hursh 2005; Lipman 2002), Canada (Leicht et al. 2009; Maroy et al. 2016), Australia and New Zealand (Codd 2005; Lingard 2010) and Latin America (Brooke 2006; Parcerisa and Falabella 2017).

The international spread of TBA as a global education policy approach is striking for at least two main reasons. First, countries from different regions of the world and with very different administrative traditions, education systems and levels of economic development seem to converge in the necessity of embracing TBA as a way to strengthen the governance of their education systems (Kamens and Benavot 2011). And secondly, countries appear to be adopting TBA despite weak and inconclusive evidence on the benefits produced by this policy technology (see Verger and Parcerisa 2017). Empirical research has reached very different and even contradictory conclusions on the effects of TBA policies on students' learning outcomes, instructional improvement and education inequalities. Education reform advocates see TBA as a way to promote transparency and quality in education. However, according to how accountability systems are designed and enacted, they might generate unexpected results and even undesired behaviours at the school level (Au 2007). Overall, there is still insufficient understanding of the circumstances through which TBA can achieve the expected results.

Faced with this reality, this chapter analyses why TBA has been disseminated and adopted as a core tool of regulatory governance in education globally. Specifically, the chapter focuses on the reasons, factors and actors behind the international dissemination of TBA. The chapter is structured into two main parts. The first part focuses on the main drivers and circumstances that, in an increasingly globalized policy and economic scenario, are conducive to the spread and adoption of TBA in education internationally, whereas the second part focuses on the particular role of international organizations in the dissemination and promotion of accountability measures in education.

Methodologically, this research is based on the scoping review method which aims to identify the main trends as well as the critical areas of disagreement and the existing 'gaps' within a specific field of the literature. The scoping review approach allows researchers to map the existing literature on a certain topic in a shorter period of time. For the purpose of this particular review, we have used mainly two scientific databases: Web of Science (WoS) and SCOPUS. Additionally, we carried out hand searching in key books and journals, grey literature and documents elaborated by international organizations. In total, fifty-one documents that focus on the international dissemination of accountability policies in education were selected. All these documents were published between 1995 and 2015.

The emergence of TBA: global drivers and contingencies

The factors that have led to the global dissemination of TBA are numerous and of a very different nature. As we show in this section, they include methodological advances in the evaluation of education, economic pressures for outputs-based educational reforms, the expansion of new public management (NPM) ideas within the education sector, the spread of global education policies that need of more intense accountability regimes and the emergence of a global industry around accountability systems in education.

Methodological advances in learning measurement

The standardized testing of students' learning outcomes is not a new phenomenon. In fact, its emergence at an international scale dates back to the post–World War period (Kamens and McNeely 2010). However, current methodological and technological advances in psychometrics and in the digitalization of testing have contributed to intensify and scale-up related assessment activities. Overall, the scientific evolution in the field of students' testing is a necessary condition for the development of more sophisticated, precise and affordable test-based accountability systems. Specifically, advances in the definition of learning standards, the measurement of learning outcomes and the design of value-added models to measure teachers' productivity have made possible an acceleration in the expansion of performance-based accountability worldwide (Gorur 2013).

The Programme for International Students Assessment (PISA) of the Organisation for Economic Co-operation and Development (OECD), as well as other international large-scale assessments (such as Trends in International Mathematics and Science Study, and Progress in International Reading Literacy Study), have become instrumental in terms of transferring the technology and the metrics that allows for assessing learning skills at the national level (Meyer and Benavot 2013). According to Lingard et al. (2016: 10), international assessments have strategically contributed to 'enhance capacities for datafication . . . by expanding the scale of assessments, the scope of what is measured, and the types of analyses that can be conducted'.

The centrality acquired by national assessments in education as an accountability tool has been reinforced by the fact that *learning outcomes* have become a commonly agreed-on proxy for 'education quality'. Many practitioners and scholars have conflated quality to the more concrete idea of students' learning, in part because learning outcomes are more concrete, comparable and measurable than other types of education quality indicators that are more context-sensitive and/or more difficult to capture through standardized measures such as education process variables, pedagogy and teachers' training (Sayed 2011).

Advances in the analysis and the visualization of the data generated by standardized tests have also contributed to make student's large-scale assessments more politically relevant. More and more politicians and policymakers tend to justify their most important decisions on the basis of education statistics on students' learning results and on their visual representations – which, among other qualities, have the capacity of condensing particular education problems and legitimize policy solutions (Williamson 2016). Here, again, international large-scale assessments such as PISA are clear examples of the persuasive power of the datafication and visualization of educational problems and realities. To a great extent, the impact of the PISA report relies in the intensive and strategic use of rankings comparing countries' performance, charts representing trends in education or figures correlating different variables with learning outcomes.

However, the current expansion of national assessments focusing on learning outcomes does not only respond to methodological and technological reasons. As we develop in the following sections, motivations of a political and economic nature are also behind the globalization of these types of assessments and related accountability measures.

Economic pressures for educational reform and learning outcomes

In a global economy, more and more countries face major *economic pressures for educational reform* and both governments and economic actors perceive learning, and particularly the acquisition of skills and competencies aligned to new labour market demands, as a key strategy for raising their economic competitiveness (Carnoy and Rhoten 2002). In fact, 'learning achievement' is considered by new human capital theory as the most significant independent variable for economic growth. For instance, according to Hanushek and Woessmann's (2008: 638) influential study on this matter, 'test scores that are larger by one standard deviation (measured at the student level across all OECD countries in PISA) are associated with an average annual growth rate in GDP per capita that is two percentage points higher' over the period that they analysed (1960–2000) (see also Hanushek et al. 2003). Similarly, de Mello and Padoan (2010: 10), in a working paper elaborated for the OECD Economics Department, argue that:

It appears that the most effective policy levers to raise GDP per capita in the long term are related to education, particularly reforms aimed at lifting the average number of years of education of the adult population and improving (students') performance.

Overall, in the current hegemonic economic discourse, basic skills are strongly linked to economic productivity and to the attraction of foreign investment. Framed by such an economic rationale, many of the ongoing education reforms conceive the increase of learning outcomes as a central goal. Accordingly, the measurement of learning achievement has become a necessary condition for establishing the level of reform success as well as the main benchmark for discovering which policies 'work' (or not) in impact evaluations. However, measuring learning outcomes has also become a central tool to find out about the level of economic competitiveness of countries. Within this context, TBA measures have become an important component of an education reform approach that situates schooling 'as the venue for increasing the economic competitiveness of the state' (Foster cited in Koyama 2013: 82).

This economic approach to education reform clearly focuses on strengthening the effectiveness of educational systems but also promotes some levels of equity. However, under this rationale, education equity is not framed by strong egalitarian principles, but is basically conceived as a way to guarantee that all students reach a minimum level of competence in core subjects.

The No Child Left Behind (NCLB) federal law, adopted in the United States at the start of the twenty-first century, is likely the most well-known and paradigmatic example of this reform approach that promotes the effectiveness of the education system in combination with soft forms of equity. The NCLB law, which was advanced by President George W. Bush Jr., promotes TBA reform in education with a focus on students' performance (mainly in two key areas, mathematics and reading). NCLB establishes learning goals that must be achieved by all students, and a system of incentives for schools that is directly linked to students' results. For instance, in schools that fail to make adequate progress during a certain amount of consecutive years, parents have the option to move to another (better performing) school or can request additional education services such as free private tutoring from the school (Stecher et al. 2003). After five years of not meeting the targets established, NCLB contemplates the possibility of the state closing the failed school or *charterizing* it (Burch 2009).

New public management and public sector reforms

The emergence and consolidation of NPM as a paradigm of public sector reform has placed greater emphasis on public services being managed more independently (in other words, through smaller managerial units) and according to the achievement of measurable outcomes (Gunter et al. 2016; Scott 2000). Overall, NPM can be broadly defined as 'an approach in public administration that employs knowledge and experiences acquired in business management and other disciplines to improve efficiency, effectiveness, and general performance of public services in modern bureaucracies' (Vigoda 2003: 813). NPM is absolutely conducive to the advance of TBA in education. NPM means that education systems need to be configured with more autonomous schools (regardless of whether they are public or private) whose actions will be scrutinized by external evaluation agencies, usually through the assessment of learning outcomes.

As mentioned above, the evaluation of students' learning outcomes in a standardized way is not a new phenomenon. It has been widely used in the past as a tool to select students for university education. What is new is the use of standardized testing as a managerial instrument, in other words as a tool to control schools' educational processes and judge their capacity to deliver desired outcomes (Kamens and McNeely 2010). Overall, TBA is a key component of education reforms informed by NPM in the sense that TBA systems are in line with more managerial governance styles at the school level and with a school leadership model oriented towards the use of performance indicators and the achievement of measurable goals and learning goals in particular (Lingard et al. 2016; Møller and Skedsmo 2013).

During the 1980s, some elements of the NPM paradigm were embraced by conservative and New Right governments aimed at making public services more cost-effective (see Tolofari 2005). However, today, NPM is accepted as a valid reform approach by a broader range of political ideologies and for a broader range of purposes. In fact, NPM measures are currently also part of the public-sector reform agenda of many social democratic governments (Verger and Normand 2015). In the 1990s, social democratic parties, under the influence of the so-called 'Third Way',[1] began adopting NPM reforms in education as a way to promote not only economic efficiency, but also equity and the diversification of public services by giving more autonomy to schools and responsibilities to local governments.

It needs to be taken into account though that beyond the role of political ideologies, accountability policies are also being adopted in many contexts because doing so is politically convenient and rewarding (Pollitt and Bouckaert 2011). Enacting accountability systems allows politicians to signal to their publics that they are working hard towards education change and that they are concerned with education results and the future of children. The fact that education systems are perceived as being in constant crisis is making governments to experience a sort of 'addiction to reform' (Merrow 2017) and more receptive towards the adoption of TBA and other types of policy solutions. TBA reforms are particularly appealing in this respect due to the fact that tend to involve low political risk (in fact, through TBA, the reform pressure is put on schools and teachers, rather than on the government), and are somehow 'cheaper and quicker than alternative reforms' (Smith et al. 2004: 50).

Alignment with other globalizing education policies

The spread of *global education policies* such as school autonomy and standards-based reform has also become conducive to the adoption of learning-outcomes accountability internationally. In current education reform packages, school autonomy and accountability tend to be conceived as inseparable. This is due to the fact that governments in their role as principal should be willing to give more autonomy to schools in organizational, budgetary and/or curricular terms, to the extent that schools accept stricter supervision and control via external evaluation and related accountability measures. As stated by the OECD, 'greater responsibilities assumed by schools imply greater accountability requirements such as external school evaluation and public reporting of student performance' (OECD 2013: 45).

Accountability is also reinforced by the so-called standards-based reform movement. This education reform approach focuses on setting very clear and measurable academic standards of what students should learn and be able to do in both terms of contents and skills. To a great extent, the development of common core standards in curricular reforms leads to an increasing emphasis on tests, rewards and sanctions (Darling-Hammond 2004). In a way, the common core standards adopted by governments define the results that schools are expected to achieve and standardized test-based evaluations are the main tool in the hands of governments to find out whether schools have fulfilled such expectations.

Finally, as education policy in many places increasingly emphasizes the market mechanisms of school choice and competition, accountability systems and national assessments are being adopted as a way to disseminate public information about the 'quality of schools' (Forsey et al. 2008). External evaluations are seen as a central mechanism in all forms of market reforms in education (Verger 2012). In the context of these reforms, standardized tests are conceived as a way to promote families becoming more well-informed education consumers. Schools are expected to react to the accountability pressures that families' choices imply by improving their education and becoming more responsive to changing societal demands.

The emergence of the testing industry

Finally, the emergence of a testing and measurement industry is another driver behind the spread of accountability reforms in many world locations. For market expansion reasons, the testing industry sector is highly interested in the deepening of TBA reforms. The testing industry has become one of the most lucrative sectors in the context of the so-called global education industry recently (Verger et al. 2016). Companies like Pearson specialize in testing preparation services and on the evaluation and tracking of children's learning outcomes. Furthermore, on the basis of these data, these companies sell education improvement services, lesson plans and/or educational platforms to countries, local governments and schools and/or families (Hogan et al. 2016). Private companies, such as the Australian Council for Educational Research (ACER) or the Learning Bar, also benefit from important contracts with governments for the administration of national assessments and/or the analysis of the data these assessments generate.

Apparently, the emergence of such economic interests in testing and measurement activities is also behind the ongoing spread of accountability reforms. According to the OECD (2013: 51), the fact that 'standardized student assessment becomes a more profitable industry' means that 'companies have strong incentives to lobby for the expansion of student standardized assessment as an education policy therefore influencing the activities within the evaluation and assessment framework'. In a similar line of reasoning, Carnoy (2016: 36) considers that 'test makers have a vested economic interest to have education systems and schools change what they define as academic knowledge or even useful knowledge to fit the particular test they sell'.

Overall, the increasing involvement of private interests within education testing regimes suggests that these regimes will expand towards new areas of education activity and education levels. This trend might be reinforced by the fact that some testing companies are increasingly embedded within policy spaces through which they can promote their agendas more effectively. We refer for instance to the Learning-metrics taskforce coordinated by Brookins, or to the Global Alliance for Monitoring Learning (GAL).

The role of international organizations

The influence exerted by a range of international organizations in the education policy field is also behind the expansion of learning-based accountability in education. International organizations have the capacity not only to fund the implementation of accountability reforms but also to promote normative emulation dynamics between member countries and a consensus around the desirability of adopting such reforms. International organizations like the OECD, The World Bank and more recently the United Nations Organization for Education, Science and Culture (UNESCO) have contributed to portray accountability measures as a key solution to address many of the problems that education systems face. In this section, we focus in these three international organizations due to the fact that are the most influential in education policy globally. However, it needs to be acknowledged that international non-governmental organizations such as the International Association for the Evaluation of Educational Achievement (IEA), the Southern and Eastern African Consortium for Monitoring Educational Quality (SACMEQ) or the People's Action for Learning Network (PAL Network) are actively involved in promoting and enacting different forms of test-based accountability globally.

The OECD and the persuasiveness of PISA

Many of the country case studies reviewed for the elaboration of this chapter coincide in pointing to the OECD – and to PISA in particular – as key driver of accountability reforms at the country level. In fact, after six editions of this influential international evaluation (2000, 2003, 2006, 2009, 2012, 2015), school autonomy with accountability measures represents one of the policy recommendations that are more consistently included in OECD/PISA reports (see for instance OECD 2011). These OECD recommendations have framed policy change within numerous education settings. According to a recent study, twenty-nine OECD country representatives (out of thirty-seven) admitted that PISA/OECD recommendations on accountability have influenced accountability reforms at the national level (Breakspear 2012).

PISA is also contributing to politicians and policymakers turning towards a 'global education race' aimed at students' achievement (Sellar et al. 2017). Within such a competitive scenario for better learning outcomes between countries, the adoption of national standardized evaluation systems is a very strategic tool in hands of governments to promote their schools achieving better learning outcomes. For instance, the 'PISA shock' that several countries have experienced – especially after obtaining bad results in the first editions of this international assessment – has also promoted the introduction of accountability reforms at the national level (Elstad et al. 2009).

The OECD division of education mainly advocates for managerial and test-based forms of accountability. However, this organization also emphasizes that accountability systems should be holistic and focus on improving classroom practices rather than placing excessive emphasis on learning outputs (see OECD 2012, 2013). The OECD is not against the publication of school results but affirms that the results need to be released in a 'fair' and 'reasonable' way. At the same time, it also considers necessary 'aligning external evaluation of schools with school self-evaluation' (OECD 2013: 8).

Aware of the fact that TBA generates controversy in many places, the OECD (2013: 14) also highlights that the adoption of accountability policies should be agreed on by key education stakeholders:

> To be designed successfully, evaluation and assessment frameworks should draw on informed policy diagnosis and best practice, which may require the use of pilots and experimentation. To be implemented successfully, a substantial effort should be made to build consensus among all stakeholders, who are more likely to accept change if they understand its rationale and potential usefulness.

The OECD, on the basis of PISA data, considers accountability and school autonomy as two policies that fit well together. According to OECD/PISA, schools with greater autonomy in resource allocation show better student results in the context of strong accountability regimes, in which governments make school achievement data publicly available. The OECD (2011: 1) also acknowledges that 'in countries where there are no such accountability arrangements, schools with greater autonomy in resource allocation tend to perform worse'.

Finally, it is worth mentioning that, since 2012, the OECD is implementing the project PISA for Development (PISA-D) to make the PISA instruments more relevant to low- and middle-income countries. This new international assessment tool might have similar effects to PISA and, by doing so, have the capacity to promote the adoption of national assessments based on PISA-related metrics in a broader range of developing countries (Addey 2017; Addey and Sellar 2018).

The World Bank: assessing learning for all

The World Bank places bigger emphasis on accountability models that promote school choice and market dynamics, as well as the empowerment of families in front of teachers and the schools (Edwards 2012). The World Bank actively disseminates these forms of accountability through its numerous knowledge products, lending operations and more recently, through the so-called Systems Approach for Better Education Results (SABER). According to the SABER framework paper on school autonomy and accountability, 'increasing school accountability is a necessary condition for improving teacher quality' (World Bank 2015: 4) and 'for improved learning because [this policy] *aligns* teacher and parent incentives' (ibid.: 2). The World Bank also echoes the OECD message on the importance of fragmenting the system in more independent and autonomous school providers at the same time that accountability is being promoted:

> School autonomy must be complemented with school accountability to promote academic excellence. This has been well documented through various impact evaluations. We also know that the highest PISA scores come from countries where autonomy and accountability are implemented together. (World Bank 2015: 36)

For the World Bank, accountability in education is a key factor in the 'systems approach' to education reform that promotes, alongside the 2020 Education Strategy *Learning for All*. This document, which defines the World Bank education policy in the 2010–2020 period, considers that 'improved performance and measurable outcomes depend on a careful balance between three policy instruments that influence the behaviour of local actors: (1) greater autonomy at the local level; (2) enforcing relationships of accountability; and (3) effective assessment systems' (World Bank 2011: 33).

This international organization considers what it calls 'the shorter route of accountability' (which operates through school choice and school-based management) to have advantages over the 'long route of accountability' (namely, the administrative and/or legal channels families have to go through in case they have complaints about the quality of their schools):

> The shorter route affords clients the power to more frequently provide feedback to providers to let them know how they are [performing] and to hold them accountable for good quality services [more directly]. (World Bank 2015: 5)

The World Bank supports the implementation of different forms of learning assessments in the developing world. Nonetheless, it is important to notice that in the 2018 World Development Report, exclusively dedicated to education policy, that World Bank (2017) warns that excessive testing and high stakes accountability practices might produce undesired behaviours among teachers and schools. This international organization is also aware of the fact that 'testing can be hard' in the low-income countries it operates due to administrative capacity issues. Thus, the World Bank does not only support bottom-up forms of accountability (such as school-based management and citizen-led assessments) because it conceives them as inherently desirable, but also because they are technically feasible (World Bank 2006; 2017).

UNESCO

The Sustainable Development Goal number 4 (SDG-4), which is the United Nations Sustainable Development Goal (SDG) focusing on education, places important emphasis on the improvement of learning outcomes. Out of the seven targets included in SDG-4, five focus on learning outcomes and on the achievement of particular skills: literacy, numeracy, global citizenship, peace culture and so forth. This shift *from school access to learning* is likely the most significant change that can be observed between the Millennium Development Goals/Education For All agenda approved in the year 2000, and the current SDGs/Education 2030 agenda approved in 2015. As a consequence, the Education 2030 Framework – which is the framework for action that was agreed on by the international community, under the lead of UNESCO, to advance the SDG-4 – promotes accountability systems that are at least partially based on the measurement of learning outcomes.

Accountability is one of the most frequently used concepts in the UNESCO Framework for Action Education 2030. For the reasons mentioned above, this framework conceives the creation of national accountability systems that focus on learning outcomes as an indispensable aspect in the monitoring and achievement of new education targets, but not only since, according to UNESCO (2015: 17), 'monitoring quality in education requires a multi-dimensional approach, covering system design, inputs, content, processes and outcomes'.

In contrast to the World Bank, UNESCO does not promote market-oriented forms of accountability. In fact, this international organization is generally sceptic about assumptions concerning the benefits of market mechanisms in education and/or sanctions for schools and teachers (UNESCO 2009). For instance, in the 2017 Global Education Monitoring report, which focuses on accountability in education, UNESCO embraces accountability as a core principle in well-functioning education systems, but also adopts a cautionary approach by emphasizing potential undesired effects of accountability. Some of its key messages are that:

> If held accountable for outcomes beyond their control, [teachers or schools] will try to avoid risk, minimize their role or adjust their behaviour in unintended ways to protect themselves.
>
> Trust is largely absent when [school] actors operate in fear of punishment. A shared purpose, which fosters trust, is central to effective accountability. (UNESCO, 2017: np)

UNESCO proposes a model of mutual accountability – that is, a model of accountability in which governments, and not only schools and teachers, are held accountable – and a model of accountability that is participatory in nature. By focusing on the importance of deliberation and participation in the definition of accountability systems, UNESCO (2015: 17) and its partners also acknowledge the contentious nature of accountability in the education policy field:

> As the primary responsibility for monitoring lies at the country level, countries should build up effective monitoring and accountability mechanisms, adapted to national priorities, in consultation with civil society. This includes building greater consensus as to what specific quality standards and learning outcomes should be achieved across the life course [. . .] and how they should be measured.

Conclusions

In this chapter, we have reflected on TBA as a key component of the rise of regulatory governance in education. The chapter has focused on the main factors behind the globalization of accountability in public education and, in particular, on the reasons why TBA has emerged as such a central device in the regulation of education in so many world locations, including more and more countries from the Global South.

As we have shown, a wide range of drivers of a very different nature (economic, technological, political, discursive and so on) are contributing to the intense dissemination of TBA solutions at the international level. To a great extent, the success of TBA relies on the fact that it is a data-driven regulatory mechanism that promotes the modernization and rationalization of education systems, at the same time that it is portrayed as a key policy solution to a broad range of problems that most education systems face in terms of efficiency, effectiveness, equity and so on.

The most relevant international organizations in the education policy field have contributed to generate such high expectations with accountability reforms in the education sector and, in fact, have portrayed accountability as a sort of 'magic bullet' in the global governance of education. Nevertheless, despite their apparent agreement around TBA as a core policy principle, there are still considerable divergences among international organizations in relation to the goals and instruments of the specific TBA models they promote. For instance, the World Bank aligns managerial forms of accountability with the promotion of market mechanisms, whereas the OECD is more inclined to use managerial accountability in combination with professional forms of self-evaluation. In contrast, UNESCO seems to be advocating for accountability systems that operate at multiple levels and in multiple directions instead of only focusing on teachers and schools as the main responsible of the delivery of good quality education.

Table 1 synthesizes the main TBA drivers (including contextual conditions, rationales and actors) that we have identified in this chapter.

Table 1 A global review of TBA drivers

Conditions	Reasons	Actors
Economic pressures for educational reform and learning outcomes	*Effectiveness:* improving the performance of schools, teachers and students	World Bank: lending and knowledge products to assess learning for all
New Public Management as a predominant public sector reform approach	*Efficiency and control:* align governmental aspirations on education to the purposes of schools	OECD: PISA as a model for national assessments, and behind an international educational race
Methodological advances in standardized testing		
Global education policies aligned to TBA	*Equity:* guarantee that all students reach a minimum level of competence in core subjects	UNESCO: promoting national assessments in the global south through the monitoring of the SDGs
The emergence of testing as an economic activity	*Transparency:* families accessing more 'objective' information about schools' performance	
International educational race		Testing industry actors increasingly embedded in new policy spaces
	Pragmatic: TBA adoption as a politically rewarding reform approach	

Source: Authors

To conclude, it is important to remark that the international dissemination of TBA policies does not necessarily mean that specific and homogeneous changes are happening on the ground. As stated by Van Zanten (2002: 302), 'states cannot avoid global pressures to change in specific directions, but they can twist and transform [these pressures] to fit national purposes and opportunities'. Thus, in real situations, TBA systems diverge considerably. Accountability systems can be high-stakes or low-stakes in terms of the consequences they imply, or more or less comprehensive in terms of the areas of knowledge they cover. TBA systems are not implemented in vacuum and interact with other forms of professional, social and/or market accountability that, in many places, have been in place for a long time. Furthermore, even when accountability systems appear to have very similar forms at the regulatory level, they may translate into very different practices according to how education actors experience and enact these systems. Overall, more research is necessary to capture the multiple trajectories and translations of TBA at the regulatory level and the way different TBA designs are conducive to different directions and results in the governance of education.

Note

1 The third way is a political ideology that seeks to reconcile socialism and capitalism and, to this purpose, combines egalitarian and individualist policies.

References

Addey, C. 2017. 'Golden relics & historical standards: How the OECD is expanding global education governance through PISA for Development'. *Critical Studies in Education*. DOI: 10.1080/17508487.2017.1352006.

Addey, C., and Sellar, S. 2018, Forthcoming. 'Why do countries participate in PISA? Understanding the role of international large-scale assessments in global education policy'. In A. Verger, M. Novelli, and H. K. Altinyelken (eds), *Global Education Policy and International Development: New Agendas, Issues and Policies*, pp. 97–118, New York: Bloomsbury Academic.

Au, W. 2007. 'High-stakes testing and curricular control: A qualitative metasynthesis'. *Educational Researcher* 36 (5): 258–267.

Barroso, J. 2009. 'A utilização do conhecimento em política: o caso da gestão escolar em Portugal'. *Educaçao & Sociedade* 30 (109): 987–1007.

Bovens, M. 2007. 'Analysing and assessing accountability: A conceptual framework'. *European Law Journal* 13 (4): 447–468.

Breakspear, S. 2012. The Policy Impact of PISA: An Exploration of the Normative Effects of International Benchmarking in School System Performance. OECD Education Working Papers, No. 71. OECD Publishing. Available at: http://dx.doi. org/10.1787/5k9fdfqffr28-en.

Brooke, N. 2006. 'The future of educational accountability policies in Brazil'. *Cadernos de Pesquisa* 36 (128): 377–401.

Burch, P. 2009. *Hidden Markets: The New Education Privatization*. London and New York: Routledge.

Carnoy, M. 2016. 'Educational policies in the face of globalization: Whither the Nation State?'. In K. Mundy, A. Green, R. Lingard, and A. Verger (eds), *Handbook of Global Policy and Policy-Making in Education*, pp. 27–42. West Sussex, UK: Wiley-Blackwell.

Carnoy, M., and Rhoten, D. 2002. 'What does globalization mean for educational change? A comparative approach'. *Comparative Education Review* 46 (1): 1–9.

Codd, J. 2005. 'Teachers as "managed professionals" in the global education industry: The New Zealand experience'. *Educational Review* 57 (2): 193–206.

Darling-Hammond, L. 2004. 'Standards, accountability, and school reform'. *The Teachers College Record* 106 (6): 1047–1085.

de Mello, L., and Padoan, P. 2010. Promoting potential growth: The role of structural reform. *OECD Economics Department Working Papers*, No. 793, OECD Publishing, Paris. http://dx.doi.org/10.1787/5kmbm6rz4dg6-en.

Edwards, D. B. 2012. 'The approach of the World Bank to participation in development and education governance: Trajectories, frameworks, results'. In C. S. Collins and A. W. Wiseman (eds), *Education Strategy in the Developing World: Revising the World Bank's Education Policy*, pp. 249–273. Bingley: Emerald.

Elstad, E., Nortvedt, G. A., and Turmo, A. 2009. 'The Norwegian assessment system: An accountability perspective'. *Cadmo* 17 (2): 89–103.

Forsey, M., Davies, S., and Walford, G. 2008. *The Globalisation of School Choice?* London: Symposium.

Grek, S., Lawn, M., Lingard, B., Ozga, J., Rinne, R., Segerholm, C., and Simola, H. 2009. 'National policy brokering and the construction of the European Education Space in England, Sweden, Finland and Scotland'. *Comparative Education* 45 (1): 5–21.

Gunter, H, M., E. Grimaldi., D. Hall and R. Serpieri. 2016. 'NPM and the dynamics of education policy and practice in Europe'. In H. M. Gunter, E. Grimaldi, D. Hall and R. Serpieri (eds), *New Public Management and the Reform of Education: European Lessons for Policy and Practice*, pp. 3–17. London: Routledge.

Hamilton, L. S., Stecher, B. M., and Klein, S. P. 2002. *Making Sense of TBA in Education*. Santa Monica, CA: Rand Corporation.

Hanushek, E. A., and Woessmann, L. 2008. 'The role of cognitive skills in economic development'. *Journal of Economic Literature* 46 (3): 607–668.

Hanushek, E. A., Kain, J. F., Markman, J. M., and Rivkin, S. G. 2003. 'Does peer ability affect student achievement?' *Journal of Applied Econometrics* 18 (5): 527–544. https://doi.org/10.1002/jae.741.

Hogan, A., Sellar, S., and Lingard, B. 2016. 'Corporate social responsibility and neo-social accountability in education: The case of Pearson plc'. In A. Verger, C. Lubienski, and G. Steiner-Khamsi (eds), *World Yearbook of Education: The Global Education Industry*, pp. 107–124. New York: Routledge.

Hursh, D. 2005. 'The growth of high-stakes testing in the USA: Accountability, markets and the decline in educational equality'. *British Educational Research Journal* 31 (5): 605–622.

Kamens, D. H., and Benavot, A. 2011. 'National, regional and international learning assessments: Trends among developing countries, 1960–2009'. *Globalisation, Societies and Education* 9 (2): 285–300.

Kamens, D. H., and McNeely, C. L. 2010. 'Globalization and the growth of international educational testing and national assessment'. *Comparative Education Review* 54 (1): 5–25.

Koyama, J. 2013. 'Global scare tactics and the call for US schools to be held accountable'. *American Journal of Education*, 120 (1): 77–99.

Leicht, K. T., Walter, T., Sainsaulieu, I., and Davies, S. 2009. 'New public management and new professionalism across nations and contexts'. *Current Sociology* 57 (4): 581–605.

Lingard, B. 2010. 'Policy borrowing, policy learning: Testing times in Australian schooling'. *Critical Studies in Education* 51 (2): 129–147.

Lingard, B., Martino, W., Rezai-Rashti, G., and Sellar, S. 2016. *Globalizing Educational Accountabilities*. New York: Routledge.

Lipman, P. 2002. 'Making the global city, making inequality: The political economy and cultural politics of Chicago school policy'. *American Educational Research Journal* 39 (2): 379–419.

Lodge, M. 2004. 'Accountability and transparency in regulation: Critiques, doctrines and instruments'. In J. Jordana and D. Levi-Faur (eds), *Politics of Regulation*, pp. 124–144. CRC Series on Competition, Regulation and Development. Cheltenham: Edward Elgar Publishing. ISBN 1843764644.

Maroy, C., and A. Voisin 2013. 'As transformações recentes das políticas de accountability na educação: desafios e incidências das ferramentas de ação pública'. *Educação & Sociedade* 34 (124): 1–24.

Maroy, C., Pons, X., and Dupuy, C. 2016. 'Vernacular globalisations: Neo-statist accountability policies in France and Quebec education'. *Journal of Education Policy* 32 (1): 100–122.

Merrow, J. 2017. *Addicted to Reform: A 12-Step Program to Rescue Public Education*. New York: New Text Press.

Meyer, H. D., and Benavot, A. (eds). 2013. *PISA, Power, and Policy: The Emergence of Global Educational Governance*. Oxford: Symposium Books.

Møller, J., and Skedsmo, G. 2013. 'Modernising education: New Public Management reform in the Norwegian education system'. *Journal of Educational Administration and History* 45 (4): 336–353.

Moos, L. 2013. 'School leadership in a contradictory world'. *Revista de Investigacion Educativa* 31 (1): 15–29.

OECD. 2011. 'School autonomy and accountability: Are they related to student performance?' *PISA in Focus, No. 9*. Paris: OECD Publishing.

OECD. 2012. Equity and Quality in Education – Supporting Disadvantaged Students and Schools. Paris: OECD.

OECD. 2013. *Synergies for Better Learning: An International Perspective on Evaluation and Assessment*. Paris: OECD.

Olmedo, A., and Wilkins, A. 2017. 'Governing through parents: A genealogical enquiry of education policy and the construction of neoliberal subjectivities in England'. *Discourse: Studies in the Cultural Politics of Education* 38 (4): 573–589.

Osborne, D., and Gaebler, T. 1993. *Reinventing Government: The Five Strategies for Reinventing Government*. New York: Penguin.

Ozga, J. 2013. 'Accountability as a policy technology: Accounting for education performance in Europe'. *International Review of Administrative Sciences* 79 (2): 292–309.

Parcerisa, L., and Falabella, A. 2017. 'La Consolidación del Estado Evaluador a Través de Políticas de Rendición de Cuentas: Trayectoria, Producción y Tensiones en el Sistema Educativo Chileno'. *Education Policy Analysis Archives* 25 (89): 1–27.

Pollitt, C., and Bouckaert, G. 2011. *Public Management Reform: A Comparative Analysis-New Public Management, Governance, and the Neo-Weberian State*. Oxford: Oxford University Press.

Sayed, Y. 2011. 'After 2015: Time for an education quality goal?' *Compare* 41 (1): 129–130.

Scott, C. 2000. 'Accountability in the regulatory state'. *Journal of Law and Society* 27 (1): 38–60.

Sellar, S., G. Thompson and D. Rutkowski. 2017. *The Global Education Race: Taking the Measure of PISA and International Testing*. Toronto: Brush Education.

Smith, W. C. 2016. *The Global Testing Culture: Shaping Education Policy, Perceptions, and Practice*. London: Symposium.

Smith, M. L., Miller-Kahn, L., Heinecke, W., and Jarvis, P. F. 2004. *Political Spectacle and the Fate of American School*. New York: Routledge.

Stecher, B., Hamilton, L. S., and Gonzalez, G. 2003. *Working Smarter to Leave No Child Left Behind*. Santa Monica, CA: Rand Corporation.

Tolofari, S. 2005. 'New public management and education'. *Policy Futures in Education* 3 (1): 75–89.

UNESCO. 2009. *EFA Global Monitoring Report 2009. Overcoming Inequality: Why Governance Matters*. Paris: UNESCO.

UNESCO. 2015. *Framework for Action Education 2030: Towards Inclusive and Equitable Quality Education and Lifelong Learning for All*. Available at: http://www.uis.unesco.

org/Education/Documents/wef-framework-for-action.pdf (last accessed: 22 April 2018).

UNESCO. 2017. *Global Education Monitoring Report 2017*. Last accessed 22 April 2018. Available at: http://gem-report-2017.unesco.org/en/chapter/introduction-accountability/.

Van Zanten, A. 2002. 'Educational change and new cleavages between head teachers, teachers and parents: Global and local perspectives on the French case'. *Journal of Education Policy* 17 (3): 289–304.

Verger, A. 2012. 'Framing and selling global education policy: The promotion of public–private partnerships for education in low-income contexts'. *Journal of Education Policy* 27 (1): 109–130.

Verger, A., and Curran, M. 2014. 'New public management as a global education policy: Its adoption and re-contextualization in a Southern European setting'. *Critical Studies in Education* 55 (3): 253–271.

Verger, A., and Normand, R. 2015. 'New public management and education: Theoretical and conceptual elements for the study of a global education reform model'. *Educação & Sociedade* 36 (132): 599–622.

Verger, A., and Parcerisa, L. 2017. 'A difficult relationship: Accountability policies and teachers'. International Evidence and Key Premises for Future Research. In M. Akiba and G. LeTendre (eds), *International Handbook of Teacher Quality and Policy*, pp. 241–254. New York: Routledge.

Verger, A., C. Lubienski, and G. Steiner-Khamsi. 2016. 'The emergence and structuring of the global education industry: Towards an analytical framework'. In A. Verger, C. Lubienski and G. Steiner-Khamsi (eds), *World Yearbook of Education: The Global Education Industry*, pp. 3–24. New York: Routledge.

Vesely, A. 2012. 'The institutionalisation of non-responsibility, efficiency or conformity? Organisational reform of public services based on accountability theory'. *Sociologicky Casopis-Czech Sociological Review* 48 (4): 757–784.

Vigoda, E. 2003. 'New public management'. *Encyclopedia of Public Administration and Public Policy* 2: 812–816.

Williamson, B. 2016. 'Digital education governance: data visualization, predictive analytics, and "real-time" policy instruments'. *Journal of Education Policy* 31 (2): 123–141, DOI: 10.1080/02680939.2015.1035758.

World Bank. 2006. *Social Accountability Sourcebook*. Washington, DC: World Bank.

World Bank. 2011. *Learning for All: Investing in People's Knowledge and Skills to Promote Development*. Washington, DC: World Bank.

World Bank. 2015. What Matters Most for School Autonomy and Accountability: A Framework Paper. *SABER Working Paper Series, 9*. Washington, DC: World Bank.

World Bank. 2017. *World Development Report 2018: Learning to Realize Education's Promise*. Washington, DC: World Bank.

Making Education News in Chile: Understanding the Role of Mediatization in Education Governance through a Bourdieuian Framework

Eduardo Santa Cruz Grau and Cristian Cabalin

Introduction

> They tried to manipulate me and I tried to manipulate them. Right? And it's [a] parasitic relationship. The parasite is useful to . . . the organism. But it's still a parasite. And they know that. (Stack 2010: 112)

Here a former Canadian Minister of Education defines his relationship with education journalists as mutual hypocrisy. This derogatory view expresses a common perception of media and journalists among education policymakers. However, the interaction between education and journalism is a complex issue in the study of education policy. Lingard and Rawolle (2004) propose working with Bourdieu's theory of 'fields' in order to examine the impact of journalism, or the 'journalistic field', on the development of education policies.

The design of education policy is a process in which various public and political actors intervene, either in state or non-state contexts, with the purpose of influencing and directing education reforms. Among these actors, and with an increasing degree of influence, is the media, which participates in shaping and guiding the development of education policy discourse, making them a central actor in the 'context of influence' (Bowe et al. 1992: 19–20). Such a view suggests that the construction of education policy discourse is neither linear nor iterative but rather a dynamic process. These relationships and practices generate new spheres of influence that stand alongside the political process of policymaking (Ball and Junemann 2012). This helps to explain the decentring tendencies underpinning education governance and the emergence of new actors, new political techniques and new practices in the governing of education systems (Olmedo 2013).

In a context of mediatization of the social and political spheres, transformations in the system of education governance cannot be understood without regard to the specific nature of media as a field of influence. Mass media has an impact on the public sphere by means of a sophisticated process of symbolic production through playing a crucial role in the circulation and legitimation of neo-liberal education discourses (Rawolle and Lingard 2010). But the media is also a space of public debate where social actors, supranational organizations, governments, politicians and various interest groups converge. The media constitutes one of the most important means for legitimizing public policies (Cabalin 2015) but it is also a field of dispute in which different social and political actors foster new ways of negotiating education politics.

In recent years, research into the impact of media discourses on the advancement of neo-liberal agendas in education reform has gathered pace and significance. These studies have gained a lot of traction in Chile (Bellei et al. 2014; Cabalin 2013, 2014, 2015; Santa Cruz 2016; Santa Cruz and Olmedo 2012) which has one of the most advanced market-oriented education systems in the world (Bellei and Cabalin 2013). Two recent student movements in 2006 and 2011 have sought to challenge the hegemony of the neo-liberal structuring of Chilean education and the media have contributed to this process through promoting student's demands as well as framing discussions about education policy in Chile.

Considering the above, in this chapter we examine the news-making process as a way to demonstrate the role and impact of mediatization in education governance. Specifically, we examine the production of education news in order to understand how the journalistic field shapes the educational field. The data for this chapter were obtained from semi-structured interviews conducted with journalists who report on education for diverse Chilean newspapers. We have relied on a purposeful selection of interviewees: only seven education journalists from three printed and one digital newspaper were considered as potential participants because they constitute major players or key influencers in discussions relating to education policy (Couldry 2012). The selected participants have at least one year of experience covering education issues for the media.

We used semi-structured interviews to address the following topics: the news criteria used in education journalism; the relationship between the media and education institutions; the role of journalists as policy actors; the definition and selection of news sources as 'newsworthy' in the coverage of education issues; the restrictions on journalist's professional work; and the editorial approach to education coverage. We identified two major themes relating to what constitutes newsworthy criteria in education media coverage: the importance of 'experts' as a significant news source, and the role of power or 'elite influence' in news production.

Education news in a mediatized policy context

The role of the media in education can be examined beyond the classical notion of the media as a pedagogical tool. In this sense, the interrelation between the journalistic and education fields can be analysed in the context of the mediatization of education (Lingard and Rawolle 2004). Mediatization is a theory used in media studies to explain the impact and power of the media in all social fields (Livingstone 2009). The mediatization of society means that the 'social order is gradually becoming a mediatized order (. . .) where the perception of politics and the perception of the world in general is based, increasingly, on the symbolic representation which the media provides' (Casero 2008: 113). According to Strömbäck (2008), this development is not uniform, so he introduces a process model of mediatization which, in its last phase, entails that media logic has gradually colonized other social spheres and institutions, among them educational and political.

Most of these studies agree that since the 1980s the media has played an active role in generating scenarios that favour the implementation of market-oriented education reforms. To this end, the media has contributed to the systematic construction of negative representations of public education or public network, and privileged the virtues of private education and private networks influencing education more generally. In this fashion, the media has conveyed a negative image of education. According to Ginsberg and Lyche (2008), this negative representation is part of a *culture of fear* as well as a strategy of *moral panic* (MacMillan 2002). These kinds of discourses acquire the manner of popular pedagogies resting on images of good and bad schools, and of good and bad students (Blackmore and Thomson 2004), while frequently ignoring the socio-cultural and material conditions under which public schools carry out their work (Simmonds and Taylor Webb 2013). In effect, the media has played a key role in promoting a discourse of the 'crisis of public education' through publishing standardized test results and establishing a ranking of schools (Mockler 2013).

The role of the media in the legitimization of market-oriented reforms has been achieved in part through the promotion of specific policies and also by disseminating certain cultural models (Goldstein and Chesky 2011). Following Bourdieu's field theory, Lingard and Rawolle (2004) maintain that there are cross effects between the education and media fields. In the case of Australia, the publication in the media of a government report titled *The chance to change* led to interruptions to the implementation of a system of competitive financing between public and private schools as well as providing a new impulse to teacher training in maths, science and technology. This is in line with a cross effect in education politics mediatization and shows that there is the need to investigate the ways in which the media contribute to agenda-setting in matters of education policy.

On this account, it is crucial to consider the complex relation that exists between the media and the formation of government education policies. The media retains a position of relative autonomy, which it exercises through endorsement of specific agendas that are either in agreement or disagreement with government education policies (Santa Cruz 2016). By definition, the media is polyphonic, even though the space occupied by the media and other social and political actors is uneven in terms of power distribution. Understood in this way, there are privileged voices, including so-called experts and think tank researchers, especially those who favour market-oriented educational policies. McDonald (2013) argues that a sophisticated system of public relations exists that allows these actors to broker a privileged access to the media. Furthermore, the marginalization of certain voices in the media is revealed in the limited presence of teacher unions (Thomas 2011) and of student organizations. Their media presence only appears to increase when they lead disruptive actions, like strikes and other forms of protest (Santa Cruz 2016). In the case of the United States, Goldstein (2010) argues that more than half of all media references to teacher unions are explicitly negative and often portrayed as resisting reforms. What the media tends to ignore are the legitimacy of their concerns.

Despite this critical opinion about the journalistic field, only some studies on the mediatization of education policies have included interviews with education journalists in order to analyse their professional routines. Goldstein (2010) argues that some education journalists are not prepared to evaluate the impact of education policy and instead simplify accounts of the reforms that take place and their consequences. Thus, different researchers note that in the media representation of and engagement with matters of education there is a striking trend towards polarization and oversimplification; the building of myths (Wallace 1993); the presence of social narratives that reveal the bias or prejudice of the media itself (MacMillan 2002); and the invocation of emotions serving to flame the fire of prejudice (Blackmore and Thorpe 2003).

The media is a key player in public discussions about education and, at the same time, reflects or constitutes a space where education discourse is negotiated. Specifically, the media plays an important role in the establishment, advancement and consolidation of market-oriented education policies.

Journalistic logic in education news

Following Bourdieu's works on journalism (1998, 2005), the journalistic field is often considered a weak autonomous field because of the political and, above all, economic fields, exercising influence on the logics of practice that make up the field of journalism.[1] Audience ratings, the struggle for advertising and the precarious state of the profession determine the dependency of journalism on generating revenue. At the same time, paradoxically, journalism exercises some independence from the economic field as it extends its influence over other fields of cultural production and politics. As a counterpoint, Bourdieu (1998) argued that the journalistic field impacts other social fields, in particular strengthening the everyday activities of diverse actors.

This understanding of journalism has impacted the formation of the professional identity of journalists and a set of core journalistic values, namely 'public service, objectivity, autonomy, immediacy and ethics' (Deuze 2005: 447). However, abundant literature in journalism studies has shown that external influences, such as organizational, economic, political and cultural factors, affect journalistic decisions (Benson 2006). News-making is a complex process that exceeds the professional identity of journalists and their core values.

The journalists we interviewed rejected the notion that extra-professional relations played any part in their work. They stated that when time came to defining the topics, arguments and approaches to reporting education, they enacted professional values related to public service ethos or public interest. From their perspective, the importance of the education system to society at large explains approaches to media coverage. For example, one journalist explained:

> You studied, your children are going to study, your parents studied, your neighbors studied, so in one way or another, education impacts us all. For example, every time the SIMCE (schooling standardized test) is taken, there are

> 230,000 children involved in a single [educational] measurement. That means, there are 80,000 families that are waiting for the results of SIMCE, from the parents to the siblings of the children who took the exam.

The journalistic value of 'public service', as Deuze (2005) indicates, is closely connected to a definition of what constitutes 'education news'. Therefore, an education news story is deemed newsworthy to the extent it speaks to the interests of the public. This logic of practice in the field of journalism is also characterized by other traditional news factors, namely conflict, prominence and power.

The journalists we interviewed agreed that the 2006 and 2011 student movements in Chile played a crucial role in the national debate about education. These movements extended debate through public scrutiny of the market principles that govern the Chilean education system (Bellei and Cabalin 2013). As education news has gained prominence in the public sphere, so has attention and prominence been paid to the 'education expert'. Indeed, the journalists we interviewed indicated that experts in education are among the most sought-after sources in their news-making practices. The government, leaders of education institutions and experts tend to be the most cited sources in media coverage and debates about education.

In their professional routines, journalists typically establish their own criteria for making judgments about whether an expert is a valid media source. Using a Bourdieuian approach (1998), education 'experts' who appear in the media acquire symbolic capital in the education debate in part due to this selection process. This symbolic capital can be understood as 'educational policy capital' (Ladwig 1994: 346) which determines the relative position of power occupied by experts in the field of education, namely their influence, credentials and presence in the media. As one journalist explained, the criterion used to define the education expert is 'prestige':

> Prestige defines who may or may not talk about education in the media. In addition, if a person has produced academically or has written papers on a given theme. Another aspect is if he or she has experience in the field and if he or she is capable of making a more systemic analysis.

Moreover, experts must have media expertise to be considered a valid newsworthy source. This expertise is evaluated in terms of their ability to explain difficult education issues in a common-sense language for a large audience, as well as meeting deadlines set by the media. Experts who comply with this 'media logic' are habitually cited by the journalists, who themselves have strong social capital.

This relationship includes the 'pedagogical role' of the experts during the news-making process. When journalists have a complicated issue on their agenda, they regularly call on these experts searching for orientation and explanations. However, this close relationship can affect the professional detachment required by both journalists and their sources, which is part of the journalistic culture (Hanitzsch 2007). As one journalist explains,

> They [experts] always want to teach you and they are always very willing to. It is because sources, like elderly academics, have time, so they give you that time, and they send me papers. They suggest themes. I go to their offices to see them, we have breakfast or lunch together and we talk about the themes.

The role of education experts in Chile – most of which are academics at universities or researchers working in think tanks – are often considered 'premium sources' by journalists and their editors. The quality of these 'premium sources' is related to their academic and expert knowledge as well as their political connections. Experts must be active participants in public debates about education and most of them experience an increase in their own symbolic capital as experts due to this continuous appearance as news source or 'op-edge' (opinion editorial) authors. Moreover, in the majority of cases at least, these experts must be quantitative researchers because journalists typically require numbers and percentages to publish education research as news. This methodological or disciplinary bias reveals itself in the scant presence of experts from the field of education and the notable dominance of experts from the fields of engineering or economics. This is complemented by a media discourse that affirms the superiority of 'objective knowledge', namely knowledge that is measurable and empirically testable and verifiable (Santa Cruz 2016).

Journalists tend to justify their predilection for quantitative studies on the basis that they want to generalize results so as to make them available to the wider population. This newsworthy criterion is also discernible in the field of education where the relative value of qualitative and quantitative research is much debated. For instance, George Bush Jr.'s administration established that only experimental research in education could be considered scientific research in the United States (Eisenhart 2006). However, for these education journalists, the distinction does not originate in a political or epistemological stance; it is only a practical way of doing news in national newspapers. As one journalist explained:

> I publish more quantitative studies than qualitative ones because the editors ask for percentages. The other day, some researchers called me to offer me a

study that was really good. It was about the incorporation of students from low-resource areas into university, but they only interviewed 25 students and didn't indicate a national trend. I need something that is systemic.

This positivist view of education news rests on the premise that news reports are based on 'impartial facts' and that these facts can be represented by numbers. This 'quantitative hegemony' also explains why school or university rankings are commonly published as news. School rankings categorize private and public schools in different levels regarding their results in the national standardized tests. The Chilean media publishes these rankings as 'objective' information about the current state of the education system. The 'best' schools, according to these rankings, are generally attended by students from a high socio-economic status. Their parents are part of the elite and they want to see their schools in the media. However, the journalists we interviewed were also critical of rankings and their competitive nature, while at the same justified the publication by saying that many parents are interested in the results of their children's schools:

> Parents like to know where their school ranks, if their school did or did not improve, if their school passed from 10th to 9th place. Extensive reports have been done on the top ten schools, which are bilingual, because parents like to see where there kids are placed and everyone calls you.

Despite the fact that journalists rely on experts as sources for their news stories, they are aware of the personal and political agendas of experts in the education debate. Many journalists we interviewed explained that government authorities and academics have particular, ideological interests in education. Thus, their relationship with these experts is largely sceptical. For the journalists we interviewed, there were no neutral agents in the public education debate. For example, experts try to mobilize their 'educational policy capital' in order to promote certain policy recommendations in the field of education, 'articulating policy agendas or politically building support for a particular educational policy or choosing to critique one or another policy agenda' (Ladwig 1994: 345). As one journalist indicated,

> Here [in education] there isn't anyone that doesn't have an agenda. So here is one part of the situation. I believe that there isn't anyone in the system that doesn't have interests. If I talk with A or B, they are both going to have a hidden agenda: ending for-profit education, for example. The system is extremely small and you know what every one of the actors is thinking.

Therefore, journalists sometimes assume that education agents compete with one another to impose their particular political agenda and gain media presence. They mobilize strategies, tactics and symbolic resources to influence debates about education in the media. Journalists therefore recognize that the interactions between the education field and journalistic field tend to operate through power relations and political interests.

Power in the education field

The education and media fields are mediated by the field of power (Bourdieu 1996). According to Swartz (2013: 62), the field of power 'is that arena of struggle among the different power fields themselves (particularly the economic and cultural fields) for the right to dominate *throughout the social order*' (emphasis added). The mediatization of education is an expression of this struggle because presenting an issue in a particular media narrative affects the framing of debates about education – the role of education, its purpose and so forth. The media framing also impacts the distribution of power in society, favouring certain social groups over others, for example (Entman 2007). Indeed, according to Fairclough (2003: 84), news itself 'is a form of social regulation'. Power is therefore key in the news-making process because organizational and structural elements influence what constitutes 'education news'.

The journalists we interviewed recognized that education is a particular issue of interest for the editors and owners of the media where they work. Journalists recognize that the editorial reframing of their news pieces do not always coincide with their personal opinions about the education system. Journalists sometimes resolve this discrepancy by evoking the journalistic culture defined by Hanitzsch (2007) in terms of their impartial and ethical professional work. Journalists recognize that education is a sphere of political and economic dispute where powerful agents exercise multiple and interrelated interests. In contrast to evidence which shows that education news coverage in Chile tends to over-represent voices that favour market-oriented policies (Santa Cruz 2016), the journalists we interviewed argued that news coverage is balanced in favour of an 'objective' presentation of education news. As one journalist describes it,

> If we are talking about the shared financing (parents pay an extra amount of money each month in voucher or subsidized schools) in elementary and secondary education, we interview people that are in favor of shared financed

schools, those that are studying shared financed schools and the people against shared financed schools. In this way, I have never had major problems in editorial terms.

However, the most evident proof of the importance of power relations in education coverage is when journalists discuss their audience. Journalists recognize that they are writing for, or behalf of, certain political and economic elites that use influential newspapers as a source of information and as a forum to discuss and shape public debates. Although initially some journalists justified education media coverage as a matter of public interest that affects all people in the same way, they also assumed that their target audience is the Chilean elite. For the journalists we interviewed, people in advantageous power and social positions are more interested in education issues than people with less power in society. As one journalist explained: 'The elite clearly have a great interest in education and that interest is even greater when it comes to higher education.'

The fact that some journalists assume that people on low income have scant interest in education has the effect of legitimizing the predominance of elite opinions and their concerns. Due to the power of the media in effecting representations of education, elite expectations, appraisals and aspirations typically become the core concerns of education governance. This elitist conception of what counts as education news has a performative effect on the dynamics of education governance. The message brought forth by the media is that education news is and must be a topic that addresses the concerns of the elite.

The news-making process is therefore an 'elitist domain' but which also includes government authorities, education experts and education journalists themselves. The elite compete to control (or shape) the circulation of policy ideas in a mediatized educational policy process. The supposed open debate about public education thus tends to be shaped and regulated by a well-educated small sector of the population. These forms of intervention reproduce the 'circular circulation of information' that Bourdieu (1998) described as a practice in the field of journalism. As another journalist explains,

> We write for the Ministry, for the experts, who are at the same time the sources and part of the elite, for the educational system actors and for other media.

These elitist forms of intervention were deeply affected by the 2006 and 2011 student movements in Chile, as many of the journalists stated. Indeed, some newspapers created special sections dedicated to reporting education after the 2006 student movement. In response to these student protests, elite social groups and the conservative media tried to placate student demands in order to avoid structural changes in the Chilean education system. This process of expanding and negotiating the boundaries of education discourse was made possible by, among other factors, the wider media coverage of the movements. This demonstrates the importance of the media in the analysis and transformation of education policy.

Final remarks

As Fairclough (2003: 85) has indicated, 'making news is a heavily interpretative and constructive process, not simply a report of "the facts"'. Indeed, the news-making process in education is a dialectical process where different actors participate, in effect trying to steer media coverage to promote certain policy issues. Hence, the discourse surrounding public education in Chile is a site of struggle where the fields of journalism and education intersect and interrelate. Many education journalists assume that actors engaged in public debates about in education in Chile are never neutral or impartial. The 2006 and 2011 student movements in Chile revealed the mediatization of education policymaking in Chile and the extent to which news-making processes have acquired the character of a political space of negotiation between different policy agents (Cabalin 2015). Education journalists have also emerged as key agents in this discussion, showing their important role in the construction of policy education discourse. Many education journalists in Chile downplay or ignore the political nature of their work, however, in effect avoiding challenging questions about their profound influence as tools of education governance and their legitimizing of certain opinions, social representations and narratives.

The journalists we interviewed recognized that media education coverage is a matter of interest for the elite because education itself is mediated by power relations. Therefore, education news is not only the material product of journalist's work; education news is the product of an array of structural and organizational factors. In the case of the most influential Chilean newspapers, certain media outlets support and promote a market-oriented structure in education (Cabalin 2013; Santa Cruz 2016). Power is also evident in the selection of news sources. According to the journalists we interviewed, 'valid' voices tend to be government actors, specific education experts and authorities representing certain education institutions. Evidence from previous research (Cabalin 2015; Santa Cruz 2016) suggests that the media, especially the written press, is a powerful space where numerous experts legitimize and augment their own symbolic power. In the Chilean case outlined here, the media also constitutes one of the links in a tortuous political chain that has advanced an array of transformations seeking to deepen market-oriented economic policies in the development of education structures and discourses (Santa Cruz 2016).

Experts possess or exercise 'educational policy capital' (Ladwig 1994: 346) which allows them to speak with authority as a source of 'authentic' knowledge. Experts and 'policy intellectuals' have acquired importance in shaping the implementation of education policies in different countries (Ball and Exley 2010). They are authorities for the media because they supposedly have the technical ability to explain education issues in a scientific and understandable manner. But experts also have political agendas and they represent certain ways of seeing and constructing the world. Moreover, some education experts have the capacity to present and interpret numbers, which is an important criterion in the news-making process. The prioritization of these expertise strengthens the dominant discourse in the Chilean education system which is that quantifiable, measurable knowledge is superior to all others. This positivist view of knowledge is far from neutral, however. Furthermore, it influences public debate, including the design of education policies and the enactment of these policies in a wide variety of contexts. The impact of the media on these practices is expressed, most notably, in the publication of the school test results and the ranking of universities. The media's validation of these new governing knowledges or technologies reaffirms the government's preference for 'governing by numbers' (Ozga 2011) and therefore implicates the media as a tool in education governance.

Note

1   Social fields are constituted by institutions, practices and social actors. Social actors develop a certain 'habitus', which describes a set of dispositions that agents acquire in their socialization processes (Bourdieu 1977: 83). In Bourdieu's conceptual scheme, habitus also relates to different forms of capital, which is understood as a 'product and process within a field' (Grenfell and James 2004: 510).

References

Ball, S. J., and Exley, S. 2010. 'Making policy with "good ideas": Policy networks and the "intellectuals" of New Labour'. *Journal of Education Policy* 25 (2): 151–169.

Ball, S. J., and Junemann, C. 2012. *Networks, New Governance and Education.* London: Policy Press at the University of Bristol.

Bellei, C., and Cabalin, C. 2013. 'Chilean student movements: Sustained struggle to transform a market-oriented educational system'. *Current Issues in Comparative Education* 15 (2): 108–123.

Bellei, C., Cabalin, C., and Orellana, V. 2014. 'The 2011 Chilean student movement against neoliberal educational policies'. *Studies in Higher Education* 39 (3): 426–440.

Benson, R. 2006. 'News media as a "journalistic field": What Bourdieu adds to new institutionalism, and vice versa'. *Political Communication* 23 (2): 187–202.

Blackmore, J., and Thomson, P. 2004. 'Just "good and bad news"? Disciplinary imaginaries of head teachers in Australian and English print media'. *Journal of Education Policy* 19 (3): 301–320.

Blackmore, J., and Thorpe, S. 2003. 'Media/ting change: the print media's role in mediating education policy in a period of radical reform in Victoria, Australia'. *Journal Education Policy* 18 (6): 577–595.

Bourdieu, P. 1977. *Outline of a Theory of Practice.* Cambridge, UK: Cambridge University Press.

Bourdieu, P. 1996. *The State Nobility. Elite Schools in the Field of Power.* Cambridge, UK: Polity Press.

Bourdieu, P. 1998. *On Television.* New York, NY: The New Press.

Bourdieu, P. 2005. 'The political field, the social field, and the journalistic field'. In R. Benson and E. Neveu (eds), *Bourdieu and the Journalistic Field*, pp. 29–47. Malden, MA: Polity Press.

Bowe, R., Ball, S., and Gold, A. 1992. *Reforming Education and Changing Schools: Case Studies in Policy.* London: Routledge.

Cabalin, C. 2013. 'Framing y políticas educacionales: Los medios como actores políticos en educación'. *Estudios sobre el Mensaje Periodístico* 19 (2): 635–647.

Cabalin, C. 2014. 'The conservative response to the 2011 Chilean student movement: Neoliberal education and media'. *Discourse: Studies in the Cultural Politics of Education* 35 (4): 485–498.

Cabalin, C. 2015. 'Mediatizing higher education policies: Discourses about quality education in the media'. *Critical Studies in Education* 56 (2): 224–240.

Casero, A. 2008. *La construcción mediática de las crisis políticas.* Madrid: Fragua.

Couldry, N. 2012. *Media, Society, World: Social Theory and Digital Media Practice.* Cambridge: Polity Press.

Deuze, M. 2005. 'What is journalism?: Professional identity and ideology of journalists reconsidered'. *Journalism* 6 (4): 442–464.

Eisenhart, M. 2006. 'Qualitative science in experimental time'. *International Journal of Qualitative Studies in Education* 19 (6): 697–707.

Entman, R. M. 2007. 'Framing bias: Media in the distribution of power'. *Journal of Communication* 57 (1): 163–173.

Fairclough, N. 2003. *Analysing Discourse. Textual Analysis for Social Research.* New York: Routledge.

Ginsberg, R., and Lyche, L. F. 2008. 'The culture of fear and the politics of education'. *Educational Policy* 22 (1): 10–27.

Goldstein, R. 2010. 'Imaging the frame: Media representations of teachers, their unions, NCLB, and education reform'. *Educational Policy* 25 (4): 543–576.

Goldstein, R., and Chesky, N. 2011. 'A twenty-first century education: The marketization and mediatization of school reform discourses'. *Educational Change* 1 (1): 16–33.

Grenfell, M., and James, D. 2004. 'Change in the field-changing the field: Bourdieu and the methodological practice of educational research'. *British Journal of Sociology of Education* 25 (4): 507–523.

Hanitzsch, T. 2007. 'Deconstructing journalism culture: Toward a universal theory'. *Communication Theory* 17 (4): 367–385.

Ladwig, J. G. 1994. 'For whom this reform?: Outlining educational policy as a social field'. *British Journal of Sociology of Education* 15 (3): 341–363.

Lingard, B., and Rawolle, S. 2004. 'Mediatizing educational policy: The journalistic field, science policy, and cross-field effects'. *Journal of Education Policy* 19 (3): 361–380.

Livingstone, S. 2009. 'Foreword: Coming to terms with "mediatization"'. In K. Lundby (ed.), *Mediatization*, pp. ix–xi. New York, NY: Peter Lang.

MacMillan, K. 2002. 'Narratives of Social Disruption: Education news in the British tabloid press'. *Discourse: Studies in the Cultural Politics of Education* 23 (1): 27–38.

McDonald, L. 2013. 'In their own words: U.S. think tank "Experts" and the framing of education policy debates'. *Journal for Critical Education Policy Studies* 11 (3): 1-28.

Mockler, N. 2013. 'Reporting the "education revolution": MySchool.edu.au in the print media'. *Discourse: Studies in the Cultural Politics of Education* 34 (1): 1–16.

Olmedo, A. 2013. 'Heterarchies and "philanthropic governance" global: Controversies and implications for social control of social policies'. *Educação e Políticas em Debate* 2 (2): 443–469.

Ozga, J. 2011. 'Governing narratives: "local" meanings and globalising education policy'. *Education Inquiry* 2 (2): 305–318.

Rawolle, S., and Lingard, B. 2010. 'The mediatization of the knowledge based economy: An Australian field based account'. *Communications: The European Journal of Communications Research* 35 (3): 269–286.

Santa Cruz, G. E. 2016. *Mediatización de las políticas educativas en Chile: El discurso de los diarios La Tercera y El Mercurio sobre la Ley General de Educación (2006–2009)* (Thesis Doctoral). Granada: Universidad de Granada.

Santa Cruz, G. E., and Olmedo, A. 2012. 'Neoliberalismo y creación de "sentido común": Crisis educativa y medios de comunicación en Chile'. *Profesorado* 16 (3): 145–168.

Simmonds, M., and Taylor Webb, P. 2013. 'Accountability synopticism: How a think tank and the media developed a quasimarket for school choice in British Columbia'. *The International Education Journal: Comparative Perspectives* 12 (2): 21–41.

Stack, M. 2010. 'Spin as symbolic capital: The fields of journalism and education policy-making'. *International Journal of Leadership in Education* 13 (2): 107–119.

Strömbäck, J. 2008. 'Four phases of mediatization: An analysis of the mediatization of politics'. *Press/Politics* 13 (3): 228–246.

Swartz, D. L. 2013. *Symbolic Power, Politics and Intellectuals*. Chicago, IL: The University of Chicago Press.

Thomas, S. 2011. 'Teachers and public engagement: An argument for rethinking teacher professionalism to challenge deficit discourses in the public sphere'. *Discourse: Studies in the Cultural Politics of Education* 32 (3): 371–382.

Wallace, M. 1993. 'Discourse of derision: the role of the mass media within the education policy process'. *Journal Education Policy* 8 (4): 321–337.

Part Four

Institutional Regimes

Preschool Teacher Agency and Professionalism: A Bourdieuian Approach to Education Governance

Ondrej Kaščák and Branislav Pupala

Introduction

As social actors, teachers inhabit a complex field of relations shaped by other important 'players': politicians enforcing a particular state doctrine, local authorities involved in school governance, parents pursuing their children's interests, professional organizations articulating the teaching community's interests and unions advocating ideas about teachers' working conditions. These complex relations are also inhabited by academics researching the education sector, teacher professionality, education policy and so on. These relations therefore exist within a complicated network of interactions.

In this chapter, we view teachers as actors in education governance and consider their 'will to participate' (Janes 2016) in matters of governance to be a key component of their professionalism. We begin with the concept of 'participatory governance' (Fischer 2006) where the aim is to ensure that the broad spectrum of actors most affected by education governance are more intensively engaged within it. The opportunities to participate are, however, bound up with the structural possibilities made possible to these professionals to wield influence. Therefore, in the first part of this chapter we describe these opportunities in relation to Slovak preschool education. To do so we draw on sociological theory, specifically Bourdieu's social field theory and its concomitant analytical tools. Then, based on an autoethnographic analysis of the debate on preschool education reform in Slovakia, we demonstrate the evolution of and potential for teacher participation in education governance. We began collating our autoethnographic experiences in 2012 with the help of funding from Slovak research grant agencies (VEGA 2/0134/18, VEGA 1/0258/18, KEGA 009TTU-4/2018). At that time, we assumed responsibility for undertaking conceptual and policy work in the preschool education sector and this prompted us to engage with the whole spectrum of professional groups in the preschool education field.

Field theory and education governance

Bourdieu's social field theory is a conscious departure from the Marxist notion of social space. It does not privilege a specific group of social actors but is primarily concerned with describing the *relationships* between actors in the social field. On this view, the social groups engaging in that field are not clearly demarcated nor is their position hierarchically static. The theory rejects a strictly economic view of the functioning of social fields and the relationships within them, and emphasizes instead the need to analytically account for the 'symbolic struggles' within social fields, that is, the 'representation of the social world' by different participating actors and/or interest groups (Bourdieu 1985: 723). It therefore provides scope for understanding education governance in the participative sense.

Bourdieu defines the social field 'as a multi-dimensional space of positions' within which 'agents are distributed . . . according to the overall volume of the capital they possess and, in the second dimension, according to the composition of their capital' (ibid.: 724). Being in possession of certain developed forms of capital is therefore strategic to maintaining or obtaining one's position in a given social field. The social field then becomes

> a field of power struggles among the holders of different forms of power, a gaming space in which those agents and institutions possessing enough specific capital (economic or cultural capital in particular) to be able to occupy the dominant positions within their respective fields confront each other using strategies aimed at preserving or transforming these relations of power. (Bourdieu 1996: 264–265)

Bourdieu's social field theory is therefore highly appropriate for understanding education governance 'as a field of contestation' and a 'technology of mistrust', as Wilkins and Olmedo allude to in the introduction to this book. In this chapter, it is mainly those who represent the 'economic fraction' and 'cultural fraction' in the field of education that often find themselves in a state of dynamic tension (Hilgers and Mangez 2015: 8). This sometimes reveals itself through clashes of interest between providers and teachers, the ministry and academics, and so forth.

In our view, the concept of education governance is based on the exercise of power among actors in a given social field of education. Education governance can be understood as a decision-making power game and as a process of creating, consolidating and transforming the power relations between different subfields representing the education social field.

Preschool subfields in Slovakia

Bourdieu's field theory (Bourdieu 1985, 1996) is based on the topological identification of the relationships and positions of the key players in social structures. To understand the network of powerful players in preschool education that forms the backdrop against which preschool teacher professionality is shaped and negotiated, it is crucial to distinguish between them. They include the political subfield, the professional subfield, the education subfield and the academic subfield, all of which are explained below (see also Kaščák and Pupala 2017).

The authoritative subfield is the political subfield. In Slovakia, the political subfield contains two divisions. The first represents the education ministry and its regulatory mechanisms and structures. Since governance of the state school sector in Slovakia occurs at the municipal level, the second division is a political subfield embodying the separate, powerful influence of ZMOS (Association of Slovak Towns and Villages), the representative body of Slovak local government that coordinates the representation of the powerful interests of regional politicians. The interests of the two political divisions often clash and therefore common regulatory mechanisms are the subject of conflictual negotiation. The regulatory actions of this group of actors (designated here as the subfield of power relations) have a direct impact on preschool teachers and their identity since they affect the setting of preschool teacher qualification requirements, pay assessments and classification, and hence teachers' social and professional status.

The second powerful subfield in preschool education is the professional subfield. The limits of this particular subfield are framed by numerous professional preschool teacher associations. In Slovakia, these associations have traditionally been the Society for Preschool Education and the Slovak branch of OMEP (since

1993) which, until 2012, were moderate associations of limited power closely linked to the political subfield. The professional subfield did not acquire its explicit power dynamics until 2014 with the emergence of the preschool section of the Slovak Chamber of Teachers (SKU) as a new professional organization and the establishment of the Slovak Association of Early Childhood Education in 2015. These two professional associations emerged out of an explicit motivation to distinguish themselves from the political subfield and to gain a voice in promoting the specific professional interests and goals of the preschool teacher community.

Despite tensions between the old and new professional associations and the fact they do not homogenously represent professional interests, they create a coherent powerful subfield that has acquired significant influence in preschool education debates. The most influential voices in these negotiations are preschool teachers under the Slovak Chamber of Teachers umbrella. Since this organization is not exclusively a preschool teacher one, its negotiating position is strengthened by the wider Slovak teacher cohort undergirding it.

Where the political and professional subfields meet, there is a relatively separate and specific subfield containing the teachers' unions who are concerned mainly with teachers' working conditions. As with the SKU, there is no separate preschool teacher union. Rather, there are three unions representing all teachers from nursery to secondary school. Although a strong opposite player to the political subfield, this powerful organization has not wielded significant influence over the development of professional preschool teacher identity. The historically complicated power relations between these powerful subfields and the political subfield more generally have led teachers to be cautious and distrustful of these key organizations. The main actors involved in clashes over politics and specialist interests are not teachers, but rather professional union leaders whose interests do not necessarily reflect teachers' interests.

The academic subfield, whose formal power is linked to tertiary preschool teacher training and to the awarding of formal qualifications, occupies a special position in the preschool education arena. Predictably its powerful tool in the field is the accumulation and distribution of knowledge within preschool pedagogy. The power to award qualifications is both immutable and important. The power accumulated in knowledge relates to expectation, but the influence exerted depends on the authority and applicability of that knowledge as well as on the willingness of other powerful groups to accept it. The academic subfield could accept its delegated position of power as awarder of qualifications and producer of specialist knowledge as its only role in the preschool education field, making it less motivated to engage further and participate in the power games directed at other subfields and preschool actors. Although possessing status in the preschool field, actors in the academic subfield do not necessarily lead powerful clashes that propel national preschool education policy, and only do so when they become active on the boundaries of several subfields.

The academic subfield is represented exclusively by academics working in university preschool pedagogy. Its delegated exclusivity may lead to it being a closed community with relatively little influence on the power games that play out in the preschool education field. This is the case where academics do not use their cultural capital to participate actively in other subfields. Sometimes the academic subfield may attract those who have obtained qualifications through that subfield, that is, university qualified preschool teachers. Clearly these are teachers rather than academics, and their professional identity is shaped through the teaching profession environment rather than the academic one. The transitionary ties between the academic environment and the university one contribute to a specific preschool teacher identity shaped by the academic subfield, nonetheless.

The academically moulded identity of the preschool teacher sometimes manifests itself in the internal professional conflicts between preschool teachers. The preschool teacher group contains those with and those without degrees – in Slovakia the minimum preschool qualification requirement is a secondary school teaching certificate. The university-educated preschool teachers tend to promote the benefits of membership of the academic subfield. Since it would be hard to defend this powerful advantage using formal qualifications, or degrees, self-definition is declarative, grounded in academic knowledge and viewed as special and unavailable to those without ties to the academic sphere.

Although the subfields are distinct, this does not mean that they are sharply demarcated or that there can be no movement between them. For example, just because the political subfield and the teachers' unions subfield are separate does not mean that only the political subfield engages in political decision-making. The unions most certainly fulfil this function as well, as do all the other subfields characterized above, and they all participate to some degree in education governance in preschool education. The overlapping of the subfields means, for instance, that teachers are always the object of power games in preschool education and, being the numerically strongest group, have strong potential to become an important subject. Teachers may therefore be manipulated through attempts to get them on side. A more obvious strategy used in these games is the switching of subfield membership. It is not unusual for education officers representing the political subfield to be former preschool teachers. State administrators responsible for preschool education nationally can be heard to utter 'I'm one of you' when seeking political power and legitimization within the preschool field. In preschool circles the political (and sometimes academic) subfield representatives are generally also members of the professional teacher associations, enabling them to declare their ties with the teaching sphere and legitimize their power.

The intersection and mutual permeability of these subfields may appear to indicate good cooperation across the preschool education field. However, more detailed analysis points to a strategic power game between the various subfields, resulting in reinforced boundaries that speak to specific needs, interests and behaviour strategies.

Research through political engagement

In research terms, it is difficult to pinpoint and describe in detail from 'the outside' the strategies and power games engaged in by the various subfields described above. The only realistic way to do so is to engage with them directly from 'the inside' as an actor-participant of these power games. Influence can then be gained over the community while pursuing research goals and obtaining a deeper knowledge of the power structures and subfields that drive the preschool community and shape the professional preschool teacher identity as we show in this study.

This kind of fertile positioning prompted us to undertake research on the powerful preschool education subfields that exist. Our identity was originally typical of the academic subfield, but in 2012 we agreed to create a new Slovak national preschool curriculum. The state (education ministry) selected us based on trust and owing to our academic expertise and suitability for a task requiring specific professional abilities and academic authority. We accepted the offer, assuming that writing and introducing the new preschool curriculum would be relatively problem-free. Early on, though, it became clear it would be far from simple and that we would encounter clusters of powerful structures in the preschool community subfield, requiring us to engage in sophisticated strategic games and disentangle the entrenched powerful ties and professional identity of the community. Consequently, it took us five long years to battle against the barriers erected through the exercise of power relations in the subfields until the new national curriculum became obligatory in 2017 for all preschools in

Slovakia. Nonetheless, it presented us with an ideal opportunity to gain an in-depth understanding of the preschool community and our position within it, and the positions of the key actors shaping it from the inside as well as the changes occurring within it during this period.

The methodological position adopted in this research was largely autoethnographic (Ellis and Bochner 2000). Having taken on the role of curriculum writers and implementers, we were still part of the academic subfield and it was on that basis that we performed this research. The data emerged from our unique experiences as academics taking on these additional roles and having to engage in strategic games and create powerful alliances. They were not necessarily collected as research data nor were they generated through the creation of a tailored research design. They were obtained from countless communicative situations and encounters occurring across all the subfields, including communication with numerous subjects participating in the discussions and power games during the reform of the Slovak national preschool curriculum and the authors' long-term direct participation in this process. Unlike in standard research approaches where the researcher occupies the position of researcher and purposefully selects the research situations or subjects, our situations and subjects did not emerge out of a clear research goal or design and so we cannot with any accuracy speak of intentional 'data collection' with a specific number of defined research subjects and research communication situations. The data generated through this study is the product of our several year-long engagement as authors in preschool education and reflects our autoethnographic experiences, much of which was recalled through memory reconstruction.

Forms of capital – entrance ticket to the subfields

The task of creating and introducing a new national curriculum is not traditionally the role of the academic subfield. It is a political responsibility mainly associated with the political subfield and its players; hence we were forced to engage and become players within this subfield. Equally, the negotiation processes required us to enter the professional subfields since achieving our goal required the acceptance of the whole professional community.

Promoting the new curriculum was a political task that set us up against the original, stable members of the two fields (political and professional), requiring us to adopt new positions and engage in power games. We were required to learn to use new resources to expand and maintain our influence, as field theory suggests: 'Bourdieu constructed his version of field theory in a dual sense in which social actors experience fields as both arenas of force and arenas of struggle' (Ferrare and Apple 2015: 48). In carrying out this task, cultural and social capital was a decisive factor. As Grenfell (2009) has shown, in social field theory the influence and mobility between subfields and fields largely depends on individuals and groups disposing various forms of capital. 'For Bourdieu, Capital is the currency of the Field: it fuels its operations and defines what is included and excluded from it' (ibid.: 19) and capital 'belongs to the field and it is the field that sets its value, but it is individuals who possess it' (ibid.: 20).

Up until 2012 the existing professional and political subfields had been based around the shared social capital that moulded the professional identity of the preschool teachers and established actors in the political field, especially state education officers, preschool controllers and state preschool pedagogic advisors. This social capital is manifested through membership of the appropriate professional preschool teacher community. Social capital plays a key role in the social field or subfield, since it denotes a network of relations. '[T]he concept of social capital is also intended to act as a moderating concept on an overly deterministic model of cultural hegemony and social dominance' (Grenfell 2009: 24). This capital is rooted in the collective professional preschool teacher identity. Former preschool teachers who become representatives in the political subfield (state officials and inspectors in particular) make particular use of it. Their position of dominance is founded on shared social capital and enables them to pursue political or economic tasks or goals in the preschool sector. The social capital widely distributed throughout the preschool community forms the basis on which hegemonic behaviour and non-conflictual interests are pursued. This appears to be key to maintaining the existing distribution of power and relationships of dominance and submission within the professional community.

However, the social capital of this community is not shared by members of the academic field nor by many of the teachers constituting the preschool community. This is partly because the power of the academic subfield is restricted by the ability to award qualifications or produce knowledge, and partly owing to the lack of links, even biographical ones, between the members of the academic field and the community and its social capital. The identity of the academic subfield representatives means they benefit as bearers of higher cultural capital. While this capital has value in and of itself, this does not mean that it is easily transferred to the preschool community, nor that the community will unconditionally accept it.

On occasions when representatives of the academic subfield intervene in other subfields, they are likely to experience the difficulty of non-acceptance because they do not share the social capital of many of those in the social community and because they are taking on roles performed by other social players whose position of power in the community is weakening. Instead, they must acquire and build up social capital before they can use their higher cultural capital to span these subfields.

Cultural capital as added value

Although higher cultural capital is highly valued, it tends to disrupt fixed power relations and introduces conflicts within specific subfields since it influences established hierarchies of dominance in the political field but also in the professional preschool teacher subfield. 'It is unsurprising . . . if, in a Field such as education, certain certificates and certain ways of thinking and doing things (Cultural Capital) were and are valued over others . . .' (Grenfell 2009: 19–20). Higher cultural capital is a general advantage within the academic profession since it provides representatives with a strategic advantage negotiating between the two subfields. In this case, preschool teachers' university education is a specific form of cultural capital that enables them to intervene in other subfields, making it easy for them to access the more accepting academic subfield. This capital brings them added negotiating value – compared to secondary school qualifications – and a position of superiority: 'The main principle behind the concept of cultural capital then is that it embodies or transmits the logic of practice of the Field in a way that differentiates and therefore establishes hierarchies' (ibid.: 20).

In the professional preschool teacher subfield, this hierarchization has led to more frequent conflict since large numbers of nursery school teachers now obtain bachelor degrees. The degree-educated and non-degree-educated groups are often careful to distinguish themselves, and there is contention over whether practical training or theory-based training is better suited to preschool work. This internal debate has no bearing on relations with other subfields (despite clarifying professionality within the subfield). University-educated teachers tend to have greater influence as they have social capital and cultural capital valued by certain fields because it is homologous to that of the academic and political fields. Hence the university-educated teachers are the leaders of the professional organization subfield. This added value is of symbolic significance:

> Every kind of capital (economic, cultural, social) tends (to different degrees) to function as symbolic capital (so that it might be better to speak in rigorous terms, of the symbolic effect of capital) when it obtains explicit or practical recognition. (Bourdieu 2000: 242)

During the negotiations related to the political goal of introducing the new curriculum, the bearers of higher cultural capital – university-educated teachers – were both in support of and resistance to these reforms. Unsurprisingly, resistance was led by the representatives of the established actors of the political subfield (the attempt to introduce the new curriculum weakening their position of power) and spilled over into the professional field, with resistance also being fomented among ordinary teachers. Support for the curriculum was mainly found among leaders of the new professional associations who had already consciously defined themselves in opposition to the continuing power hierarchies, blurring the line between the professional and political subfields. They intentionally used their cultural capital to create new ties and counterbalance the existing preschool community power hierarchy.

The distribution of power in the various preschool education subfields, their boundaries and the actions of their representatives began to be mirrored in and played out through the media, with both traditional and new media being used in attempts to influence the community. Notably, although the media have traditionally been a tool of the academic subfield, preschool teachers – especially those wielding higher cultural capital – began engaging with this sphere. The power games over the new preschool curriculum led a group of teachers to emerge out of their professional subfield and into the political and academic fields. They published articles in academic journals (e.g. Vargová 2014/2015) hoping to influence any decisions about the new curriculum and accepted offers to speak to the media or meet senior state officials. One interesting and effective way in which the power games were reflected through the media was the use of Facebook, with teachers creating a discussion group that would later become the main mediator and source of friction for the different actors representing the various subfields affected by the negotiations.

In the clash between the traditional hierarchies, Facebook proved to be a highly motivating arena to facilitate diverse views. It enabled all those who participated to move rapidly from one subfield to another, liberating them from the well-trodden power structures and encouraging leaders to emerge from the professional preschool teacher community. The professional subfield was therefore given the opportunity to extend its influence into the political and academic subfields.

The open discussions on Facebook that loosened the boundaries of the subfields occurred in parallel with the power games associated with our entrance into the political and professional subfields. They were not limited simply to this theme, but spawned many others, and through these the hitherto hidden professional dimensions of the internally differentiated preschool teacher community were revealed. On a methodological note, an analysis of the teachers' discussions in the Facebook group can be found in some of our previous work on professional preschool teacher identity (Kascak et al. 2016; Tesar et al. 2017).

Teacher agency and strategies of the professional subfield

Perhaps the best way of understanding and describing teacher engagement in the field of education governance is to identify the clashes that emerged between other subfields in the education field. As indicated above, engagement is dependent on the level of cultural and social capital held by the teachers or their subfield representatives. This also applies to other representatives from other subfields who sometimes directly participated in the debate. This was evident in the preschool teacher debates on Facebook.

In the professional subfield, there is an ongoing debate among teachers about whether teachers should increase their cultural capital by obtaining a degree. One university-educated teacher with a high level of cultural and social capital in the teacher community responded to a colleague asking whether she should study:

> [Name], you definitely won't regret studying. I can only encourage you. Besides in the future we can finally expect the minimum requirement in this country to be at least stage 1 of higher education. You wouldn't have to catch up because you'd already have it.

Another teacher joins in:

> I really don't know what you mean by 'finally', I think a secondary school teaching certificate is enough for nursery school teachers.

A third teacher, well known in the community, with an equally high level of cultural and social capital, responds:

> not even stage one primary school teachers needed a degree, a couple of years at a teaching institute was enough, today they have to have a master's. Introducing the bachelor degree for nursery schools would help move preschool teacher education in Slovakia forward. So long of course as it's a quality university course.

What is important to note here is that when an argument appears in favour of the need for preschool teachers to have a degree, the most influential teachers – university educated – spring into action. These teachers take control of the conversation, actively encouraging discussion and directing it from within the community. They generally 'silence' the more critical, traditional voices of the predominantly older members.

Teachers with high levels of cultural and social capital are also much more accommodating of academics who attempt to enter the teacher subfield and engage in discussion. The membership base of the professional subfield is, however, more suspicious, frequently rejecting their attempts at social networking:

> I'm really surprised and can't understand where our female preschool experts have got to and why it is men – university professors, doctors etc – who think more about the economics than about the child and the conditions of learning that are making these important decisions. I know that you invited female teachers with experience to the consultations, but shouldn't it be the other way round?

Apart from the attempt to create distance between them and the academic representatives in the university and medical subfields, one can also identify stereotypes that still inform professional preschool teacher identity in Slovakia: gender identity linked to female emotional closeness to children. Male academics are frequently portrayed as incapable of understanding such emotional closeness and stereotyped as prioritizing impersonal and emotionally bare 'economic' criteria. This is a paradoxical view, since Bourdieu demonstrates that the intellectual field of power has traditionally been in direct opposition to the economic field. The comment continues:

> This should be dealt with by a group of female experts, of whom there are many, even in the OMEP at the education offices etc. If this group of experts were to propose changes to the curriculum all female teachers would definitely support them!!!!!!!!

The above comment clearly demonstrates that elements of social power in the preschool teacher community is wielded by women, namely 'female experts' with a high level of cultural capital, that is, university educated, which enables them to manage the behaviour of the whole community. The proposal itself is unimportant, but what matters is who makes it and how strongly it is received.

Economic versus cultural fractions

As Bourdieu states, in the field of power the economic and cultural fractions continually fight one another. In the specific field of preschool education these are ZMOS with its economic agenda and the professional subfield which rejects the economic view of preschool education. The conflict is especially heated since the economic motives of ZMOS, as the representative of one division of the political subfield, directly block further teacher professional development. In Slovakia, the school authorities, that is, the political subfield of education governance, prefer to employ cheaper, less-qualified teachers. The economic fraction in the field of power thus directly opposes teachers' attempts to build up cultural capital.

> Hello there, girls, do you think university educated teachers tend to get selected for vacancies? I'm thinking about continuing my studies but I don't want to neglect my children . . .

Another teacher responds directly:

> I've twice experienced them choosing me for my secondary schooling over a university-educated one – because of the pay.

The leader of the community, with a high level of cultural capital, replies:

> There are towns/villages where it's more of a barrier because nursery school teachers still only need secondary school education and so for them the benefit is a cheaper workforce. On the other hand – we are only one of four countries in the EU that doesn't require higher education, min. bachelor degree (everywhere else you need a bachelor or master's). And as long as ZMOS have their say, so it will be for a long time.

It is the leader who introduces the issue of academically comparable knowledge (or lack of) and a strategic awareness of power. She points out that it is because of ZMOS, representing the economically oriented political subfield, that less-educated nursery school teachers are employed. Furthermore, she actively opposes the economic fraction and seeks strategic political tools with which to intervene. This type of engagement could be seen when ZMOS proposed that the ministry should no longer ringfence regional nursery school funding for resources and equipment. ZMOS wanted local government to be able to use the resources ringfenced for five-year old nursery school children for other purposes. The subsequent conflict was won by the professional community and ZMOS's proposal was dropped. In correspondence with us, the leader of the professional community stated:

> we've won the battle over the dedicated nursery school resources ☺ Those communist throwbacks (ZMOS) got it on the nose today. So it pays to fight. And I'm having deja vu about the battle over the national curriculum – even when it looks like all's lost, it isn't ☺

Conclusion

The preschool teaching profession can be depicted from many perspectives. When looked at in conjunction with education governance, a much broader, all-encompassing perspective can be obtained, in which teacher engagement is not just about classroom teaching or making decisions within the school setting. Preschool teachers do not operate merely at this level but are involved in various subfields that define the preschool sector generally. Their professional toolset is therefore much larger and can extend to political or academic circles. Equally their level of engagement is dependent on the level of their social and cultural capital. Teacher professionality is therefore multifaceted and evolves through dynamic social interaction and negotiation. It is not simply determined by pedagogic factors but through engagement with the various subfields shaping the preschool sphere. Teachers are frequently active and influential players in conceptual and political decision-making, and therefore expand their action radius or field of influence to shape forms of expertise, policymaking and their overall professional status. It has been demonstrated in this chapter that their influence is significant when practised on the basis of principles of democratic, open social discourse.

It appears that as events unfolded from 2012 onwards, Slovakia was able to strike out on the path to participatory education governance. The conditions for this were laid down by the greater engagement of academics (approach to drafting the national curriculum) and teachers and their professional organizations in the discussions on preschool education reform. Opportunities to enter the field of power in preschool education sector are also structurally dependent. The landscape of preschool education has changed, shaped by new political tasks, new discourse, new forms of accountability and professionalism. These changes are captured by Ball (2009) under the term 'the governance turn' and time will tell whether the new conditions will continue to encourage participation or not.

Bourdieu's field theory shows that improving teachers' social and cultural capital is a key element of participation because they enable mobility between the preschool education subfields. A natural alliance has emerged between the academic subfield and the development of effective resistance against a purely economic reading of education governance. Hence the 'governance turn' need not be a neo-liberal trap. It also creates arenas of engagement, participation and freedom and it is the role of teachers to learn to make use of these tools of engagement and to ensure that they remain firmly part of their professionality.

References

Ball, S. 2009. 'The governance turn!' *Journal of Education Policy* 24 (5): 537–538.

Bourdieu, P. 1985. 'The social space and the genesis of groups'. *Theory and Society* 14 (6): 723–744.

Bourdieu, P. 1996. *The State Nobility: Elite Schools in the Field of Power*. Stanford: Stanford University Press.

Bourdieu, P. 2000. *Pascalian Meditations*. Stanford: Stanford University Press.

Ellis, C., and Bochner, A. P. 2000. 'Autoethnography, personal narrative, reflexivity: Researcher as subject'. In N. Denzin and Y. Lincoln (eds), *The Handbook of Qualitative Research*, pp. 733–768. Thousand Oaks: Sage.

Ferrare, J. J., and Apple, M. W. 2015. 'Field theory and educational practice: Bourdieu and the pedagogic qualities of local field positions in educational contexts'. *Cambridge Journal of Education* 45 (1): 43–59.

Fischer, F. 2006. 'Participatory governance as deliberative empowerment. The cultural politics of discursive space'. *The American Review of Public Administration* 36 (1): 19–40.

Grenfell, M. 2009. 'Applying Bourdieu's field theory: The case of social capital and education'. *Education, Knowledge and Economy* 3 (1): 17–34.

Hilgers, M., and Mangez, E. 2015. 'Introduction to Pierre Bourdieu's theory of social fields'. In M. Hilgers and E. Mangez (eds), *Bourdieu's Theory of Social Fields. Concepts and Applications*, pp. 1–36. New York: Routledge.

Janes, J. E. 2016. 'The "will to participate": Governmentality, power, and community-based participatory research'. *Intersectionalities* 5 (1): 110–125.

Kaščák, O., and Pupala, B. 2017. 'Topography of power relations in Slovak preschool sector based on Bourdieu's field theory'. *Journal of Pedagogy* 8 (1): 57–76.

Kascak, O., Pupala, B., and Mbugua, T. 2016. 'Slovak preschool curriculum reform and teachers' emotions: An analysis of Facebook posts'. *Early Childhood Education Journal* 44 (6): 573–580.

Tesar, M., Pupala, B., Kascak, O., and Arndt, S. 2017. 'Teachers' voice, power and agency: (un)professionalisation of the early years workforce'. *Early Years* 37 (2): 189–201.

Vargová, M. 2014/2015. 'Poznámky učiteľky k inovovanému štátnemu vzdelávaciemu programu pre predprimárne vzdelávanie v MŠ' ['Teachers comments on the innovative state preschool education programme for nursery schools']. *Predškolská výchova* 69 (5): 5–14.

Ever Greater Scrutiny: Researching the Bureaucracy of Educational Accountability

Mark Murphy

Introduction

Meier and O'Toole (2006: 1) in their book *Bureaucracy in a Democratic State: A Governance Perspective* suggest that governance has a 'bureaucracy problem'. The problem for them resides in the persistent and never-ending challenge of reconciling the 'demands of democracy with the imperatives of bureaucracy' (ibid.). This problem has been codified in the narrative of 'red tape' – a set of policies regulations, protocols and procedures which, so critics of bureaucracy insist, stifle creativity and innovation in favour of a desire for control and surveillance.

While it is indeed the case that governance has a bureaucracy problem, it is also true that bureaucracy has a governance problem. This governance problem is especially pronounced when employing the definition of governance as 'governing without government' (Rhodes 1996). This approach to managing public services in more decentralized regimes, which employs techniques of 'steering at a distance' (Kickert 1995; Marginson 1997) to achieve public sector reforms, has come at a substantial cost, as the emphasis on accountability mechanisms to ensure compliance and surveillance has reduced governance to a 'technology of mistrust' (Rose 1999: 154). This is joined by concerns over the impact of this technology on policy outcomes: there is an ever-widening list of unintended consequences of accountability (Liff 2014; Mendez and Bachtler 2011; Monfardini 2010; Murphy and Skillen 2015; Papadopoulos 2010), the cumulative evidence pointing to the inherently flawed nature of this 'new' bureaucratic approach to public service delivery (Travers 2007).

This is a significant issue for the field of education, as the complex and multifaceted bureaucracy surrounding accountability in particular has altered the landscape of education governance since its development in the last several decades (Murphy 2010). In particular, the implementation of quality assurance mechanisms – audit, inspection, performance indicators and evaluation – has opened up the education sector to ever greater scrutiny. The education profession is under increasing pressure to evidence accountability to the public and the public purse, with educators working in varied fields such as schools, colleges and universities subject to a heightened level of surveillance, regulation and bureaucratic scrutiny. There is a constant demand for legitimation and justification from the political sphere in the form of highly visible accountability mechanisms (Schwier 2012; Shore 2008), with mounting levels of paperwork required to account for their professional capacity, judgment and competence.

This trend towards ever-increasing accountability is part of a broader agenda of regulation in relation to public sector reform initiatives. But like all reform initiatives, this level of education surveillance has itself been subject to scrutiny from researchers, who aim to detail the consequences of such accountability-led reform. The evidence suggests that this bureaucratic mode of governance has questionable impacts on education practice, and overall tend to support Meier and O'Toole's (2006) assertion that a tension exists between bureaucracy and democracy.

This tension has itself long been a focus of attention of a strand of social theory indebted to the work of Max Weber and his writings on bureaucracy (Weber 1958). Most notable in this vein is the work of Jürgen Habermas, particularly in his more sociological writings exemplified in the *Theory of Communicative Action* (1984, 1987) and his critique of lifeworld colonization.

The purpose of this chapter is to explore the connections between Habermas' Weber-inspired critical sociology and the field of education accountability research. What understandings can be applied from his work? What kinds of methodological implications can be drawn out regarding this specific strand of education governance? In order to achieve this purpose, I will first outline Habermas' methodological position, followed by a summary of his contribution to the debate over governance. I will then draw on case studies from the research literature, exploring the ways in which Habermas' post-positivist 'critical sociology' has influenced the debate over educational accountability. The chapter will also cast a critical eye over the ways in which his classic system/ lifeworld distinction has been used to bridge the gap between social theory and research methodology. Specifically, the chapter examines the ways in which this distinction both opens up and also closes down avenues for research exploration, and the chapter turns to the concept of *street-level bureaucracy* (Lipsky 1980) for further refinement of Habermas' ideas around governance.

It should be noted that, compared to other social theorists such as Bourdieu and Foucault, there has been a less visible association between Habermas and education research. That being said, the field of education has been engaging in fruitful debate with Habermas for decades now, a debate that is still ongoing (see e.g. Bouchard and Morris 2012; Caspersz and Olaru 2014; Huttunen and Murphy 2012). I draw on some of this work in the following sections and also on my own work and previous arguments (see in particular Murphy 2010, 2013, 2017). It should also be noted that Habermas was not one to use the term 'governance' in relation to his ideas on power, the state and capitalist modernization. His conceptual apparatus, however, offers much to current theories of education governance, especially given his focus on steering mechanisms and the pathologies of bureaucratic interference in the 'lifeworlds' of citizens and institutions. This steering at a distance via power and money can be classified as elements of a shift from government to governance.

Habermas and social research: between theory and method

Ongoing dialogues with Habermas' intellectual positions and the existence of numerous applications of his core concepts (see Murphy 2017) testify to his relevance to the field of social research. At the same time, less attention has been paid to Habermas' *own* take on theory, method and research, which has tended to occupy a less privileged position compared to debates over discourse ethics and deliberative democracy. This neglect is partially a result of the passage of time, as his extended arguments on methodology were first published in the 1960s and have been somewhat forgotten in the face of his subsequent publications. Later translated into English, *Theory and Practice* (Habermas 1974) and *On the Logic of the Social Sciences* (Habermas 1988) together provide a comprehensive outline of his empirical and normative approach to theory-driven research, one that has governed his thinking to the present day. There are two aspects to this position. The first aspect concerns his critique of positivism, in the face of which he makes a case for what he calls a 'critical sociology' (Habermas 1974: 10). This critical sociology, when confronted with the objectivism of the behavioural sciences, 'guards itself against a reduction of intentional action to behaviour' (Habermas 1974: 10).

This position is clarified further in *On the Logic of the Social Sciences* (1988) where Habermas argues that there 'are no uninterpreted experiences, neither in everyday life nor, especially, within the framework of scientifically organized experience' (Habermas 1988: 97). Habermas argues that the research process cannot be removed from the various factors (economic, political and cultural) that to him inevitably impinge on the research process itself. This awareness and critique of the limitations of positivism as a social science research paradigm was allied to a strong political agenda in Habermas' work, a commitment to 'an interest in emancipation going beyond the technical and the practical interest of knowledge' (Habermas 1974: 9). As a disciple of Frankfurt school critical theory, Habermas viewed research as a tool of emancipation, as a way of furthering democratic practices by revealing the existence of damaging pathologies in late capitalist society.

As a result of this two-pronged approach to critical sociology, Habermas' approach to the study of governance is far from politically neutral. Questions of sovereignty, nationhood and territory (core issues in Political Science) take something of a back seat in Habermas' social theory, where instead the role of the state in relation to social equality takes centre stage. Here, the functions of state governance as they are commonly considered – public administration, resource allocation, wealth re-distribution, boundary maintenance (territory, population) policy prioritization and the maintenance of order – are viewed as secondary questions to those that concern issues of freedom and justice. And because of these concerns with freedom and justice, the approach to state governance in Habermas' social theory has avoided becoming bogged down in procedural or juridical affairs, its hinterland instead a world of power, inequality, elites, identity and, above all else, social change.

From legitimation crisis to lifeworld colonization

To best understand Habermas' conception of governance, it make sense to place it within its rightful theoretical and historical context; and this, regardless of how far modern-day critical theory has travelled, still demands a reference to the work of Karl Marx. This is because Marx looked to uncover and identify pathologies at work in the machine of capitalist modernization – which as an objective comes close to explaining the remit of the Frankfurt School more generally. A classic of this is Marx's own concept of alienation (Marx 1959), closely followed in significance by commodification. Early Frankfurt school in the shape of Theodor Adorno and Max Horkheimer put forward the concept of the 'totally administered society' (1973) – an idea of an over-bearing reason that managed to encompass both of these pathologies. Habermas was and is certainly part of this tradition but his contribution to the literature on social pathologies has distinct elements that managed to both update and also transform our understandings of capitalism and state governance in late modernity.

Habermas tended to avoid the Marxist critiques of the state that were popular when he established his own conceptual apparatus. The 1960s and 1970s saw a concerted effort on the part of thinkers like Louis Althusser, Ralph Miliband and Nikos Poulantzas to detail and analyse the extent to which modern Western states acted as the handmaiden of capitalism. This was the key debate at the time and has arguably never quite disappeared – the power of 'big business' to usurp state-bounded democracy is a persistent theme in discussions over globalization (e.g. see Jones 2000).

Comparing Habermas to Marxist and neo-Marxist theories of state governance helps to illustrate the distance he created between his own ideas and that of Marxist orthodoxy. Habermas was never fully convinced of the conflation at work here regarding the state-economy nexus, and sidestepped fashionable approaches to the state based on ideology and hegemonic power. In this he was influenced heavily by not just the likes of Weber but also the work of Talcott Parsons (1937). Although never quite a functionalist, Habermas was more interested in crafting a theoretical take on the state and the market that managed to keep them conceptually separate while also making a more nuanced space for action-oriented approaches. The importance he placed on the steering media of power and money has a strong functionalist element, which helps Habermas build a theory that reassessed Marxist historical materialism as well as providing a way out of restrictive and deterministic approaches to theory.

This understanding opened up a new intellectual and methodological space for Habermas in his attempts to grapple with twentieth-century problems of governance. He set his sights especially on the welfare state compromise, steered this way to some extent by the conundrum so often highlighted by Marxist critics – how did the capitalist system manage to avoid a working-class revolution? In his book *Legitimation Crisis* (1976), Habermas theorizes that legitimation crises arose from states overreaching their boundaries. In a similar fashion to Claus Offe (1984), Habermas argues that the more responsibility states assume over welfare services as well as consumption, the greater the chance that crises of social integration will occur in the lifeworld. Consequently, if the state cannot manage the pathologies of capitalist modernization, it therefore ends up paying a price and the 'price for this failure is withdrawal of legitimation' (Habermas 1976: 69).

This withdrawal of legitimation occurs in the lifeworld, part of Habermas' new two-level conception of society, a conception that now allowed him to construct both an action-theoretic and a systems-theoretic analysis of the process of societal rationalization. The concept of the lifeworld referred to the background consensus of everyday lives, the stock of taken-for-granted definitions and understandings of the world that provide coherence and direction to people's lives, while the system was a concept used to define that aspect of society where political and market imperatives take precedence; that is, the state administrative apparatus (steered by power) and the economy (steered by money). This two-level concept of society allows Habermas to examine the 'growing autonomy of systematically integrated action contexts over against the socially integrated lifeworld' (1987: 305).

This dual-perspective methodological reconstruction allowed Habermas to tackle the core issue at the heart of Weber's theory – bureaucratization and the iron cage of modern public administration. According to Weber, bureaucratization signified the institutionalization of purposive-rational action. Habermas (1987: 307), however, argues that bureaucratization 'should be regarded as the sign of a new level of system differentiation'. It is the anchoring of the steering mechanisms of the economy and the state – money and power, respectively – in the structures of the lifeworld that signifies bureaucratization for Habermas.

Habermas reconfigured this bureaucratization thesis in terms of a clash between social and system integration. Heavily indebted to the classic work of David Lockwood (1964), this distinction identifies the co-existence of two sets of relationships, one between actors and one between parts of the system. For Habermas, the clash between these sets of integrative relations has implications for state governance and its effects on the lifeworld. Phenomena related to the iron cage now count as 'effects of the uncoupling of system and lifeworld' (Habermas 1987: 318). As the media of money and power function independently of language, they are not tied to the communicative structures of the lifeworld, which are dependent on language as the means to reaching understanding. As a result, these media allow the uncoupling of formally organized domains of action from the structures of the lifeworld, which in turn unleash their functionalist reason of system maintenance onto the lifeworld structures. It is this pathological side-effect of societal rationalization that Habermas refers to as the 'colonization of the lifeworld'.

Habermas qualifies his most famous thesis on bureaucratic governance by arguing that bureaucratization, in the shape of separate formal domains of action, has to be seen as an ordinary and to some extent legitimate component of modernization processes. Because of this, Habermas must make a distinction between functional and dysfunctional forms of bureaucratization. He must be able to distinguish the normal mediatization of the lifeworld from the pathological colonization of the lifeworld. According to Habermas (1987), it is only when the economic and political system, via the media of money and power, attempt to reify the symbolic structures of the lifeworld that pathologies arise.

It is this 'systematically induced reification' (ibid.: 327) of the symbolic structures of the lifeworld that Habermas views as constituting colonization. The capacity to act communicatively is under threat from systemic imperatives, which, via the media of money and power, reify those structures of the lifeworld that are based on communicative action. Habermas (ibid.: 326) terms this reification of everyday communicative practice a 'one-sided rationalisation', a restricted rationality ushered in by the process of capitalist modernization. This is a process with origins in 'the growing autonomy of media-steered subsystems, which not only get objectified into a norm-free sociality beyond the horizon of the lifeworld, but whose imperatives also penetrate into the core domains of the lifeworld' (ibid.: 327).

Colonization, bureaucratization and education research

This critique of colonization resonates with recurring debates over managerialism and new education governance as well as consumerism and the ways in which these policy-driven responses to crises have created unforeseen consequences in the education sector. In the field of education, Habermas has been used to form normative judgments on the success or otherwise of public sector modernization processes, and has been used to generate critiques of the new bureaucracy of accountability and its damaging and colonizing effects on the teaching professions and the management of education institutions. The distinctions between instrumental and communicative reason, and pathological and non-pathological forms of bureaucracy, have facilitated the development of critical perspectives in relation to the education reform agenda that has driven change in countries such as the United Kingdom, United States and Australia. This is especially the case when it comes to the manner in which Habermas-inspired authors have delineated the limitations of the new bureaucracy. A good example of this is provided by Deakin Crick and Joldersma's work on Habermas and citizenship education (2007). According to them, instrumental rationality has come to dominate the ethos of education, through the over-emphasis on measurement and performance targets. This domination has resulted in a 'discourse of accountability', which sees core school activity – the curriculum, teaching and learning – 'all taking on the language of bureaucratic relationships' (Deakin Crick and Joldersma 2007: 84).

The limits of accountability and its colonizing tendencies are also evident in a set of case studies of further education colleges, conducted by Oakes and Berry (2009), who used Habermasian theory as a heuristic devise to explore the impact of accountability measures. The limitations outlined in their study were caused in part by the data demands of accountability – the need to account on a regular basis placing increased time pressure and work demands on an already time-strapped education sector. The over-bearing nature of accountability had the effect of 'distorting the lifeworld of some of the managers' (Oakes and Berry 2009: 355), with one manager suggesting bureaucratic mechanisms of accounting were creating more bureaucracy in the college:

> There is a lot of bureaucracy around and I suppose until we have actually got systems that are giving us information that you are confident in, then not having that tends to create bureaucracy by having to do special exercises to go and collect data. (FE manager, quoted in Oakes and Berry 2009: 355)

Another related theme that emerges from the literature is the manner in which these damaging effects get played out in the key interpersonal relations across the education field. This issue provides an effective link between the complex grand theory of Habermas and the day-to-day concerns of professionals across the sector. While the nature of professionalism is of course a topic of much debate, one of the key elements of professional life, at least in the education sector, is the relationship between the professional and the non-professional. Unlike much of the literature on professionalism, however, which tends to focus more on interprofessional relations or relations between professionals and institutions/ government, the Habermas-inspired work focuses on the key relations between educator and student. In the field of education, concern has been raised over the encroachment of accountability demands into this relationship. Aper (2002: 13) in a critique of accountability in US schools, utilizes Habermas' framework to explain that, while student achievement is a rational goal of schools, 'when intense emphasis is placed on limited measures of this objective at the expense of the intersubjective lifeworlds of schools, serious distortion of the system and lifeworld occur' (ibid.).

This theme is developed by Lee in a case study of standardized testing and literacy education (Lee 2014). Here, the colonization thesis is used to identify the damaging effects of instrumental rationality on both the capacity of teachers to teach and the ability of students to learn skills such as critical thinking. Using the example of DIBELS (Dynamic Indicators of Basic Early Literacy Skills), Lee (2014: 91–92) argues that this form of education governance has pathological effects on both sides of the relationship:

> DIBELS decouples itself from the lifeworld domain and becomes a systemic force that comes back to encroach on or colonize the lifeworld by replacing communicative rationality with instrumental rationality . . . It facilitates and dictates how reading should be taught [and learnt].

Such a view arguably reflects those of a significant proportion of education professionals, and their attitudes towards the dysfunctionality of hyper-instrumentalist logic applied to education, particularly via testing (West 2010).

Critical reflections on colonization and bureaucratization

My own work (e.g. Murphy and Skillen 2013) suggests that caution should be exercised when applying the abstract theory of colonization to specific workplace contexts and specific education policy reforms. Not all pathologies in education governance can be explained away by recourse to specific theories designed to explain other contexts and situations. It also should be noted that Habermas' focus on the welfare state compromise and the crisis of legitimation paved the way for a critique of capitalist modernization, not necessarily a critique of education governance.

This is a significant point, as it identifies something of a blind spot in Habermas' conceptual apparatus. A more sustained analysis of education governance would entail an examination of bureaucracy as mediated by education *professionals* – by those who engage with the public and deliver education services. This would inevitably require a close look at bureaucratic and regulatory governance at the level of the 'street' – as highlighted by Michael Lipsky (1980) in his famous text *Street-level bureaucracy*. Working at the level of the street, the argument goes, allows professionals such as teachers and academics to 'make policy' through their capacity to exercise judgment and use discretion when dealing with students. No bureaucratic regime can be that all-encompassing where the activities of professionals can be so regulated that their role as policy filters can be overridden.

It is precisely this aspect, the intersubjective dimension, that Lipsky saw as core to the work of street-level bureaucrats. According to him, the 'essence of street level bureaucracy is that they require people to make decisions about other people' (Lipsky 1980: 161). Lipsky's original notion was designed to acknowledge and identify such a function for professionals, as a way of understanding how they are active players themselves in the process of forming policy (Hupe and Hill 2007: 280). Understanding bureaucracy at the level of the 'street' offers a powerful rejoinder to systems-level approaches to government regulation and control. It also offers an intellectual space from which to explore how educators manipulate official policy in the context of their relationships with students – an aspect ignored by Habermas. While Lipsky was clearly aware that street-level bureaucrats operated within the context of significant external constraints, not least the tendency of demand to increase to meet the supply of public services, their position at the level of the street secured them a position of influence.

The introduction of the street-level into the analytical framework surrounding education governance also has the added value of highlighting the highly regulated nature of professional life in educational institutions such as schools, colleges and universities, and the existence of other regulatory mechanisms that act in tandem alongside the overbearing state-economy apparatus. One of these highlighted in the literature is the role of law. The author's own work examined the prevalence of legal forms of accountability in the education sector (Murphy and Skillen 2016). Recent years have seen the spread of an American-style litigation culture in the United Kingdom, with members of the public increasingly seeking recourse to the law to appeal or complain, or to achieve compensation (Allsop and Jones 2008). The increasing tendency of people to resort to litigation suggests that recourse to the law is seen as a more immediate form of taking education services to account. Numerous aspects of work in the education sector work have been affected by the spread of a litigation culture, with the sector seeing steady rises in the number of lawsuits (Furedi and Bristow 2012). The evidence suggests that the mechanisms of quality assurance, through the need to document and measure quality, can also act as the mechanisms of legal exposure, providing evidence for both forms of regulation.

The findings of the study by Murphy and Skillen (2016) evidence the conflicting effects of evidential exposure. The evidential requirements of accountability constitute a double-edged sword: evidence providing a platform for calling individuals and educational institutions to account, while also opening up teachers to liability exposure. The evidential nature of accountability mechanisms is fertile ground for exposure to legal risk in schools, colleges and universities (Power 1997). What the bureaucracy of quality assurance contributes to professional life is a magnification of this legal risk, evidential exposure prone to highlighting incompetence and the dangers of unchecked professional discretion and judgment. A culture of mistrust and suspicion, alongside strategies of containment and professional obfuscation attached themselves to this form of bureaucracy early on, a set of values that have never quite been shaken off. Magnified legal risk inevitably helps to strengthen this culture, a culture in which 'watching your back' and 'covering your tracks' are paramount, and where emotions such as fear and doubt are never far from the surface.

Both of these concerns identified in the literature – around professional discretion and the multiple sources of regulation – point to the importance of bringing the professional level into the analytical framework. They also point to significant weaknesses in Habermas' conceptual apparatus and the incapacity of the colonization thesis to incorporate education professionals into the theory of system-level steering. This suggests that the dual methodological approach favoured by Habermas works only in certain circumstances – and needs tweaking in order to deliver a more accurate representation of education governance. After all, the scrutiny and the debate that has evolved around accountability is to a great extent a product of boundary disputes – who gets to make professional decisions, where does judgment and discretion lie and to what extent should it be deployed in education settings? Regulatory oversight asks questions of education autonomy but must also grapple with the consequences of this oversight as well as the myriad ways in which policy can be manipulated at the level of the street.

This angle – the role of mediated governance via professional discretion – is an important qualifier of Habermas' core approach. But a more general question for his approach relates to the relevance of his central thesis in the twenty-first century: Is it still fit for purpose in the current era of neoliberal globalization? It could be argued that austerity has ushered in an era in which the theory of the overreaching state no longer applies. The 'mid-century compromise' – that is, the welfare state and the gains won by unions – has been eroded to a great extent, resulting in a state that does not necessarily have the authority or the power to overreach itself anymore. So instead of a crisis of legitimation, what is potentially occurring in neo-liberal societies is a 'crisis of responsibility' (Della Porta 2015: 119). Today's legitimacy crisis is not necessarily the result of market regulation in support of labour, but could instead be viewed as the result of market deregulation and its restrictive effects on civic, political and social rights. The social movements that have sprung up since the financial crisis are arguably a response to what Della Porta calls the 'abdication of responsibility' on the part of the state in the face of privatization, liberalization and deregulation – with political competency stripped away from the state, leaving only mistrust and suspicion to fuel the anger that drives these social movements. Although this is quite an abstract thesis and needs further examination in applied settings, it is important to reconsider theories such as Habermas' in historical contexts which appear to be undergoing rapid transformation once again.

Conclusion

This chapter aimed to assess the relevance of the colonization thesis for education governance, specifically in relation to accountability-driven reform agendas. It sought to explore the efficacy of a Habermasian critical sociology of bureaucracy, one which aims to take a highly normative analytical position and apply to a dual-perspectivist methodology. The chapter also explores the ways in which the colonization thesis could benefit from a more street-level approach to bureaucratic governance.

The thrust of this chapter should, I hope, suggest to the reader that the social theory of Habermas, while immensely useful to understandings of education governance, is as open to critique as any other theoretical approach. Those who wish to incorporate his work should feel able to adopt a critical stance to his ideas, and not be wary of questioning his positions and to incorporate other thinkers into their own data analysis. Such a stance offers a timely reminder to the reader that theories are there to be applied and not set in stone (Murphy 2017: 13). Contrary to what theory purists might think, hybridization – combining elements of different theories to form another – is a crucial tool for theory building in the field of education governance. Habermas is himself undeniably a master of hybridization, an intellectual strength which is no more evident than in the two volumes of *The Theory of Communicative Action*. Here he expertly weaved together a complex theory via measured critiques of Durkheim, Weber, Marx and Mead, among others. Extolling the virtues of hybridization is an important activity when it comes to the theory–method relationship, as too often education researchers approach theories such as those developed by Habermas as if they were immune to modification. This is a mistake, as the best applied work is not afraid to question the theory it is applying, opening it to critique while combining it with other socio-theoretical concepts. This kind of intellectual creativity is at the core of social theory – without such hybridity it would be difficult to see how modern theoretical developments could occur. This is certainly the case when it comes to further developing our current understandings of education governance in a highly complex and constantly evolving political landscape.

References

Adorno, T., and Horkheimer, M. 1944/1973. *Dialectic of Enlightenment*. New York: Verso Press.

Allsop, J., and Jones, K. 2008. 'Withering the citizen, managing the consumer: Complaints in healthcare settings'. *Social Policy and Society* 7 (2): 233–243.

Aper, J. 2002. 'Steerage from a distance: Can mandated accountability systems really improve schools?', *Journal of Educational Thought* 36 (1): 7–26.

Bouchard, N., and Morris, R. 2012. 'Ethics education seen through the lens of Habermas's conception of practical reason: The Québec education program'. *Journal of Moral Education* 41 (2): 171–187.

Caspersz, D., and Olaru, D. 2014. 'Developing "emancipatory interest": Learning to create social change'. *Higher Education Research & Development* 33 (2): 226–241.

Deakin Crick, R., and Joldersma, C. W. 2007. 'Habermas, lifelong learning and citizenship education'. *Studies in Philosophy and Education* 26: 77–95.

Della Porta, D. 2015. *Social Movements in Times of Austerity: Bringing Capitalism Back Into Protest Analysis*. Cambridge: Polity Press.

Furedi, F., and Bristow, J. 2012. *The Social Cost of Litigation*. London: Centre for Policy Studies.

Habermas, J. 1974. *Theory and Practice* (trans J. Viertel). London: Heinemann.

Habermas, J. 1976. *Legitimation Crisis*. Oxford: Blackwell Press.

Habermas, J. 1984. *The Theory of Communicative Action, vol 1: Reason and the Rationalization of Society*. Boston: Beacon Press.

Habermas, J. 1987. *The Theory of Communicative Action, volume 2: Lifeworld and System: A Critique of Functionalist Reason*. Boston: Beacon Press

Habermas, J. 1988. *On the Logic of the Social Sciences* (trans. S. Weber Nicholson and J. Stark). Cambridge: Polity Press.

Hupe, P., and Hill,M. 2007. 'Street level bureaucracy and public accountability'. *Public Administration* 85 (2): 279–299.

Huttunen, R., and Murphy, M. 2012. 'Discourse and recognition as normative grounds for radical pedagogy: Habermasian and Honnethian ethics in the context of education'. *Studies in Philosophy and Education* 31 (2): 137–152.

Jones, R. 2000. *The World Turned Upside Down? Globalisation and the Future of the State*. Manchester: Manchester University Press.

Kickert, W. 1995. 'Steering at a distance: A new paradigm of public governance in Dutch higher education'. *Governance: An International Journal of Policy and Administration* 8 (1): 135–157.

Lee, C. G. 2014. 'Systemic colonization of the educational lifeworld: An example in literacy education'. *Educational Philosophy and Theory* 46 (1): 87–99.

Liff, R. 2014. 'Unintended consequences of NPM drive the "bureaucracy"'. *International Journal of Public Administration* 37 (8): 474–483.

Lipsky, M. 1980. *Street-level Bureaucracy: Dilemmas of the Individual in Public Services*. New York: Russell Sage Foundation.

Lockwood, D. 1964. 'Social integration and system integration'. In G. Zollschen and W. Hirsh (eds), *Explorations in Social Change*, pp. 244–256. Boston: Houghton Mifflin.

Marginson, S. 1997. 'Steering from a distance: Power relations in Australian higher education'. *Higher Education* 34: 63–80.

Marx, K. 1959. *Economic and Philosophic Manuscripts of 1844*. Moscow: Progress Publishers.

Meier, K., and O'Toole, L. 2006. *Bureaucracy in a Modern State: A Governance Perspective*. Baltimore: John Hopkins University Press.

Mendez, C., and Bachtler, J. 2011. 'Administrative reform and unintended consequences: An assessment of the EU cohesion policy "audit explosion"'. *Journal of European Public Policy* 18 (5): 746–765.

Monfardini, P. 2010. 'Accountability in the new public sector: A comparative case study'. *International Journal of Public Sector Management* 23 (7): 632–646.

Murphy, M. 2010. 'Forms of rationality and public sector reform: Habermas, education and social policy'. In M. Murphy and T. Fleming (eds), *Habermas, Critical Theory and Education*, pp. 78–93. New York: Routledge.

Murphy, M. (ed.). 2013. *Social Theory and Educational Research: Understanding Foucault, Bourdieu, Habermas and Derrida*. London: Routledge.

Murphy, M. (ed.). 2017. *Habermas and Social Research: Between Theory and Method*. Oxon: Routledge.

Murphy, M., and Skillen, P. 2013. 'The politics of school regulation: Using Habermas to research educational accountability'. In M. Murphy (ed.), *Social Theory and Educational Research: Understanding Foucault, Bourdieu, Habermas and Derrida*, pp. 84–97. London: Routledge.

Murphy, M., and Skillen, P. 2015. 'The politics of time on the front line: Street level bureaucracy, professional judgement and public accountability'. *International Journal of Public Administration* 38 (9): 632–641.

Murphy, M., and Skillen, P. 2016. 'Exposure to the law: Accountability and its impact on street level bureaucracy'. *Social Policy and Society* (published online). Available at: https://www.cambridge.org/core/journals/social-policy-and-society/article/exposure-to-the-law-accountability-and-its-impact-on-streetlevel-bureaucracy/C7CAD84020C5D9A0D3B60A20827865B2.

Oakes, H., and Berry, A. 2009. 'Accounting colonization: Three case studies in further education'. *Critical Perspectives on Accounting* 20: 343–378.

Offe, C. 1984. *Contradictions of the Welfare State*. London: Hutchinson.

Papadopoulos, Y. 2010. 'Accountability and multi-level governance: More accountability, less democracy?' *West European Politics* 33 (5): 1030–1049.

Parsons, T. 1937. *The Structure of Social Action*. Glencoe, IL: The Free Press.

Power, M. 1997. *Audit Cultures: Rituals of Verification*. Oxford: Oxford University Press.

Rhodes, R. 1996. 'The new governance: Governing without government'. *Political Studies* 44 (4): 652–667.

Rose, N. 1999. *Powers of Freedom: Reframing Political Thought*. Cambridge: Cambridge University Press.

Schwier, R. 2012. 'The corrosive influence of competition, growth, and accountability on institutions of higher education'. *Journal of Computing in Higher Education* 24: 96–103.

Shore, C. 2008. 'Audit culture and illiberal governance: Universities and the politics of accountability'. *Anthropological Theory* 8 (3): 278–298.

Travers, M. 2007. *The New Bureaucracy: Quality Assurance and Its Critics*. Bristol, UK: Policy Press.

Weber, M. 1958. 'Religious rejections of the world and their directions'. In H. Gerth and C. W. Mills (eds), *From Max Weber*, pp. 323–359. London: Kegan Paul.

West, A. 2010. 'High stakes testing, accountability, incentives and consequences in English schools'. *Policy and Politics* 38 (1): 23–39.

Transformation and Control: What Role for Leadership and Management in a 'School-Led' System?

Howard Stevenson

Introduction

Education policy in the English state school sector has seen substantial and often rapid reforms over a period of at least three decades. The broad pattern of these reforms is not unique to England although the English system has often played a vanguard role in implementing policies which have been reproduced in different forms in many different contexts.

I locate these reforms, in terms of their form and the intentions established for them, as a deliberate attempt to push back against the welfarist education policies of the post-war period in which a fully comprehensive school system, provided through democratic local government institutions, was beginning to emerge (Ranson 2012). As indicated, education was one part of the wider struggle about the role and future of the welfare state. However, because of the unique role education plays in reproducing labour power and its key ideological function, it can be considered as at the centre of this struggle. The purpose of this pushback against post-war welfarism has been to reconfigure English state education along market-driven lines, opening up public education to large-scale privatization and reframing service users as individual consumers.

This contestation of the purposes and form of English state education has often played out as a struggle between the central state and professional interests such as teacher unions and local government (the latter being the traditional providers of education in the English state system). This has become a struggle focused on an apparently simple question – who governs education? In this chapter I argue that a key element of the state's response to that question has been to mobilize new actors in a transformed governance system that simultaneously combines centralizing and decentralizing tendencies and a complex mix of public and private sector agents. One of the key features of this new settlement has been a hugely transformed role for school leaders who have been mobilized as a key driver of institutional and system change. My aim in this chapter is to set out how the role of school leaders has changed over an extended period of system reform and how headteachers have become central to the governance of the new, increasingly marketized school system. However, this is not about school leaders becoming transformational leaders in a 'school-led system', but rather becoming managerial functionaries in a system designed to deliver control and compliance.

In order to address these issues, I will draw on a theoretical tradition broadly rooted in critical labour and management studies and which sees work, and the way in which work is managed and controlled, as central to understanding organizations. Labour process theory underpins much of this approach (Braverman 1974), with its emphasis on work as an exploitative activity in which relations between employer and employee are intrinsically antagonistic. Although this tradition has a base in the broad sociology of work it also had a specific focus on teaching and the application of labour process theory to teachers' work (Connell 1985; Ozga and Lawn 1981). The value of such an approach is its ability to illuminate new forms of control in teaching (Reid 2003) and specifically the changing role of school leaders in a transformed school system.

This chapter provides an analysis of English school sector education policy over an extended period of time (broadly from the mid-1970s to the present time) and views the changed role of the school leader as both a consequence and a driver of the restructuring of state education along neo-liberal lines.

Who governs? The collapse of consensus

In February 1974, the Conservative Prime Minister at the time called a General Election following extended industrial action by mineworkers and the election was subsequently framed by the government around a single question – 'who governs – politicians or the unions?' The government lost the election. However, although defeated, the questions raised by the election remained. The miners' industrial action highlighted the growing tensions between labour, capital and the state as escalating economic crisis began to unravel the post-war settlement that had existed between the three parties to that settlement and which had provided the basis for the welfarist consensus.

The question of 'who governs?' translated directly into the educational context when a conflict at the William Tyndale primary school in North London became a national media story (Davis 2002). The dispute emerged between teachers at the school and their employer, the Inner London Education Authority, and focused on the curriculum in the school and the pedagogical approaches adopted by the teachers (Ellis et al. 1976). More fundamentally it opened up the question of control in the education system more widely and who should be able to determine what is taught and how it is taught (Lowe 2007).

The question of 'who governs' raised by events at William Tyndale were then further highlighted when the Labour government launched a *'Great Debate'* (Callaghan 1976) focused on the purposes of education but inevitably raising wider questions of accountability and control. The principal problem was identified as a system that was not aligned with the wider needs of society (framed largely in terms of the needs of the labour market) (Finn 1987), while the cause was identified as a teaching profession that was out of touch and that lacked accountability. The curriculum was presented as a 'secret garden' (Lawton 1982) from which parents, for example, were largely excluded.

Labour's precarious grip on political power at that time, combined with growing economic crisis, ensured that the so-called Great Debate is remembered historically more for the questions it raised, than the answers it provided, let alone the policies it generated. In this chapter I argue that the questions raised by the Great Debate, and which have continued to lie at the heart of the struggles over the future of education policy in England, as elsewhere, are in essence questions of education governance. I see these questions of governance as fundamentally questions of management and control in relation to the key features of the learning process – who decides what is taught and how it is taught? Who decides how education institutions are organized and what are the mechanisms and processes through which decisions are made and, crucially, enforced. A focus on governance more widely necessarily requires a focus on the multiple mechanisms through which control within education systems is exercised, and a recognition of the multiple influences that play out in the struggles over what is taught and to whom. However, within such an approach it is essential to recognize the centrality of teachers' work and the need to understand the mechanisms by which that work is managed and controlled. In locating my own approach to working within this tradition, I draw on the work of Goodrich (1920) and his interest in the 'frontier of control' as the point of contestation between managerial authority and worker autonomy. My own interest in governance questions in education is concerned with better understanding the 'frontier of control' between school leaders and classroom teachers and how this frontier shifts over time as the struggles over the purposes of education play out as a struggle over the control of teachers' work.

Thatcherism: the emergence of managerialism

Labour's defeat in the 1979 general election brought with it a Conservative government and the premiership of Margaret Thatcher. 'Thatcherism' (Hall and Jacques 1983) represented an explicit repudiation of post-war welfarism and the end of any claim to consensus across the major political parties. The political ideas that underpinned the New Right had already been incubating for many years, developed by leading thinkers such as Friedrich Hayek (1944) and Milton Friedman (Friedman and Friedman 1980), but nurtured in a myriad of think tanks, such as the Adam Smith Institute (Pirie 2012), the Institute for Economic Affairs and the Centre for Policy Studies, in which academics and leading Conservative politicians exchanged ideas and analysis. Education featured prominently as a focus for this new thinking, most obviously in the Black Papers (see Cox and Boyson 1975). Much of this analysis focused on the concept of 'producer capture' – the notion that state enterprises default to bureaucratization and monopolization and that those who work in them act in their own self-interest rather than in the interests of users (Demaine 1993). The 'political' nature of public systems privileged those able to mobilize collective strength within political processes (through organized lobbying, industrial action, etc.) and the response was to seek to dismantle this power by subjecting public sector workers to market forces (Friedman and Friedman 1980).

This objective was to be advanced most dramatically by the passage of the 1988 Education Reform Act which in a single piece of legislation threw the post-war welfarist settlement in education into reverse and set state education in England on an entirely different trajectory (Stevenson 2011). This legislation represented a significant challenge to local government as the basis of democratic community control of schools and signalled the emergence of quasi-market mechanisms as the principal form of school accountability (Ranson 2008). The 1988 Act had many interdependent features relating to both curriculum and governance issues which, when taken together, created a quasi-market underpinned by increased consumer information and choice. One key feature of this new quasi-market was the introduction of a form of site-based management in which key local authority responsibilities were devolved to school level, reinforced by a pupil-driven funding formula that linked school funding directly to pupil numbers.

These explicitly political efforts to fragment the school system were supported by a range of academic writers who advocated the decentralization of education systems and the introduction of site-based management. In the United States, such calls were led by committed market fundamentalists such as Chubb and Moe (1990), while elsewhere similar demands were framed in less explicitly ideological language, often drawing on an emerging discourse of school effectiveness and improvement. Perhaps the most influential contributors were the Australian academics Caldwell and Spinks whose book *Leading the Self-Managing School* (1992) provided academic cover for the shift to system fragmentation advocated by the New Right.

These policy changes inevitably brought about a shift in power within the school system even if some of the changes were more apparent than real (Stevenson 2013). The explicitly stated intention of the 1988 Act was to shift power to parents, increasingly recast as 'consumers', where parent power was to be exercised in two forms – as customers exercising choice in a market and as members of school governing bodies, now with significantly increased responsibility.

Arguably the most appreciable shift in power however was to the headteacher whose role reflected the significant increases in responsibility at the school level. At the same time, and significantly, the term 'educational leadership' becomes increasingly common in both academic literature and education policy papers. In the opening chapter to their edited collection *The Principles and Practice of Education Management*, Bush and Bell (2002) make a case for using the term 'management' in the title, as the overarching term that includes both leadership *and* management; however, they acknowledge that the concept of 'leadership' was increasingly being privileged. This shift in language was significant because it emphasized the increased responsibilities being placed on headteachers in particular. 'Management' was often presented as maintenance of the *status quo*, in contrast to leadership with its emphasis on change. Such analysis fitted well with a narrative that presented state education as 'broken' and in need of radical restructuring (Wallace 1993).

Much of the material presented in academic programmes at this time reinforced the notion of the school leader as the new educational entrepreneur steering the school in a complex market environment (signalled by the branding of many postgraduate educational management programmes as MBAs or Master of Business Administration). Course texts often focused on the headteachers' role in managing human resources (Bush and Middlewood 1997), school budgets (Coleman and Anderson 2000) and relations with 'stakeholders'. Many texts explicitly sought to draw on business principles such as Total Quality Management and apply these to educational contexts (Murgatroyd 1993). Developments such as Grant Maintained Schools (GMS, schools removed from local authority control) were largely viewed as exciting manifestations of Caldwell and Spinks' (1992) 'self-managing school' with little critical attention devoted to the shift from a public service model underpinned by some notion of democratic participation (through local government elections) to a market-driven model based on notions of consumer 'choice' (Davies and Anderson 1992).

In a similar way schools were presented as relatively straightforward organizations in which the interests of all could be easily reconciled. The role of leaders was to articulate a 'vision' and to mobilize 'stakeholders' in support of that vision. Discussion over educational 'ends' was often rendered invisible as educational objectives were considered unproblematic. School leadership and management was firmly located within a unitarist paradigm in which the interests of all were aligned. Conflict was considered aberrant.

This approach contrasted sharply with those who presented education institutions as much more complex organizations in which tensions over educational ends was considered inevitable and conflict in some form was the norm – an argument presented by Ball (1987: 19):

> I take schools, in common with virtually all other social organizations, to be *arenas of struggle*; to be riven with actual or potential conflict between members; to be poorly co-ordinated; to be ideologically diverse. I take it to be essential that if we are to understand the nature of schools as organizations, we must achieve some understanding of these conflicts.

One manifestation of the airbrushing of conflict out of mainstream educational leadership and management literature was the almost total absence of any serious discussion of union organization within schools, despite teachers being one of the most highly unionized occupational groups and with long-established industrial relations structures based on collective bargaining. At this point it is possible to see how an explicitly political agenda to weaken teachers' collective organization (through mechanisms such as site-based management) is in turn reinforced by an academic literature that reframes the employer–employee relationship, with all its inherent conflicts, as a matter of human resource management in which tensions are internalized and individualized. This invisibilizing of teachers' collective organization out of the education management literature when it was so obviously part of the daily life of school organization cannot be seen as simple error of omission. Rather it reflects the recasting of the headteachers' role as the unchallenged school leader, with power concentrated in the hands of 'management' rather than with classroom teachers. Schools are not to be seen as complex organizations in which a plurality of 'visions' and interests co-exist, sometimes comfortably, but oftentimes not. Rather schools are framed as relatively simple, unitary, organizations in which goals are self-evident and uncontested. Those who challenge, and who generate conflict as a result, do not belong.

New Labour: leadership transformed

In 1997, the Conservative government that had introduced the 1988 Education Reform Act was defeated decisively, and for a moment it looked as though the education policy narrative was about to shift. Prior to the election it was becoming clear that the new education market that had been introduced through the 1988 Act was facing considerable difficulties. This was most clearly illustrated by the case of The Ridings School in Halifax (Murch 1997). The Ridings School was a struggling school in a working-class community that was suffering badly in the new education market. As a GMS there was no local authority able to intervene and break the vicious circle of falling rolls and shrinking budgets. The school was on the brink of collapse with no prospect of support.

The election of a Labour government in 1997 opened up the possibility of change, and one of the first steps it took was to bring GSM back into local authority control. However, while the discourse shifted, and there were some high-profile policy changes, the under-pinning analysis of state education, and its problems, remained remarkably consistent. New Labour's analysis continued the narrative that state education was 'broken' and in need of 'fixing'. It also maintained the view that 'producer interests', namely local authorities and teachers (or more specifically, teachers' unions) were at best incapable of bringing about the necessary changes. In some analyses these groups were presented as actively resisting government reforms (DfEE 1988). The challenge for New Labour therefore was to 'drive' radical and substantial change, while finding ways to circumvent the established power blocs of local government and teacher union organization (Barber 2007).

New Labour's strategy was to retain the architecture of the 1988 Act (a quasi-market based on standardized tests, league tables, parent choice policies and funding systems linked closely to student enrolments) but to reinforce this through a centralized system of target-setting and benchmarking (Ball 2017). This in turn was strengthened through an increasingly powerful national inspectorate whose judgments became correspondingly more influential. The so-called naming and shaming of poorly performing schools also emerged at this time as a key feature of government policy.

However, there was also a recognition of the limits of policy mechanisms focused narrowly on punitive measures, and that if change was to be secured then consent within the system needed to be cultivated more assiduously. In particular, school leaders, increasingly seen as key to the success of system change, needed to take on a more supportive role within the system. In the period since 1988 many headteachers had been reluctant to embrace the thrust of post-1988 Act policy and some had been at the forefront of opposition (on issues such as curriculum reform, testing and opted-out schools) (Stevenson 2000).

The 'reculturing' of school leadership was to be secured principally through the establishment of the National College of School Leadership (NCSL), set up in 2000 as the provider of professional development for school leaders. At the centre of this provision was the National Professional Qualification for Headteachers (NPQH), a qualification aimed directly at headteachers and aspiring headteachers. Initially it was non-mandatory but in 2004 it became a requirement for all new headteachers to hold NPQH (this requirement remained until 2012 when the Coalition government merged the NCSL into a new National College of Teaching and Leadership and made the NPQH non-mandatory). By 2004 NPQH was part of a 'suite' of leadership qualifications aimed at 'middle' and 'senior' leaders as well as headteachers.

Significantly, when the Labour government identified the need for leadership training for headteachers it specifically chose to establish a new 'College' rather than, for example, look to the large number of existing postgraduate programmes offered through universities. One possible explanation for this was that the creation of a specific institution, located in a prestigious building on the Jubilee Campus at the University of Nottingham (but, significantly, not part of the University) itself signalled the new emphasis on 'leadership'. Not only were leaders 'important' in terms of their status within the developing decentralized school system but they were 'separate' too. The new national college therefore simultaneously signalled the importance of leadership and the separation of leaders and the leadership function from the practice of teaching. Moreover, by establishing a separate college the government of the time was also deliberately rejecting the notion of universities and their education departments having any appreciable input into the training of new school leaders (a move that anticipated the later downgrading of universities' role in training future teachers – see Mutton et al. 2017).

What was soon apparent was that the NCSL had a key role in re-engineering school leadership in the English school system. As has been indicated, universities were largely excluded from the process of formal leadership professional development, while *within* NCSL programmes such as NPQH the content of learning materials was heavily filtered in ways that favoured mainstream school improvement literature and made invisible the work of more critical scholars (for a detailed study of the ways in which NCSL programmes sought to reinforce particular notions of school improvement, while rendering alternative perspectives invisible, see Thrupp and Wilmott's 2003 analysis).

One example of the National College's dependence on mainstream school improvement literature was its promotion of 'transformational leadership' (Leithwood and Jantzi 1990; 2005) as a form of leadership orthodoxy within its programmes and especially NPQH. Transformational leadership had emerged as central to the new educational leadership movement in universities and fitted well with New Labour's narrative of a broken state education system in need of radical reform. Transformational leadership emphasized the role of vision and values in educational leadership and the role of leaders in mobilizing teachers and others in schools in support of that vision. Transformational leadership was counterposed to transactional leadership with the former emphasizing action, commitment and dynamism, while the latter was associated with leadership as an exchange process in which employee commitment was secured through a transactional relationship with the workforce. The former was about 'buying in' while the latter was presented as 'buying off'.

The reinforcement of these ideas within the NPQH programme was pivotal to securing the culture shift among headteachers that New Labour saw as critical. Transformational leadership emphasized change and agency with everything becoming possible when the 'right' leadership was in place. Often framed in a language of 'moral purpose' the view of leadership presented in the NPQH programmes was entirely aligned with the arguments for system fragmentation presented by Caldwell and Spinks (1992) and Chubb and Moe (1990). In this 'no excuses' culture schools that were unable to compensate for the wider structural inequalities in society clearly had weak leadership. Such a judgment would be confirmed officially through the power of the inspectorate and the identification of the school as failing. In such cases headteachers were increasingly removed from their position.

New Labour: old scientific management

During this period, the language of transformation and values-driven change was the clear message to aspiring school leaders (see Fullan n.d.). I want to argue, however, that this was the period when a very different reality emerged. Although official discourse emphasized school autonomy and the importance of agentic leadership, school leaders found themselves functioning in an increasingly centralized system. Not only was the quasi-market introduced in 1988 retained but control mechanisms were strengthened by new policy technologies in which national targets for school performance were cascaded through the school system – at local authority, individual school and individual teacher level. All of this was to be buttressed by the national inspectorate that was taking on increased powers and whose judgments were becoming increasingly high stakes for schools and which in turn was fed by the industrial production of performance data in order to make judgments about 'effectiveness'.

This had little to do with transformational leadership, as the introduction of national strategies with centrally promoted pedagogical strategies and buttressed by national targets meant headteachers had only limited opportunities to set the direction for their school. Rather what emerged was a modern form of scientific management in which headteachers had restricted autonomy, but were expected to assume increased control over the labour process of teachers (Carter et al. 2010).

The case for English school leadership as a twenty-first-century form of scientific management, more than a century after Taylor (1911) presented his arguments, requires a brief restatement of Taylor's original arguments. Central to his thesis was that any work task could be reduced to a set of mathematical rules and formulae, as the scientific basis for designing the work in such a way as to maximize efficiency (defined as the relationship between the value of inputs and the value of outputs). Taylor's argument was that every task was reducible to the 'one best way' and that it was the task of management to identify the one best way and then to scientifically match the ideal employee to the necessary technology, and the scientifically designed workflow in order to manage production. The final element of this analysis was that workers needed to be incentivized to perform appropriately and therefore a system of payment by results was essential. This in turn required employers to be able to quantify the output/contribution of individual workers in order to be able to link pay and performance.

There is a temptation to see Taylor's ideas as a quirky feature of a rapidly industrializing age and with little contemporary relevance, especially outside of traditional manufacturing processes. Such a response fails to appreciate the wider politics of scientific management and in turn its continued relevance. Scientific management was above all a strategy for management to take control of the labour process and to wrest that control from workers (individually and collectively) (Braverman 1974). Taylor's argument was that as long as workers enjoyed autonomy in the exercise of their craft skills management were unable to sufficiently control their labour. However, by transforming complex labour processes into numerical formulae the control of the labour process passes from the worker to the manager. Designing work in this way has the added advantage of allowing 'low-skill' elements of work to be identified and reallocated to less qualified, and cheaper, labour. Such a division of labour not only drives down labour costs but further reinforces managerial control as workers lose labour market power in a fragmented labour process in which labour substitution is made easier. Scientific management, in its traditional Taylorian form, can therefore be seen as a key strategy for shifting the frontier of control in a favour of management.

Many of the processes described above, fundamental to scientific management, became increasingly visible in the English school system during the period of the New Labour government. As has been indicated, the national literacy and numeracy strategies were introduced and presaged an unprecedented degree of centralization in teaching methods, certainly by the standards of English state education. In some form, it is possible to see these developments as the emergence of a 'one best way' approach to teaching even if the actual experience fell some way short of the type of scripted curricula that might be said to reflect classic Taylorism (Horn 2014). More significant at this time was arguably the growing 'datafication' of teaching whereby increasing aspects of the educational process were transformed into a numerical score for the purpose of ranking, comparison and reward or sanction (Ball 2003; 2015). For teachers, this was experienced as relentless target-setting reinforced by the newly introduced system of performance-related pay. National pay systems had been under attack in the English school system since at least 1987 during which time increasing discretion for pay issues had been devolved to school level. Although there was considerable debate as to whether performance related pay could be linked to crude student performance scores in standardized tests, it was clear from an early stage that this was a common practice in many schools. The final element in this latter-day version of Taylorism was the introduction of a National Workload Agreement (agreed with most teachers' unions) that allowed for the use of Teaching Assistants to undertake a number of roles that had previously only been undertaken by qualified teachers, such as covering the classes of absent teachers. This was intended to reduce the amount of time qualified teachers spent performing 'cover duties', but it also opened the door to the use of Teaching Assistants to undertake a range of roles previously only performed by qualified teachers.

It was during the period that the contradictions in the experiences of educational leaders emerged most starkly. The discourse of transformational leadership continued to resonate with the rhetoric of school autonomy and the self-managing school. Headteachers were encouraged to believe in their own agency and capacity to bring about change. At the same time however, centralized targets, policed by an increasingly powerful inspectorate, served to exclude any meaningful agency in relation to educational ends. Rather school leaders' 'freedoms' were confined to managerial functions intended to assert increased control over the education system in general and individual teachers within it. In this sense school leaders emerged as a key element in new governance structures, playing a key role in ensuring teachers taught appropriate content using approved methodologies. As such they might be considered at the front line of the frontier of control, playing a key role in managing the work of teachers but lacking any meaningful agency over their own work.

Transformational leadership and system transformation: the privatization of English state education

The New Labour government was defeated in 2010 and replaced by a Coalition government dominated by the right-wing Conservative Party, with centre party support. There can be no question that the shift in government education policy that this presaged was substantial (DfE 2010). Since the 2010 election it is difficult to identify a single aspect of school sector education policy that has not experienced substantial reform – curriculum, assessment, school organization and governance have all been affected. However, once again the continuities are at least as striking as the disruptions, in particular those that can trace a lineage back to 1988.

Given the focus of this chapter, the issue of most interest in the period since 2010 has been the commitment to make all English state schools academies (schools within the state system but outside of local authority control). This first emerged after the 2010 election when the new government made clear that academies were no longer to be 'special cases' – schools in areas of deprivation with a long history of poor performance, but that all schools were to be encouraged to become academies. High-performing schools could choose such a route, while so-called failing schools were to be required to become an academy (sometimes 'forced') under the oversight of a sponsor (either another school or a Multi-Academy Trust, MAT). Since 2010 the Conservative Party has won two elections (in 2015 and 2017) but struggled to deliver an initial commitment to make all schools academies.

As with many key policy developments since 1988, the approach of governments since 2010 can only be understood as a complex mix of simultaneous centralizing and decentralizing tendencies. The drive towards academization can be seen as a further move towards school autonomy and the expansion of the self-managing school more widely across the system. However, this must be seen in the context of the pressures on school leaders identified above, combined with additional curriculum and assessment reform that has further undermined the scope for school-level decision-making.

Moreover, all these developments must be located within the move towards what is now referred to as a 'school-led system' in which schools are increasingly 'networked' with other schools in order to capitalize on economies of scale and develop cross-institution support. Much of the support for this approach draws on the work of David H. Hargreaves who authored a series of four 'think pieces' for the NCSL in which he set out his ideas for a 'self-improving school system' (2010, 2011, 2012a, 2012b). In essence Hargreaves (2010: 5) argued that school improvement should come from *within* the school system:

> At its core, the notion of a SISS [self-improving school system] assumes that much (not all) of the responsibility for school improvement is moved from both central and local government and their agencies to the schools.

For this to be able to work effectively Hargreaves argued a number of conditions needed to be developed. First, schools needed to find ways to work together; secondly, they needed to develop their own solutions to their own specific problems and to work together to operationalize these solutions; and finally, it was necessary for school leaders to work across schools (in other words, to develop 'system leaders'). A number of features of this approach are now clearly visible in the English state school system. These include the formation of networks of schools (such as Teaching School Alliances, TSA), the creation of leaders working across schools (National Leaders of Education, NLE) and the increased emphasis on school-based teacher training and leadership development.

What is significant about the Hargreaves analysis is the acknowledgement that a school system based on independent self-managing schools, without any mechanisms of support, was unlikely to bring about system improvement. Therefore, at the same time the government of the day was trying to drive all schools towards Academy status, it was simultaneously seeking to drive all academies into groups of schools – MATs.

At the time of writing it is not clear what the balance of academies and local authority maintained schools is likely to be in the future. What is clear is that stand-alone academies will become increasingly rare as government policy drives such schools into MATs. MATs therefore are likely to become increasingly important in the governance of the English state school system with other bodies, including local authorities, becoming correspondingly peripheral. What is also evident is that new governance structures are emerging in which the traditional school-based powers of governing bodies are being transferred to Trust-level Boards, and individual governing bodies are either abolished or transformed into consultative bodies with little meaningful power.

At present the implications of these policy developments for school leaders are unclear. What seems likely, and is already evident, is that increasing numbers of headteachers working within the context of MATs will find that they have limited scope for school-level decision-making as key decisions will increasingly become Trust-level decisions. At the time of writing, the experience of headteachers appears to vary considerably with some MATs working as loose confederations in which individual schools retain considerable autonomy while others experience a much more centralized model in which headteachers are expected to work within very tight parameters, with their role largely ensuring that MAT-level decisions are implemented at school level (Gibson 2016).

Conclusion

For nearly thirty years the dominant discourse in the English state school system has emphasized school autonomy and the agency of school leaders. Decision-making, it has been claimed, has been devolved to school level and headteachers. Those on the ground and closest to the point where decisions need to be made have apparently been empowered to exercise their judgment.

My argument is that these developments need to be analysed much more critically. Three decades of school reform has seen a systematic effort to marginalize the professional voice of classroom teachers while also seeking to close down spaces for democratic community control of education. Governance in education has been transformed from a tri-partite partnership model involving the central and local state and teacher organizations, with teachers in schools enjoying considerable professional autonomy, to a model that appears more complex in its range of actors and in the balance between central control and local autonomy. The school leader has emerged as a central figure in this new landscape, at one and the same time personifying the new autonomy while simultaneously acting as a key enforcer of the centralizing tendencies in English state education.

Co-opting a key section of the teaching profession, school leaders and securing their support and mobilizing them in pursuit of this reform agenda has been a central strategy of those driving these changes. This has in part been achieved through the twin pressures of the market and the national inspectorate which have combined to create a powerful force driving compliance with centrally determined policy. However, co-option has also relied on the manufacturing of consent and support in more complex ways. Key to this process has been the promotion of a particular approach to leadership, promoted through the NCSL and the training programmes that are its legacy. This approach to school leadership has often emphasized values and moral purpose together with the role of headteachers as transformational leaders.

My argument is that this strategy has been extremely successful in re-engineering state schooling in England along marketized and increasingly privatized lines as school leaders have been central to driving this reform agenda 'from within'. However, this has not been through a process of transformational leadership but rather by transforming leaders into a new cadre of scientific managers focused on maximizing teacher output and controlling almost every aspect of their work. The final irony is that school leaders have now fallen prey to the very same processes of deskilling that they have been imposing on teachers. In current governance structures a small number of school leaders are elevated to the status of Chief Executive Officers with increased numbers reduced to the status of branch managers – acting as managerial functionaries in a hierarchy which affords them little agency.

References

Ball, S. J. 1987. *The Micro-Politics of the School*. London: Routledge.
Ball, S. J. 2003. 'The teachers' soul and the terrors of performativity'. *Journal of Education Policy* 18 (2): 215–228.

Ball, S. J. 2015. 'Education, governance and the tyranny of numbers'. *Journal of Education Policy* 30 (3): 299–301.

Ball, S. J. 2017. *The Education Debate*. Bristol: Policy Press.

Barber, M. 2007. *Instruction to Deliver: Tony Blair, Public Services and the Challenge of Achieving Targets*. London: Methuen Publishing Ltd.

Braverman, H. 1974. *Labor and Monopoly Capital: The Degradation of Work in the Twentieth Century*. New York: Monthly Review Press.

Bush, T., and Bell, L. (eds). 2002. *The Principles and Practice of Educational Management*. London: Sage Publications.

Bush, T., and Middlewood, D. (eds). 1997. *Managing People in Education*. London: Sage Publications.

Caldwell, B., and Spinks, J. M. 1992. *Leading the Self-Managing School*. London: Routledge.

Callaghan, J. 1976. *The Great Debate*. Available at: http://www.educationengland.org.uk/documents/speeches/1976ruskin.html, accessed 10 October 2017.

Carter, B., Stevenson, H., and Passy, R. 2010. *Industrial Relations in Education: Transforming the School Workforce*. London: Routledge.

Chubb, J. E., and Moe, T. M. 1990. *Politics, Markets and America's Schools*. New York: Perseus.

Coleman, M., and Anderson, L. (eds). 2000. *Managing Finance and Resources in Education*. London: Sage Publications.

Connell, R. 1985. *Teachers' Work*. London: HarperCollins.

Cox, C. B., and Boyson, R. 1975. *The Fight for Education*. London: Dent & Sons.

Davies, B., and Anderson, L. 1992. *Opting for Self-Management: The Early Experiences of Grant-Maintained Schools*. London: Routledge.

Davis, J. 2002. 'The inner London education authority and the William Tyndale Junior school affair, 1974–1976'. *Oxford Review of Education* 28 (2–3): 275–298.

Demaine, J. 1993. 'The new right and the self-managing school'. In J. Smyth (ed.), *A Socially Critical View of the Self-Managing School*, pp. 35–48. London: Routledge.

Department for Education (DfE). 2010. *The Importance of Teaching: The Schools White Paper*. London: HMSO.

Department for Education and Employment (DfEE). 1998. *Teachers Meeting the Challenge of Change*. London: HMSO.

Ellis, T., McWhirter, J., McColgan, D., and Haddow, B. 1976. *William Tyndale: The Teachers' Story*. London: Writers' and Readers' Publishing Cooperative.

Finn, D. 1987. *Training Without Jobs: New Deals and Broken Promises*. Basingstoke: Macmillan Education.

Friedman, M., and Freidman, R. 1980. *Free to Choose*. London: Penguin.

Fullan, M. n.d. *Moral Purpose*. Available at: https://www.nationalcollege.org.uk/cm-mc-ssl-resource-moral-purpose.pdf, accessed 10 October 2017.

Gibson, M. 2016. 'Sponsored academy school principals in England: Autonomous leaders or Sponsor Conduits?' *International Studies in Educational Administration* 44 (2): 39–54.

Goodrich, C. 1920. *The Frontier of Control: A Study in British Workshop Politics.* Harcourt, Brace and Howe: New York.

Hall, S., and Jacques, M. (eds). 1983. *The Politics of Thatcherism*, pp. 19–39. London: Lawrence and Wishart.

Hargreaves, D. H. 2010. *Creating a Self-Improving School System.* Nottingham: NCSL.

Hargreaves, D. H. 2011. *Leading a Self-improving School System.* Nottingham: NCSL.

Hargreaves, D. H. 2012a. *A Self-Improving School System in International Context.* Nottingham: NCSL.

Hargreaves, D. H. 2012b. *A Self-Improving School System: Towards Maturity.* Nottingham: NCSL.

Hayek, F. 1944. *The Road to Serfdom.* London: Routledge and Kegan Paul.

Horn, B. 2014. 'Moments or a movement? Teacher resistance to neoliberal education reform'. *FORUM* 56 (2): 277–286.

Lawton, D. 1982. *The End of the Secret Garden? A Study in the Politics of the Curriculum; an Inaugural Lecture, Delivered at the University of London, Inst. of Education, on 15. Nov. 1978.* London: University of London Inst. of Education.

Leithwood, K., and Jantzi, D. 1990. 'Transformational leadership: How principals can help reform school cultures'. *School Effectiveness and School Improvement* 1 (4): 249–280.

Leithwood, K. and Jantzi, D. 2005. *Transformational Leadership. The Essentials of School Leadership.* London: Sage Publications.

Lowe, R. 2007. *The Death of Progressive Education: How Teachers Lost Control of the Classroom.* London: Routledge.

Murch, I. 1997. 'Behind the headlines: Learning lessons from The Ridings'. *Education Today and Tomorrow* 49 (1): 9–10.

Murgatroyd, S. 1993. 'Implementing total quality management in the school: Challenges and opportunity'. *School Organisation* 13 (3): 269–281.

Mutton, T., Burn, K., and Menter, I. 2017. 'Deconstructing the Carter review: Competing conceptions of quality in England's "school-led" system of initial teacher education'. *Journal of Education Policy* 32 (1): 14–33.

Ozga, J., and Lawn, M. 1981. *Teachers, Professionalism and Class: A Study of Organized Teachers.* London: Falmer Press.

Pirie, M. 2012. *Think Tank: The Story of the Adam Smith Institute.* London: Biteback Publishing.

Ranson, S. 2008. 'The changing governance of education'. *Educational Management Administration & Leadership* 36 (2): 201–219.

Ranson, S. 2012. 'Governing education: Remaking the long revolution'. *FORUM* 54 (2): 185–204.

Reid, A. 2003. 'Understanding teachers' work: Is there still a place for labor process theory?' *British Journal of Sociology of Education* 24 (5): 559–573.

Stevenson, H. (2000). *Shifting Frontiers: Trade Union Responses to Changes in the Labour Process of Teaching.* University of Keele, unpublished PhD thesis.

Stevenson, H. 2011. 'Coalition Education Policy: Thatcherism's long shadow'. *FORUM* 53 (2): 179–194.

Taylor, F. W. 1911. *The Principles of Scientific Management*. London: Harper.

Thrupp, M., and Willmott, R. 2003. *Educational Management in Managerialist Times*. London: Open University Press.

Wallace, M. 1993. 'Discourse of derision: The role of the mass media within the education policy process'. *Journal of Education Policy* 8 (4): 321–337.

Index

accountability
  accountability infrastructures 9, 12
  accountably to the centre 7
  accountability regimes 139, 142, 145,
    150, 194
  downward accountability 11
  horizontal accountability 2
  test-based accountability 13, 64, 104,
    140
  upward accountability 11
achievement gap xxii
actor network theory 11, 103–9, 114,
  116
adaptive
  adaptive curriculum 53
  adaptive learning xxi, 30, 31, 34, 43
  adaptive technologies 44, 52, 56
administrators xxi
Adorno, T. xx, 197
algorithmic
  algorithmic calculation 44
  algorithmic governance 12, 33, 35
  algorithmic governmentality 22, 25, 38
analysis
  critical analysis xxiii
artificial intelligence xxiii, 21, 32, 36,
  56, 74
assessment
  comparative-competitive frameworks 9
  educational assessment 105
  high-stakes testing 7
  performance benchmarks 8
  performance related pay 219
audit
  audit of the population 25
  auditor 1
authoritarianism
  authoritarian pedagogies xxi
  elites 13, 36, 168
  far right xix
  hierarchy xix, xxi, 1, 186–7
  ruling class xviii

autoethnography 183
automated feedback 25

Ball, S. 44, 106, 123, 214
Bauman, Z. xxi
behaviour management 10, 25
behavioural psychology 51, 54
Bevir, M. 67–8
Boltanski, L. 67
Bourdieu, P. 11, 14, 159, 163, 178, 184
business: business leader 3
business networks 22

capital xviii
  cultural capital xxiil, 184–5
  educational policy capital 164
  forms of capital 183
  human capital 35, 143
  social capital 164, 184
  symbolic capital 164
CDDAAL 30
Chicago School of Economics 83, 86
choice 5
citizenship education 200
colonization 199
complexity
  complexity regulation 9
conduct of conduct 22
consensus-building 11
conservative media 168
constructionist approach 90–1
consultant 1, 24, 106
consumerism
  consumer 5, 126
  consumption xxii
context of influence 159
control society 44, 211
crises
  crises of democracy xxiv
  crises of responsibility 204
critical inquiry 4
critical logics approach 13

critical sociology 194
cultural production 163
cultural workers xxii

data
  big data 12, 24, 32, 37, 43, 50
  cognitive computing 33
  cognitive technologies 33
  data-driven audit 9
  data analytics xxiii, 31
  data dashboards 52
  data infrastructure 12, 63–4, 72, 75
  data mining 25, 33
  data management 63
  data monopoly 22
  data politics 21, 36
  data production 63
  data regimes 12
  data science 30
  data visualization 21, 28, 29, 36
  data warehouses 25
  digital architecture 27
  digital data 12
  digital disruption 50
  digital learning management 53
  digital learning platform 27
  digital learning products 27
  digital personalization 50, 52
  digital policy instruments 23, 24, 37
  digital technologies 12, 21, 49
  educational data 21, 22
  visual analytics 28, 143
decentralization 5, 6, 8, 22
Deleuze, G. xviii, 2, 44–6
democracy
  citizens xviii, 5
  counter-hegemonic xxi
  egalitarianism xxi, xxiv
  emancipatory xxiii
diagnosis
  programmatic solutions 10
digital governance 21, 24–6, 32, 36,
    73, 77
digitizing governance 24, 36
discourse
  dialogue xxiv
  political discourse theory 124–5
  rhetoric xxii
disintermediation 6
disorientation 49

dispositif 67
disposition 65–6

e-learning 26
economy 198
edu-business 26, 31, 106
education
  critical education xxi
  cultural education xxiii
education governance xxi, xxii, xxiii, xxiv,
    1, 2, 3, 12, 21, 22–3, 28, 32, 37, 44, 58,
    63–4, 76, 99, 116
education leadership 14, 209
  transformational leadership 218,
    220
education management 10, 209
  scientific management 218
education planning 5, 52
efficacy xxi, 10
efficiency 46, 59
EIU 28, 29
epiphylogenetic 48
episteme 46
epistemology 4, 11
ethical dilemmas 58
ETIN 50
evaluation
  assessment metrics 113
  comparison 24
  evaluation regimes 12
  league tables 28, 83
  numerical assessments 111, 114
  performance appraisal 1, 11
  performance management 7, 31, 221
  performance measurement 21
  ranking 24, 36, 45, 50, 110, 162
  target setting 50
  technologies of measurement 24
  testing companies 25
expertise 1, 22, 27, 33, 36–7, 58
  experts 164, 170

Fairclough 167, 169
fake news
  alienation of fact xx
  conspiracy xx
fast policy 24, 29
field of contestation 3
Foucault, M. xviii, 4, 22, 36, 67,
    85, 115

Giroux, H. xxiv
global education governance 13,
    140, 146
global testing regimes 8
good governance 2, 8
governance 194
    biopolitical xviii
    bureaucratic governance 199
    charities 2, 7
    extrastatecraft 66, 73
    extra-state organizations xxiii, 7
    global governance 13, 104, 106, 114
    governance hegemony 7
    governing at a distance 7, 193
    governing by numbers 170
    governing knowledge 28
    governing without government 193
    participatory governance 177
    regulatory governance 139
    soft biopolitics 26
    spatialities of governance 109
    stree level bureaucracy 201
    temporalities of governance 109, 115
government
    brokering 1
    civil servants 2
    commissioning 1
    councillors 2
    local government 1, 6, 209
    municipality 1
    national government 1, 8, 26, 106,
        113
    regional office 1
    welfare planning 5
governmentality 22, 28, 85
governors xxiii, 1, 6, 7

Habermas, J. 11, 14, 194
hard governance 7
head teacher 3, 92
hegemony 123, 130
    hegemonic economic discourse 144
heterarchy 5
high-reliability organization 11
HMI 93, 95
Horkheimer, M. 197
hybridization 14 *see also* hybridity 98
hypostatization 4

IBM 33, 34, 35, 74

identities
    class position xxii
    cultural position xxii
ideology 197
individualism
    private worries xxi
    self-interest 5
informatic power 64
infrastructure studies 12
inspection
    inspection policy 12
    inspection systems 83, 113
    inspector training 96
    monitoring 1, 7, 87
    school inspector 1, 13, 83–4, 87, 92–3,
        96–8
interconnectivity 10
intermediary associations 2
interoperability 69, 76
interpretivist governance
    studies 12
interviewing 90

journalistic field 159

Keynesian
    bureaucracy xix, 193, 198
    fordist xviii
    post-fordist xviii

labour process theory 14
Laclau and Mouffe 124
late-developing country 6
leadership
    cults of personality xx
    leaders 1
    transformational leadership 14
learning
    learner behaviour 32
    learning achievement 143
    learning analytics 12, 30
    learning curve 28–9, 35
    learning information management 71
    learning outcomes 107
    learning pathways 30
libertarian 5
lifeworld 197–8
local authorities 215
local school boards 63
logic

counter-hegemonic discourses 135
   fantasmatic logic 128, 133
   political logic 128, 132
   social logic 128, 130
logistics of engagement 54

machine intelligence 21
machine learning 21, 27, 29, 30–1, 34, 35
managerialism 236
   managerial authority 14
markets
   competition xix, 7, 123, 126
   consumerism xix, 199
   discourse 124
   equivalences xx
   hidden hand 1
   quasi-market xiv, 13, 84, 126, 212, 215
marketization
   customers 72
   suppliers 72
Marx, K. 196
media 49, 83, 94, 161, 162
   mediatisation 160
memory 47, 49, 55
metagovernance 9
methodological
   methodological globalism 106
   methodological nationalism 106
merit xxii
Microsoft 75
middle leader 3
militarization xxi
missing middle 6
mode of intervention 1
multiplicity 4

NAPLAN 8
narrative approach 13, 84, 88–92, 95, 97–8
nation state xxiii
neoconservative 4
neoliberalism xix, xxi, xxiii, 1, 83, 86, 160
networks
   governance networks 103
   horizontal networking 9
   interorganizational networks 63, 66, 72
   network analysis 23
   policy networks 2, 34, 106, 123
   state governance 197
   transnational policy networks 114
neurotic government 7

new public management 3, 144–5
New Right 145
news structuring 13
No Child Left Behind (NCLB) 144
non-human
   non-human actors 21, 24, 37, 104,
      106–7, 116
   non-human technologies 24, 37, 104,
      106–7, 114, 116
normative commitment 1, 3
NSIP 65, 69–70, 72–3

OECD 1, 8, 26, 27, 28, 63, 83–5, 105–6,
      142, 148
Ofsted 84, 87–8, 94–5
ontology 4, 66

parents 3
Pearson 21, 22–4, 26, 31, 32–7, 73, 75, 147
pedagogy
   curriculum xviii
performance pay 3
personalized learning xxi, xxiii, 12, 30–1,
      33–4, 44, 54, 57
phenomenology 90
PISA 8, 83, 86, 106, 110, 112–13, 142, 148
policy
   policy actors 23, 159
   policy analysis 29
   policy assemblage 23–4, 28
   policy community 5
   policy implementer 88, 92, 97
   policy instruments 23–4
   policy makers 36
   policy networks 23, 37
   policy shaper 88, 92
   policy strategy 1, 5, 6
   policy technology 141
policy network analysis 22–3
political-economic project 1, 8
politics xxi
polyvalence 1
positivism 166, 195
   disinterest xxii
   equivalence 9
   materiality xx
   neutrality xx
   objectivity xx
   objective facts 21
   objective instrument 9

quantification 9, 166
  scientific management 14
  solidity xx
  statistical knowledge 25
  universalized knowledge xxii
post-structuralism 12
power 167
  distribution of power 186
  hegemonic power 197
  power games 182
  power relations 168
  power struggles 178
precarity xx
prestige 164
privatization 161, 220
  commercial business 86
  commercial interests 73–5
  commercial organisations 36, 72
  consultancy xix
  contracting xviii
  corporations xviii, xxi, xxiii,
    44, 58
  deregulation xxiii, 8
  for-profit xix
  investors xviii
  ownership xviii
  philanthropy xix, xxiii, 43
  post-politics xix
  private monopoly 22
  profiteering xx, 31
  public-private partnerships 12, 69
  social enterprises 2
problematization
  problematics of government 5
  problematizing activity 10
professionalism 200
  professional communities 76
  professional conversations 83
  professional discretion 8
  professional group 114
  professional judgement 3, 14
progress xxii
public
  collective agency xxiv
  publics xviii, xix
  public criticism 75
  public entities 58
  public problems xxi, xxiii
  public sector xix
  public service 164

quality
  education quality 142
  quality assessment 113
  quality assurance 194
  quality management 113

real-time data analytics 21, 25, 31, 35, 54,
    57–8
reason
  instrumental reason 199
  communicative reason 199
regulatory gap 6
rhetoric xxii
Rhodes, R.A.W. 98, 193
Rose, N. 4, 22, 44, 193

scaling technique 1, 10
school board 1
school governance 3
school improvement 83–4
science
  evidence xx
  technology xxiii
self-governance 7, 11, 45
self-improvement 134
self-regulation xviii, 11, 45, 140
shareholders 31
SIIA 50
situated
  situated accounts 68
  situated agency 65
  situated narratives 77
social actors 170, 177, 198
social field 170, 179, 184
  academic subfield 180
  authoritative subfield 179
  professional subfield 179
social justice activist 5
social movements xxiv
social space 178
social theory xxi, xxii, xxiii, 4, 14
socio-cybernetic systems 57–8
soft governance 7
software studies 22, 23
stakeholder 5, 11
standardization xx, xxii, 9, 31, 55, 75, 142,
    162, 201
  standard-based reform 146
state monopoly 6, 22
Stiegler, B. 12, 44, 46–7, 55, 57, 59

struggles over meaning 3
students xxi, xxiii, xxiv
student engagement 52, 54
subjectivities 4
Systems Approach for Better Education
    Results (SABER) 150

talent xxii
Taylor 218
    Taylorism 219
teachers xxi, xxiii, xxiv, 3, 36, 75
    teacher agency 187, 220
teaching machines 51
technics 45, 47, 57
technology 46, 57, 76
techno-logical 48
technology of government 2, 3
technology of mistrust 7, 193
technology studies 64
think tank 24, 106
Third Way 145

time 48
transnationalism 103
transparency 11
trust 3, 5, 37
types of schools
    academies 3, 8, 86, 126–7, 222
    charter schools 3
    converter academies 129
    free schools 3
    independent public schools 8

UNESCO 105, 151
Unions
    teacher unions 209, 214

vehicle of empowerment 1, 11

Weber, M. 194
World Bank 1, 2, 103, 105, 109, 111–12,
    150
Wright Mills, C. xxi